Using
Turbo Pascal ®

Using
Turbo Pascal®

Steve Wood

Osborne **McGraw-Hill**
Berkeley, California

Published by
Osborne **McGraw-Hill**
2600 Tenth Street
Berkeley, California 94710
U.S.A.

For information on translations and book distributors outside of the
U.S.A., please write to Osborne **McGraw-Hill** at the above address.

CP/M is a registered trademark of Digital Research Corp.

IBM is a registered trademark of International Business Machines.

Turbo Pascal and Turbo Toolbox are trademarks of Borland International.

USING TURBO PASCAL®

1234567890   DODO   898765

ISBN 0-07-881148-1

Brad Hellman, Technical Editor
Deborah Wilson, Composition
Jan Benes, Text Design
Yashi Okita, Cover Design

Contents

PREFACE

Using Your Turbo Pascal

Commenting on Turbo Pacal's many enhancements, a reviewer described Turbo Pascal as not really Pascal but a new, Pascal-like language. Certainly it is true that Turbo Pascal permits, indeed facilitates, activities never intended by Professor Niklaus Wirth, the creator of Pascal. On the other hand, it is quite possible to write programs in the Turbo Pascal environment that conform to the ISO Pascal Standard.

Turbo Pascal is much more than just a compiler. It combines an editor, a compiler, and a debugger to create a very productive software development environment. The purpose of this book is to help you make yourself at home in this environment and to demonstrate how Turbo Pascal may be used to best advantage as you create a complete application program.

While the Turbo Pascal reference manual is better than most, it is still just what the name implies, a reference manual. It makes no attempt to instruct you as to when or even how you would use Turbo Pascal's many unique features. Most of these features are illustrated in the examples presented in the following pages.

This book assumes that you've had at least some previous programming experience. Some exposure to Pascal or another structured language will be helpful but not essential. The objective is to help you get comfortable with the Turbo environment and help you become a productive Pascal programmer.

You will notice that the book is divided into two parts. Part I—THE LANGUAGE concentrates on Pascal in general and Turbo Pascal in particular. The emphasis here is on structured program development and the syntax requirements of Pascal. Early on, you will be loading the Turbo system and checking it out. Even if you are a veteran Pascal programmer, you will want to skim this part to pick out those areas that discuss Turbo Pascal enhancements. You will find a thorough discussion of the features that make Turbo Pascal such a remarkable software development system. There are lots of examples, so you will learn by doing.

The next part, Part II—THE APPLICATION, involves developing a complete, useful application program. While it isn't practical to include every Turbo feature in one application, you will find that by the time you've finished, most of the Turbo tools will be familiar. As an added bonus you will have the application itself and dozens of useful routines that can be used as building blocks in future programs.

Because of the emphasis on examples and particularly on the development of a complete application program, you will find that this book contains many source code listings. Readers who would like to have these listings on diskette may order such a diskette directly from the author. Send your order to:

> precision logic systems
> Attn: Steve Wood
> 2012 Lake Air Drive
> Waco, TX 76710
>
> (817) 776-3100

The cost is $19.95, plus $3.00 shipping and handling. Most MS-DOS and CP/M diskette formats are available. Visa and Master Charge are accepted.

-------------------------- cut along this line ----------------------

Please send me the Using Turbo Pascal source code listings on disk. My $19.95 payment plus $3.00 for shipping and handling is enclosed.

_____ check   _____ money order

Name _____

Address _____

City _____ State _____ ZIP _____

precision logic systems, Attn. Steve Wood, 2012 Lake Air Drive, Waco, TX 76710

PART I

ONE

Introducing
The Language

This book is divided into two parts. Part I will introduce you to the Turbo Pascal programming language. In Part II you will put the language to work as you develop a complete loan amortization program.

If this is your first exposure to Pascal, you will find Part I essential. Along with a review of the syntax and semantics of the language, Part I discusses design methods that take advantage of Pascal's unique block structure. At the end of Part I, you'll know how Pascal's block structure can affect the programs you write. The many examples give you a complete, basic review of Turbo Pascal's powerful and advanced capabilities.

If you are already an experienced Pascal programmer, you too should review Part I. There are two reasons for this: one, since Turbo Pascal is a complete, integrated development system, including a Pascal compiler, editor, and debugging tools, you will need to read about how they work together. The second reason is that Turbo Pascal offers a large number of extensions to the standard Pascal language. All of these extensions, including special directives used to control the compiler, will be reviewed in Chapters Two through Eight.

Pascal as a Language

Named after a 17th-century mathematician and philosopher, Blaise Pascal, Pascal is a relative newcomer as a programming language since its introduction in the early 1970s. Pascal was developed by professor Niklaus Wirth as a simple language to be used in an educational environment. Because Dr. Wirth felt that programming should be approached systematically, Pascal was designed in this way. The result was a simple yet powerful language.

In the ensuing years, the power of the language became evident to computer manufacturers and language developers. The result has been a proliferation of Pascal language systems, most of which include many different extensions to the standard definition of the language. Because Pascal was not designed to develop business applications, standard Pascal offers only limited input and output facilities and lacks formal provisions for text strings. Commercial versions of Pascal are usually enhanced to overcome these weaknesses.

Since many languages are incapable of executing directly on the computer, they must undergo further processing. The nature of that processing depends on the type of language system used. (The term *language system* refers to how a language is implemented, not to the language itself. For example, BASIC may be implemented as a compiled system or as an interpreted system.) An overview of the four types of language systems follows.

Assemblers

The source code for an assembly language program is converted directly to machine-readable code by a program called an assembler. The resulting code, called *object code*, is a series of binary values (ones and zeros) that can be executed directly by the computer. Because there is a direct relationship between source code and object code, the object code produced by an assembler is usually very compact and efficient. Unfortunately, writing the source code is tedious, time-consuming, and error prone. To the uninitiated, assembly language source code may be as unreadable as the machine code that it represents.

Compilers

A compiler is a program to translate the source code of a high-level language, which is more or less like English, into executable object code. Unlike the source code for an assembler, a compiler's source code is not directly related to the object code that is produced. As a result, the object code is usually bulkier and less efficient than that produced by an assembler. On the other hand, the source code can be developed much faster and maintenance is easier.

Interpreters

Like assemblers and compilers, interpreters are programs that process source code; however, the objective of an interpreter is not to produce executable object code, at least not permanently. In simple terms, an interpreter reads the source code one statement at a time and executes each statement as it goes along. Of course, in order to execute the source code, the interpreter must convert it to executable object code, but that code is not saved. When a statement needs to be executed again it must be reconverted to machine code. For many applications this results in very slow execution. The advantage of an interpreter is that the programmer can easily experiment with the program. Most interpreters permit interrupting the program, modifying the program, and then restarting without having to start a compiler phase.

P-Code

You may have seen the term p-code associated with Pascal. P-code is a language system that, in effect, combines the compiler and interpreter concepts. High-level source code is processed by a program similar to a compiler. The difference is that the code produced is not executable object code. It is an intermediate code, called p-code. This p-code can then be processed by a program much like an interpreter.

At first glance it may be hard to see the advantage in such a system. The objective is portability. In the world of computer programs, portability refers to the ability to run a program on a number of different computer systems without changing the program. P-code-based systems are promoted as being portable to any system that has a p-code interpreter available to it. The drawback to p-code is that it is slow, like interpreters, but without the advantages.

Source Code Examples

Figure 1-1 shows two segments of code that print the letter "A" in the top-left corner of the screen; one is in 8086 assembly language and the other in Turbo Pascal. Unless you are an 8086 assembly language programmer who is familiar with IBM PC hardware, you probably wouldn't know from the assembly language source code what result it would produce. Source code written in a low-level language, like assembly language, works directly with the computer system for which it is written. It follows that a language a computer can understand is bound to be difficult for a programmer to understand. A program written in assembly language is hard to decipher without extensive comments. The source code for a high-level language, on the other hand, is relatively easy to follow. Although you may have never seen Turbo Pascal before, the operation of Figure 1-1 should be clear. In addition, a high-level language can usually be compiled or interpreted on a variety of computer

8086 assembler source code to display an "A" in the upper-left corner of
the video screen on monochrome IBM PC or compatible computer
systems.

```
MOV    AX,741H
MOV    DI,0B000
MOV    [DI],AX
```

Turbo Pascal source code to display an "A" in the upper-left corner of the
video screen.

```
GoToXY(1,1);
Write('A');
```

Figure 1-1.   Examples of 8086 and Turbo Pascal source code

systems, since the compiler or interpreter takes care of the details of control-
ling the hardware.

Knowing the variations in programming languages can help you evaluate
Turbo Pascal as a language system. In addition, a comparison illustrates the
tradeoffs that are made during the development of such a system. The ideal
language system might be described as having some of the following
features:

- Produces compact, efficient, object code.

- Uses a high-level source code that is easy to understand.

- Allows the programmer to make changes and see the results quickly and
  easily.

- Produces portable code that can run on any computer system.

Unfortunately, such a language system does not exist and may never exist.
Nevertheless, you may want to compare this wish list with various other
languages.

Here's how Turbo Pascal rates in each area.

The code produced by the Turbo compiler is very compact and efficient
compared to other compiled systems, regardless of the high-level language

used. When properly formatted and structured, Pascal source code is very readable.

The editor and debugging tools are integrated with the compiler. Moving from program to editor to correct errors or to modify operations is quick and easy. Though it is not quite the same as with an interpreter, the speed of the compiler combined with its powerful editor make it a very productive development system.

For portability there are versions of Turbo Pascal available for most CP/M, MS-DOS, and XENIX microcomputer systems as well as most systems that use the Motorola 68000 microcomputer processor. The source code for one system should compile and execute on any other system for which a Turbo compiler is available, assuming system-dependent routines are not used.

Installing Turbo Pascal

The best way to become familiar with Turbo is to use it to write some simple programs. Before you can do that, you will need to install the system. Installation is performed by the TINST.COM program on your Turbo master disk. If you haven't done so already, follow this procedure to create an installed Turbo master disk:

1. Make a backup copy of the original Turbo Pascal master disk.
2. Place the copy in Drive A; type TINST, and press RETURN.
3. Now configure your computer's screen for the Turbo system. The menu that appears will vary, depending on the type of computer system and the version of Turbo Pascal you are using. In all cases, one of the choices will be **Screen Installation**. Make that selection by pressing S.
4. The selections offered will vary depending on the version of Turbo you're using. Select the terminal or monitor description that matches your system. If your system is not included, you must select N for **None of the above**. Refer to the terminal installation section of your Turbo reference manual for details on adding a new terminal definition to the list.

After you have selected or defined a terminal configuration, the initial installation selection screen will be displayed again. One of the selections will be **Command Installation**. Read the next section before deciding to use this option.

Configuring the Editor

When you buy a Pascal compiler, you may not receive an editor to use in preparing your program files. Turbo not only includes an editor, but it also integrates the editor with the compiler.

Since you will configure the editor, you should arrange the editor's functions in a way similar to those of your favorite editor. With Turbo Pascal's Command Installation program, this can usually be accomplished. The Turbo editor is a *command-based editor*, which means that you indicate an edit function by pressing a control key combination. You will have to relearn a little if you are used to a *mode-based editor*, where commands are only recognized when you are in a command or edit mode. Microsoft's BASIC editor and a number of mainframe editors fall into this category. Since you don't have to change modes to perform editing functions, editors like the one included with Turbo Pascal are sometimes called *modeless editors*. Chances are you will learn to love modeless editing, especially if you are using a system that has function keys.

Of course, to use a command-based editor effectively you must learn the control key combinations. Learning can be shortened by modifying the control key sequences to match those of your favorite editor or word processor. Even if you don't have a favorite editor, you should consider modifying the default commands if your keyboard has function keys or other dedicated editing keys.

If you are a veteran WordStar user, you'll be satisfied without making any changes since the default configuration uses most of the command key sequences popularized by that word processor. IBM PC users will find that there is a secondary set of default command keys that make use of the keypad cursor control keys and a couple of the function keys for the most common operations. Table 1-1 shows the default command keys, including the optional keys for the IBM PC.

For the reader who is not familiar with the command structure of Word-Star, it is based on pressing the CONTROL (CTRL) key in conjunction with one or two other keys. In an effort to make this a one-handed operation, the keys used are generally those that can be reached by the left hand. The major complaints are that the commands are not mnemonic.

If your system has function keys, you will be best served by making full use of the single key commands. You may associate the various editing functions with selected keys by selecting Command Installation from the installation menu. A word to the wise on using this installation program: take time to go through the list of commands in the Turbo reference manual and decide in advance which key you want to assign to which task. For obvious reasons you can't assign the same key to two different commands.

Table 1-1. Turbo Pascal Default Editor Command Keys

Cursor Control	Default Control Key Combination	IBM PC Optional Key
Left One Character	CTRL-S	LEFT ARROW
Right One Character	CTRL-D	RIGHT ARROW
Up One Line	CTRL-E	UP ARROW
Down One Line	CTRL-X	DOWN ARROW
Up One Video Page	CTRL-R	PGUP
Down One Video Page	CTRL-C	PGDN
Left One Word	CTRL-A	CTRL-LEFT ARROW
Right One Word	CTRL-F	CTRL-RIGHT ARROW
Scroll Up	CTRL-W	None
Scroll Down	CTRL-Z	None
Left End of Line	CTRL-QS	HOME
Right End of Line	CTRL-QD	END
Top of Screen	CTRL-QE	CTRL-HOME
Bottom of Screen	CTRL-QX	CTRL-END
Top of File	CTRL-QR	CTRL-PGUP
Bottom of File	CTRL-QC	CTRL-PGDN
Beginning of Block	CTRL-QB	None
End of Block	CTRL-QK	None
Restore Cursor Position	CTRL-QP	None
Tab	CTRL-I or TAB	TAB
Auto Tab On/Off	CTRL-QI	None
Insert or Delete		
Insert On/Off	CTRL-V	INS
Backspace and Delete	DEL or BACKSPACE	BACKSPACE
Delete Character	CTRL-G	DEL
Delete Word	CTRL-T	None
Insert Line	CTRL-N	None
Delete Line	CTRL-Y	None
Delete to End of Line	CTRL-QY	None

Table 1-1.   Turbo Pascal Default Editor Command Keys (*continued*)

Block Commands	Default Control Key Combination	IBM PC Optional Key
Mark Start of Block	CTRL-KB	F7
Mark End of Block	CTRL-KK	F8
Mark One Word	CTRL-KT	None
Hide/Display Block	CTRL-KH	None
Copy Marked Block	CTRL-KC	None
Move Marked Block	CTRL-KV	None
Read Block From File	CTRL-KR	None
Write Block to File	CTRL-KW	None
Search and Replace		
Find Search String	CTRL-QF	None
Replace Search String	CTRL-QA	None
Repeat Find/Replace	CTRL-L	None
Miscellaneous		
Insert Control Character (x)	CTRL-P, CTRL-X	None
Abort Command	CTRL-U	None
Restore Line	CTRL-QL	None
End Edit	CTRL-KD	None

The installation program doesn't check for duplicates until you are finished, and then it only notifies you of the first duplication it finds. If you haven't done this before, you may have to repeat the process a few times before getting it right. Other potential problems could be the way some keys send the scan code to the processor or how a key you have selected sends the same code as a selected key combination. You can catch these errors during the first configuration pass by noting the video representation of the keys as you enter the definitions.

Writing a Turbo Program

Before writing your first program you should make a working copy of your Turbo Pascal development system. Your working Turbo disk should be a system disk; that is, it should contain the files necessary to start up your computer when you first turn it on. If you're not sure how to create such a disk, check your operating system manual. Copy the files TURBO.COM and TURBO.MSG from your *installed* Turbo master onto the system disk. When you have finished you will have a Turbo development disk with plenty of room for the source and object code files you will be creating.

Since you will be spending most of your development time in the editor, it is a good idea to take some time to learn its features well. Here is the procedure for loading Turbo Pascal and creating a source code file using the Turbo editor. These instructions are designed to work with any system supported by Turbo Pascal. If you have a hard disk or prefer to use different disk drives, you will need to alter the procedure. If you are already familiar with the editor, you may skip this section.

1. Start your computer system with your work disk in drive A.

2. When the system prompt appears, type TURBO and press RETURN.

3. Press Y in response to **Load error message?** and the TURBO.MSG file will be loaded into memory. Programming errors will now be referenced with a descriptive message rather than a number.

4. The Turbo Pascal main menu, similar to the one in Figure 1-2, will be displayed. There may be some variations depending on the version of Turbo you are using.

    The options presented in the Turbo menu will be covered in detail later. For now, you want to get into the editor. To do that, simply press E.

5. You will be prompted to enter a name for the file to be edited. Type TEMP and press RETURN. The screen will clear and the cursor will move to the left corner of the second line. The top line is reserved as an editor status line. Take a moment to review the information that is presented here.

6. Using Table 1-1 and the Turbo Pascal reference manual as guides, experiment with the editor and become very familiar with the edit functions and the keys used to invoke them.

Logged drive: A

A> Copy B: PROGRAM, PAS   LPT1;]

Active directory: \PAS

Work file:
Main file:

Edit   Compile Run Save
Dir   Quit compiler Options

Text: 0 bytes
Free: 62024 bytes

Figure 1-2.   Turbo Pascal main menu screen

7. When you feel comfortable with the Turbo editor, here is how to start over. First, exit the editor by pressing CTRL-KD. At this point you have only left the editor; the file has *not* been saved.

8. Next press the SPACEBAR to display the menu. Note that TEMP.PAS is shown to be the current work file.

9. Change to a different work file by pressing W. Because the current work file TEMP.PAS has been edited but not saved, you are first asked whether you wish to save it before assigning a new file. Since there is no need to save the text that was entered while you were experimenting with the editor, press N.

10. In response to the prompt for a new work file name, enter KEYS, press RETURN, and then press the SPACEBAR to update the menu. The work file will now be KEYS.PAS. The .PAS extension is added automatically unless you specify a different extension. If you need to work with a file that has no extension, you must terminate the file name with a period.

11. Next press E to edit the current work file. When you pressed E in step 4, you were prompted for a file name. That will only happen when there is no current work file. If you have specified a work file, that is the file that will be edited when you press E. In this case it is a new file.

12. You are now ready to enter your first Turbo Pascal program. Enter the program exactly as it is shown.

```
program Display_Keys;

  const QUIT = ^Q;

  var   inchr : Char;

  begin
    ClrScr;
    WriteLn('Press a key to display its ASCII Code');
    WriteLn('Press <CTRL><Q> to QUIT');
    repeat
      Read(Kbd,inchr);
      WriteLn('The ASCII code for ',inchr,' is ',Ord(inchr));
    until (inchr = QUIT);
  end.
```

The purpose of this exercise is to familiarize yourself with the Turbo editor and the basic operation of the compiler. Don't be concerned with understanding the syntax of the program at this point. By the time you finish Chapter 8, it will all make sense.

13. After you have entered the source code, exit the editor by pressing CONTROL-KD.

14. Press S to save the file. It is a good idea to get in the habit of saving your work when you exit the editor. When you start using Turbo's advanced features it is possible to write programs that cause the computer to lock up. You will then have to reset the system to regain control. If that happens and you haven't saved your work file, any changes will be lost. By the way, system lock-ups are not caused by problems with the Turbo compiler, but by problems with the program being tested.

15. To compile and test, run your program in one step by pressing R. Any typing errors will be apparent when you try to compile or run the program. In either case, compilation or execution of the program will halt with the cursor located at the error. Press ESC to enter the editor and correct the error by comparing the listing with your program.

16. Before you know it, the screen will clear and you will be asked to press a key. Each time you press a key other than CTRL-Q, the character that is produced by that key will be displayed followed by the ASCII value of the character. When CTRL-Q is pressed the program will end.

17. Save the corrected version of the program and exit Turbo Pascal. Return to the operating system by pressing Q.

That's all there is to it. You have entered the source code, compiled it, and executed the resulting object code. All without having to leave Turbo Pascal. The Turbo editor will be discussed more in Chapter 5.

A Structured Approach to Programming

In most curriculum handbooks, computer programming is classified as a science; however, there is no step-by-step procedure for writing a good computer program. In fact, there is much controversy over what constitutes a good computer program. One might even argue that if it works it's good. That is not to say that programming in Pascal cannot be approached systematically. In fact, Pascal was developed with the idea of promoting a systematic method of programming. The basis of this method is the concept of block structured programs.

What exactly is structure in programming? It might be defined as the way the parts are put together to form the completed work. In a painting, primary colors are combined to produce shades. Various shades are combined to form an object. Objects are positioned and combined to create the finished work.

In a similar manner, a structured program is made up of basic *functions* and *procedures*, which are combined to create routines according to the rules of the language. These routines are then positioned and combined to create a working program. Block structured languages, like Pascal, take this concept a step further. The routines created using the basic functions of the language can themselves be used to create still larger routines. These routines created by the programmer are sometimes called *blocks*, in that they are used to build other routines and, finally, the program itself. In Pascal these blocks are called *subprograms*.

There is a distinct advantage to this programming approach. Subprograms take advantage of the divide and conquer method of problem solving to break a problem into smaller and smaller pieces until you are working with a routine that can be coded and tested with ease. A number of easily debugged programs may be combined to create a complete application such as a general ledger or inventory management system.

This concept of modularity leads to increased productivity. Once you have perfected the routines that are used to accept and edit user input, you can simply copy those routines into any future project that involves user input. After a while you will have a whole library of tested subprograms.

Another advantage is the ease with which errors are located and corrections made. The context of the error usually leads you directly to the offending subprogram. Because subprograms are made up of smaller subprograms, it is easy to narrow the possibilities down to the statement that caused the problem.

Most programs require modifications and additions from time to time. Changes and additions can usually be made to a structured program without leading to side effects that cause things that used to work to stop working. If you have ever updated a BASIC program and inadvertently used a variable that was already being used for something else, you have experienced the problems caused by side effects. Structured languages limit such problems by limiting the effect of an action, such as a variable assignment, to the subprogram in which it takes place. As a result the subprograms, called *procedures* and *functions* in Pascal, are relatively independent of one another. When interaction between subprograms is desired, it is controlled and obvious. This will be demonstrated as you build your own procedures and functions in the following chapters.

TWO

The Basics

In this chapter we'll discuss the parts that make up a simple Pascal program. A simple Pascal program is one in which only predefined subprograms are used to build the program. As was mentioned in the first chapter, Pascal subprograms are known as *procedures* and *functions*, but as you will discover, the subprograms are really simple programs with some minor adjustments. The difference between procedures and functions will be covered in Chapter 4. When you purchase a Pascal compiler, a number of subprograms have been predefined. For example, the Turbo Pascal program in Chapter 1 used the WriteLn procedure to write information to the screen and the Read procedure to read information from the keyboard.

Parts of a Pascal Program

As you develop a Pascal program or subprogram, you will find that it can be divided into three parts:

- The *header*, which is optional, announces or names the program, like a title of a book.
- *Definitions* and *declarations*, which are also optional, can be categorized as

        type definitions
        constant definitions
        variable declarations
        label declarations
        subprogram definitions.

  The first four will be discussed in this chapter; subprogram definitions will be covered in Chapter 4.
- *Statements* define the action of the program. Assignment statements, flow control statements, and so on are grouped in this part. The state-

ment part starts with the reserve word **begin** and finishes with the reserve word **end**. Since the simple program has only one statement part, end also indicates the end of the program and should be appended with a period (.). Every Pascal program or subprogram is required to have a statement part.

The Header

No matter how small or large, every program should begin with a program header. The program header, which is always the first line in a program, begins with the reserved word **program** followed by a name and a semicolon (;). Although optional, the program header is highly recommended as it announces the program and gives it an identity. For example, from a glance it is possible to determine that the following is a complete program:

```
program DoLittle;
   begin
      WriteLn ('Do what?');
   end.
```

The header indicates that this is a program, not just a procedure or function, and is identified as DoLittle. Incidentally, procedures and functions also have headers, which are required and are very similar to program headers.

Definitions and Declarations

In order to write a program that does more than print silly phrases, you will almost always need some data. A data item is any piece of information that will be manipulated by a program and require storage space in the computer when the program is executed. Data that never changes is called *constant* data and the everchanging kind is called *variable*. Not only do you define data in a Pascal program, but you must reserve space in memory for variables by a variable declaration. You must do the same for constant definitions. When you need to refer to a specific data item, you must have some way to identify it.

One purpose of constant definitions and variable declarations is to assign names, or *identifiers*, to a specific data item. If definitions and declarations were added to the DoLittle program, they would appear between the header and the statement part. Turbo Pascal does not require that the definitions and declarations appear in any particular sequence.

Before listing the various types for the declaration and definition part, there are a few things you should know about identifiers. When it comes to naming, Pascal permits the use of long, meaningful names for variables, constants, headers, subprograms, and other program parts.

1. Identifiers must begin with an alphabetic character or an underline character.
2. The first character may be followed by up to 126 additional characters, which must be alphabetic characters, numeric characters, or the underline character.

The case (upper or lower) of alphabetic characters is not significant. For example, TURBO, turbo, and Turbo are considered to be identical.

The rules concerning identifiers are liberal enough so you can use meaningful names to describe the purpose of the data item being identified. By taking advantage of this, you will make your programs easier to understand, which will result in better programs with fewer errors.

Although you are only limited by your imagination when creating identifiers, Turbo Pascal reserves the identifiers listed in Table 2-1 for its own use. If you attempt to use any of those words as user-defined identifiers, the compiler will issue an error message.

Types

In addition to providing identifiers for variables, you must indicate the type of data that will be used by the variable. In Pascal, the type of a data item serves two major purposes. One is to indicate how much storage is to be allocated for a data item of a particular type. The other is to prevent type mismatches. A mismatch occurs when you attempt to assign a value of one type to a variable of another type. Before this can be illustrated you will need to know what data types are available in Turbo Pascal.

In Pascal, types can be categorized as predefined and user-defined. User-defined types will be described in Chapter 3. Pascal's predefined types, listed in Table 2-2, can be described as *scalar* types, with the exception of the Text type, which will be covered in the next chapter. Although Real is not scalar, Pascal considers it as a scalar type. The term scalar refers to an ordered set of values that fall within a limited, definable range. For example, the letters A-Z form a range of 26 specific values. Here are short descriptions of the five predefined scalar types available in Turbo Pascal.

Boolean   The ordered set of values FALSE and TRUE define the Boolean type. This means that data items declared to be of this type may be assigned only one of those values. A Boolean data item will be allocated one byte of storage. Boolean variables are most often used in conditional test statements and program loops.

Table 2-1.   Turbo Pascal Reserved Words

Identifier	Standard Pascal	Usage
absolute	N	Variable declaration.
and	Y	Boolean and arithmetic operator.
array	Y	Type definition.
begin	Y	Logic control. Used with end.
case	Y	Logic control. Used with of, else and end.
const	Y	Marks start of constant definitions.
div	Y	Arithmetic operator.
do	Y	Logic control. Used with for, while and with.
downto	Y	Logic control. Used with for.
else	Y	Logic control. Used with if and case.
end	Y	Logic control. Used with begin and case. Type definition. Used with record.
external	N	Subprogram definition.
file	Y	Type definition.
forward	Y	Subprogram definition.
for	Y	Logic control. Used with to, downto and do.
function	Y	Subprogram definition.
goto	Y	Logic control.
inline	N	Statement control.
if	Y	Logic control. Used with then and else.
in	Y	Set operator.
label	Y	Marks start of label declarations.
mod	Y	Arithmetic operator.
nil	Y	Pointer to nothing.
not	Y	Boolean and arithmetic operator.
overlay	N	Subprogram definition.
of	Y	Logic control. Used with case. Type definition. Used with array, file, and set.
or	Y	Boolean and arithmetic operator.
packed	Y	Not used in Turbo Pascal.

Table 2-1. Turbo Pascal Reserved Words (*continued*)

Identifier	Standard Pascal	Usage
procedure	Y	Subprogram definition.
program	Y	Program definition. Optional in Turbo.
record	Y	Type definition. Used with end.
repeat	Y	Logic control. Used with until.
set	Y	Type definition.
shl	N	Arithmetic operator.
shr	N	Arithmetic operator.
string	N	Type definition.
then	Y	Logic control. Used with if.
type	Y	Marks start of type definitions.
to	Y	Logic control. Used with for.
until	Y	Logic control. Used with repeat.
var	Y	Marks start of variable declarations.
while	Y	Logic control. Used with do.
with	Y	Record variable field access. Used with do.
xor	N	Boolean and arithmetic operator.

Table 2-2. Turbo Pascal Predefined Types

Identifier	Standard Pascal	Turbo	Description
Boolean	Y	Y	TRUE and FALSE
Byte	N	Y	Integer value 0 to 255
Char	Y	Y	ASCII set of characters plus #128—#255
Integer	Y	Y	Integer values −32768 to 32767
Real	Y	Y	Real numbers
Text	Y	Y	External file of Char type structure, which is enhanced over the standard

Char The values that make up this type are all of the characters in the ASCII set (see the ASCII table in the Turbo reference manual) plus the characters, if any, represented by character codes 128-255. The characters represented by codes 128-255 are implementation-dependent; that is, they may vary from one computer system to another, or they may not be used at all. Char type values use one byte of memory for storage.

Any character may be represented in Turbo Pascal by its ASCII code in decimal, preceded by the pound sign (#), or hexadecimal, preceded by the pound and dollar sign ($). For example, this program

```
program Write_Cat_Three_Times;
  begin
      Write(#67#97#116#32);
      Write(#$43#$61#$74#$20);
      Write('Cat');
  end.
```

will produce

Cat Cat Cat

In the first Write statement, the characters "C" "a" "t" " " are represented by their decimal ASCII codes preceded by the pound sign (#). The second statement represents the same characters using hexadecimal values to indicate their ASCII codes. As this illustrates, Turbo Pascal uses a leading dollar sign ($) to denote hexadecimal values. In the third statement the characters themselves are enclosed in single quote marks, which is how character strings are *delimited* in Pascal. There will be more on strings in Chapter 3. While not appropriate as used here, the first two forms provide a convenient way to represent values that cannot be entered from the keyboard. Another alternate form is available to represent the ASCII control characters. Just enter the circumflex (^) followed by a letter (A-Z) or [, \,], ^, _, which happen to be the special characters represented by character codes 91-95. Therefore, CTRL-C may be represented as

^C or #3 or #$3

At first glance it might appear that all of these options are overkill, but in practice each has its place. It's up to you to pick the one that makes the most sense for the value being represented.

Integer The range of values defined for the Turbo Pascal Integer type is −32768 through 32767. Two bytes are required to store an integer value. Integer values are represented as signed values, meaning they may be used to hold numeric values less than 0. There are times when Integer type data items are used to hold values with a range of 0 through 65535, which is the range of *unsigned* values that can be stored in two bytes. This is a common practice with memory addresses. You cannot assign a value to a data item if that value is outside the defined range of the item's type. For example, if **item** is an Integer variable, the statement

item := 40000;

will cause the compiler to complain because 40000 is greater than 32767. However, the compiler will accept the statement

item := $9C40;

where $9C40 is the hexadecimal equivalent of 40000. This will allow you to assign values greater than 32767 to Integer type variables. However, you should be aware that following such an assignment, the value is stored as a signed integer. As a result, this statement:

Write(item);

will result in −25536 being output rather than 40000. Notice that 40000 − 65536 equals −25536. As long as you are aware of this and allow for it in your code, you can use Integer type data items to manipulate unsigned integer values.

You should also be aware that Turbo Pascal does not check the result of an expression before assigning it to an Integer variable. For example, the following statements will compile and execute without generating an error, assuming **item** is an Integer variable.

item := 30000 * 3;
Write(item);

The result, however, will be 24464 instead of 90000, which is the remainder when 90000 is divided by 65536. In other words, when a value in excess of 65536 is stored in an Integer type variable, the result will be that value mod 65536. While this can be useful in some cases, if it happens inadvertently it will cause problems.

Byte   The Byte type is not included in standard Pascal and is a predefined *subrange* of the standard Integer type. You'll learn more about subranges when user-defined types are discussed. The range of type Byte is 0 to 255, and as you might suspect, each item of Byte type data uses one byte of memory. If you know that the value of a data item will never fall outside this range, you will save storage by declaring it as a Byte type data item. Finally, if the value of an expression exceeds 255 and is assigned to a Byte type variable, the variable will contain the value modulo 256. If **item** is a Byte type variable in the following statement:

$$\text{item} := 255 * 3 + 3;$$

item will have a value of 0, which is the remainder when 768 is divided by 256.

Real   Real types are allotted six bytes of storage and hold values in the range 1E−38 to 1E+38. While this is a wide range of values, you must remember that these values are only accurate to 11 decimal places. If you are developing business applications, you might prefer to think of the range as −99,999,999.99 to 99,999,999.99 rounded to the nearest penny. This range of values can be represented with relative accuracy using Real type data items.

As with all floating-point systems, this accuracy may be compromised by a chain of calculations that propagate the rounding errors inherent in the system. If you require absolute accuracy for such calculations, you should use the *BCD* (binary-coded decimal) option that is available for Turbo Pascal version 3.0 or later. BCD stores decimal values without the loss of accuracy that may occur when the standard floating-point system is used. Using the BCD option, Real type values may have 18 significant digits.

Constants

In Pascal constants are used to associate a fixed value with an identifier. The identifier may be user-defined, or it may be the *literal* identifier that describes the value. For example, FALSE and TRUE describe Boolean values; "A","*", #7 and $0D describe Char values; and 1, 28, 3987, and −32768 describe integer values. All of these are examples of literal constants. On the other hand, user-defined constants, called *named constants*, must be defined in the constant definition part as illustrated here:

$$\text{const COMMPORT} = 56;$$

With the constant definition, you are telling the compiler, "Any time you see COMMPORT in this program, I want you to substitute the number 56."

Notice that the reserved word **const** must introduce the constant definition part. Every definition below **const** is a constant definition until a different definition or declaration, such as variable declaration, or until the beginning of the program. Any number of constant definitions may follow; each is terminated with a semicolon.

There are a couple of advantages to using named constants. It makes your source code easier to understand. When you see COMMPORT in the source code, you will know right away that you are referring to the communications port. On the other hand, seeing 56 is not too informative. The other advantage becomes apparent when you need to modify the code. For example, what if you have made 26 references to the communications port in your program and decide to recompile it on a system that uses port 14 instead of 56 for communications? If you have used a named constant to make those references, you will only have to make the change in the constant definition.

const COMMPORT = 14;

If you used the literal value 56 for each reference, you'll have 26 changes to make.

Turbo Pascal also offers a third, nonstandard, type of constant. It is called a *typed constant*. Should you decide that the constant COMMPORT would serve your needs better as a typed constant, you could define it as follows:

const COMMPORT : Integer = 56;

In a sense, a typed constant functions like a variable; its value can be changed within the statement part of the program. To appreciate how this differs from a regular named constant, it will help to understand what the compiler does with each one.

When a standard named constant is defined, the compiler simply makes note of the fact on an electronic scratch pad called a *symbol table*. In essence the compiler establishes a relationship between the identifier and the value you have assigned it. When the compiler is compiling the code and finds the identifier, it substitutes the constant value associated with the identifier. The resulting machine code will be the same whether you use named constants or literal constants.

In the case of a typed constant the compiler has more to do, but the resulting machine code will sometimes be smaller. When the definition is encountered, the compiler sets aside enough space in memory to hold the data indicated by the type specified. In the preceding example, it would have reserved two bytes to store an integer, and next initialized that space to the value indicated—56 in this case. Now the symbol table can be updated as before, only this time it relates the identifier to location of the value in memory rather than to the value itself. Finally, whenever the identifier is found in the source code, the compiler generates code that references the value indirectly via the address where it is stored.

In the example, a typed constant would not result in any saved space because it takes more code to access an integer value indirectly using an address than it does to store the integer itself as a literal value. A typed constant doesn't save space unless the type involved uses more than four bytes of storage. You should also avoid using typed constants inside loops, where speed is important, because of the additional processing required for indirect referencing. On the positive side typed constants can save a significant amount of space when referencing large user-defined types.

Table 2-3 lists the two named constants, MAXINT and PI, that are predefined in Turbo Pascal as well as indicating the literal constants that describe each of the predefined types.

The MAXINT constant is required in standard Pascal. The value it represents indicates the maximum permissible value of an integer, which is 32767 on all systems for which Turbo Pascal is presently available. Also of interest, but not available as a predefined constant, is the minimum valid integer value. It may be calculated as $-(MAXINT + 1)$, which is -32768 on systems that use Turbo.

As you might suspect, PI holds a value of 3.1416 to 11 decimal places. As noted in Table 2-3, it is nonstandard.

The remaining predefined constants make up the set of literal constants for the predefined types. They include the numeric representation of Integers and Reals as well as the alphabetic characters that represent Char. Also in this group are TRUE and FALSE, which are the literal constants of the Boolean type.

Variables

When a variable is declared, memory is allocated, providing a place to put a particular type of data. A variable declaration also provides a name for that place. The rules for declaring variables are straightforward: variables are usually declared in the variable declaration part. The variable declaration

Table 2-3.   Turbo Pascal Predefined Constants

Identifier	Standard Pascal	Turbo	Description
MAXINT	Yes	Yes	Contains the integer value 32767
PI	No	Yes	Pi value 3.1415926536
Numbers	Yes	Yes	Literal constants for Integer and Real types with decimal and hexadecimal representation
Characters	Yes	Yes	Literal constants for the ASCII set plus nonstandard special characters
TRUE and FALSE	Yes	Yes	Literal constants for the Boolean type

part is denoted by the appearance of the reserved word **var**. Following that, one or more variable identifiers may appear. Each identifier (or group of identifiers separated by commas) of a given type must be followed by a colon (:), a valid type identifier, and a semicolon (;). Here is an example of a variable declaration part:

```
var     interest_rate,
        payment_amt,
        principal      :  Real;
        current_year   :  Integer;
        current_month  :  Byte;
        inchr          :  Char;
        exit_flag      :  Boolean;
```

The format used for the source code is flexible. The three Real type variables could also be declared like this:

```
var interest_rate, payment_amt, principal: Real;
```

The advantage of the first format is that it leaves room for comments to the right of each declaration.

Pascal variables are not initialized when they are declared. Until you assign it a value, the storage represented by a declared variable contains garbage.

Typed Constants

Typed constants, in addition to being used to save storage space, can be used as initialized variables. In fact, typed constants actually *are* initialized variables. If you want them to be constants, you shouldn't change their values. You may use a typed constant identifier anywhere you would use a variable identifier. Type constants are defined in the constant section but are declared similar to variables with values assigned to them. Here is an example of some typed constant definitions:

```
const   TEXT           =  'T';
        UPPER_CASE     =  'U';
        video_width    :  Byte =   80;
        input_type     :  Char =   UPPER_CASE;
        scaling_ratio  :  Real =   0.50;
```

Here, typed constants used as initialized variables are lowercase letters;

regular constants are in uppercase. When user-defined types are introduced, you will see even greater possibilities for the use of typed constants as initialized variables. In the final analysis it would appear that typed constant is a misnomer. They should probably be called initialized variables.

Turbo Pascal provides a number of variables that have been predeclared. Since most of them are used in advanced features, they will be discussed along with their features. A complete summary is given in Appendix A.

Table 2-4. Turbo Pascal Arithmetic and Relational Operators

Identifier	Standard Pascal	Description
Arithmetic Operators		
− {unary minus}	Y	Reverses the sign of its operand
not	Y	Boolean **not** operation and Integers
*	Y	Integer or Real number multiplication
/	Y	Real number division
div	Y	Integer division
mod	Y	Modulus operation; result equals remainder after integer division
and	Y	Boolean **and** operation and Integers
shl	N	Bitwise shift left operation
shr	N	Bitwise shift right operation
+	Y	Integer or Real number addition
−	Y	Integer or Real number subtraction
or	Y	Boolean **or** operation and Integers
xor	N	Boolean **xor** operation and Integers
Relational Operators		
$val1 = val2$	Y	TRUE if values are equal
$val1 <> val2$	Y	TRUE if values are not equal
$val1 < val2$	Y	TRUE if $val1$ less than $val2$
$val1 <= val2$	Y	TRUE if $val1$ less than or equal to $val2$
$val1 > val2$	Y	TRUE if $val1$ greater than $val2$
$val1 >= val2$	Y	TRUE if $val1$ greater than or equal to $val2$

Labels

The purpose of a label is to mark the destination of a **goto** statement, which will be discussed with the logic control statements later in this chapter. As such, labels do not play a significant part in building programs. In fact, a properly designed program should not need labels. However, if you write a program that uses them, they must be declared. This is done in the **label** declaration part. This part is marked by the reserved word **label** followed by one or more valid **label** identifiers separated by commas and terminated with a semicolon. The following is a valid Turbo Pascal label declaration part:

> **label** ErrorExit, AbortExit, 1234;

The last label identifier is permitted in Turbo Pascal to maintain compatibility with standard Pascal, which requires that labels consist of 1 to 4 numeric characters. Turbo Pascal allows both letters and numbers.

Operators

Much of the data manipulated in the statement part of a program or subprogram is performed by operators. Before examining the statement part, it will be helpful to review the operators available in Turbo Pascal. Pascal operators fall into three categories: arithmetic operators, logical operators, and relational operators, which determine the logic flow of a program (see Table 2-4).

The term *expression* refers to any combination of one or more literal or named constants or variable identifiers, with one or more operators. Here are some examples of valid expressions:

> -22 (*unary minus*)
> (8 + 3)
> (big <> small)
>
> (not exit)
> (item / 5 + cost)
> ((a + b) * c)

Literal or named constants and variables that appear in an expression are called *operands*.

When more than one operator appears in an expression, the evaluation sequence depends upon their *precedence*. The operator with the highest precedence will be evaluated first. Where two or more operators have the same precedence level, evaluation proceeds from left to right. There are five precedence levels as follows:

1. − (Unary minus)

2. not

3. *, /, div, mod, and, shl, shr

4. *, −, or, xor

5. =, <>, <, >, <=, >=, in

Parentheses alter the precedence of operators by forcing the program to evaluate the expression within parentheses first. Addition will be evaluated before multiplication, as in 5 * (3 + 4). In *nested* parentheses, which are parentheses within parentheses, the innermost expression will be evaluated first.

The following discussion will illustrate how Turbo Pascal's arithmetic, logical, and relational operators are used and what type of operands may be used with them. You will find that the result of an expression may vary depending on the type of its operand or operands.

Arithmetic Operators   In the following lists of operators, the operand types will be indicated in italic next to the operator.

− (Unary Minus) *Integer or Real*

The unary operator negates, or reverses the sign, of its single operand. For example,

> If int__var equals 12, −int__var equals −12
> If real__var equals −9.63, −real__var equals 9.63

not *Integer*

The integer is converted to its binary equivalent, each bit is then complemented, and the result is reconverted to an integer. For example:

> If int__var equals 12, **not** int__var equals −13

which in binary terms is

> **not** 0000000000001100 = 1111111111110011

* *Integer or Real*

In multiplying, if either operand is a Real type, the result will be a Real type value; otherwise the result will be an Integer. Note that Turbo Pascal does *not* check for integer overflow.

/*Integer or Real*

The left operand is divided by the right operand. The result for division will always be a Real type value. If the right operand equals 0, an error occurs.

div *Integer only*

The result of integer division will always be an integer value. Any remainder is discarded. Division by 0 results in an error.

mod *Integer only*

The left operand is divided by the right operand and the result is the remainder, which will always be an Integer type value. The right operand must not be equal to 0.

shl *Integer only*

The form for **shl**, for shift left, is *integer1* **shl** *integer2*. The binary equivalent of *integer1* is shifted left the number of positions indicated by *integer2*. This is the equivalent of *integer1* * (2 ^ *integer2*) — in other words, multiplication by powers of 2. Since the result will always be an Integer type stored in a 16-bit word, any value of *integer2* over 15 will shift the value to 0.

If **int_var** equals 256, **int_var shl 3** equals 2048, which is the same as

$$256 * (2*2*2) = 2048$$
or
$$0000000100000000 \text{ shl } 3 = 0000100000000000$$

shr *Integer only*

The form for **shr**, for shift right, is *integer1* **shr** *integer2*. The binary equivalent of *integer1* is shifted right the number of positions indicated by *integer2*. This is the equivalent of *integer1* **div** (2 ^ *integer2*) — in other words, integer division by powers of 2. Since the result will always be an Integer type, any value of *integer2* over 15 will always produce a result of 0.

If **int_var** equals 2048, **int_var shr 3** equals 256, which is the same as

$$2048 \text{ div } (2*2*2) = 256$$
or
$$0000100000000000 \text{ shr } 3 = 0000000100000000$$

and *Integer*

Both operands must be Integer type. The form for arithmetic **and** is *integer1* **and** *integer2*. When the operands are Integer types, the value of both operands is converted to binary, and each bit in the left operand is logically **and**ed with the corresponding bit in the right operand.

If int_var1 equals 12 and int_var2 equals 15,
int_var1 **and** int_var2 equals 12

which is the same as

$$1100 \text{ and } 1111 = 1100$$

Note that **and** is used to reset (switch off) bits in **int—var2** that are reset in **int—var1**.

or *Integer*

Both operands must be Integer type. The value of both operands is converted to binary, each bit in the left operand is logically **or**ed with the corresponding bit in the right operand, and the result is reconverted to Integer type.

> If int—var1 equals 12 and int—var2 equals 15,
>
> int—var1 **or** int—var2 equals 15

which is the same as

$$1100 \text{ or } 1111 = 1111$$

Note that **or** is used to set (switch on) bits in **int—var1** that are set in **int—var2**.

xor *Integer*

xor, for exclusive or, requires that the two operands be of Integer type. Each operand is converted to binary, and each bit in the left operand is logically **xor**ed with the corresponding bit in the right operand. The result is reconverted to Integer.

> If int—var1 equals 12 and int—var2 equals 15
> int—var1 **xor** int—var2 equals 3

which is the same as

$$1100 \text{ xor } 1111 = 0011$$

Note that **xor** is used to reverse the state of bits in **int—var1** that correspond to bits that are set in **int—var2**.

+ *Integer or Real*

If either operand is a Real type, the result will be Real; otherwise the result will be an Integer type. Note that Turbo Pascal does *not* check for integer overflow.

— Integer or Real

If either operand is a Real type, the result will be Real; otherwise the result will be an Integer type.

Logical Operators   Turbo supports four logical operators: **not**, **and**, **or**, and exclusive or, or **xor**. Table 2-5 lists the truth table for these operators.

not

The result of an expression using the **not** operator depends on the type of the operand. **not** reverses the truth of any Boolean variable. For example, if **inp—ok** equals TRUE, **not inp—ok** equals FALSE.

and

The only time the results of an **and** operation are TRUE is when both operands are TRUE. For example, if the Boolean variable **inp—ok** equals TRUE and the Boolean variable **port** equals FALSE, the statement **inp—ok and port** equals FALSE.

or

Again, both operands must be of the same Boolean type. If either operand is

Table 2-5.   Truth Table for **not, and, or, and xor**

First Value	Operator	Second Value	Result
TRUE	not	—	FALSE
FALSE	not	—	TRUE
TRUE	and	TRUE	TRUE
TRUE	and	FALSE	FALSE
FALSE	and	TRUE	FALSE
FALSE	and	FALSE	FALSE
TRUE	or	TRUE	TRUE
TRUE	or	FALSE	TRUE
FALSE	or	TRUE	TRUE
FALSE	or	FALSE	FALSE
TRUE	xor	TRUE	FALSE
TRUE	xor	FALSE	TRUE
FALSE	xor	TRUE	TRUE
FALSE	xor	FALSE	FALSE

TRUE and a logical **or** is performed, the result is TRUE. For example: if **inp—ok** is TRUE and **port** is TRUE, **inp—ok or port** is TRUE.

xor

One operand must be TRUE and the other FALSE to produce a value of TRUE. For example, if **inp—ok** is FALSE, and **port** is TRUE, **inp—ok xor port** is TRUE.

Relational Operators

Relational operators are used in conditional expressions, which will be fully discussed later, to compare scalar values. These operators always produce a Boolean result. The two values compared must be of the same type except that Real, Integer, and Byte values may be compared with each other; that is, a Real value may be compared to a Byte value and so forth.

Operator			Result
value1	=	*value2*	TRUE if both values are equal.
value1	<>	*value2*	TRUE if both values are not equal.
value1	<	*value2*	TRUE if *value1* less than *value2*.
value1	<=	*value2*	TRUE if *value1* less than or equal to *value2*.
value1	>	*value2*	TRUE if *value1* greater than *value2*.
value1	>=	*value2*	TRUE if *value1* greater than or equal to *value2*.

Statements

The statement part is where the logic of a program or subprogram is defined. It is here that data described by the preceding parts is manipulated to produce the result desired by the user of the program. Statements can be categorized as follows:

1. Assignment statements.
2. Compound statements.
3. Logic control statements.

Subprogram statements belong on the list, but they will be covered in detail in the next chapter.

In Pascal the semicolon is used primarily as a statement separator. As a general rule, each Pascal statement is followed by a semicolon, which separates it from subsequent statements. There are a few exceptions to this rule that will be discussed as the need arises.

Assignment Statements

An assignment statement consists of a variable (or function) identifier followed by the assignment operator (:=) followed by an expression. Here are some examples:

> item := 0;
>
> exit := FALSE;
>
> interest_rate := 12.5;
>
> payments := principle / payment_periods;

Of course, it makes no sense to assign a value to a constant. The primary thing to remember when using assignment statements is that the type of the result of the expression must be compatible with the type of the variable receiving that value. If it is not, you will get a type mismatch error when you attempt to compile the code.

Compound Statements

In addition to marking the start and finish of the statement part, **begin** (without a semicolon) and **end** (with a semicolon appended) form a statement pair that is used to combine any number of statements into a compound statement. A compound statement may be made up of all types of statements, including other compound statements. A compound statement may be used as the statement part of any logic control statement, as will be illustrated by the **begin-end** pair for the while statement. The following discussion on the **while** loop will illustrate the principle of compound statements.

Logic Control Statements

Table 2-6 summarizes the statements you may use to control the logic of your programs. Be sure to enter, compile, and run the example programs that are presented here. Experiment with them and spend as much time as you need to master the operation of these control structures.

The While Loop   The while loop executes one statement repeatedly until the condition of the loop evaluates to FALSE. The form of the while loop is

> **while** *condition* **do** *statement*₁

If *condition* is initially FALSE, *statement*₁ is never executed. Changing

Table 2-6. Turbo Pascal Logic Control Statements

Logic Control Statements		
Identifier	**Standard Pascal**	**Description**
while-do	Y	Conditional loop—test at top
repeat-until	Y	Conditional loop—test at bottom
for-do	Y	Predetermined loop—test at top
if-then-else	Y	Two-way branch—else part is optional
case-of-else	Y	Multi-way branch—else is optional
goto	Y	Transfer control to a labeled statement

*statement*₁ into a compound statement effectively changes the form to

$$\begin{aligned}
&\textbf{while } \textit{condition } \textbf{do}\\
&\quad \textbf{begin}\\
&\qquad \textit{statement}_1\\
&\qquad \textit{statement}_2\\
&\qquad\quad .\\
&\qquad\quad .\\
&\qquad\quad .\\
&\quad \textbf{end};
\end{aligned}$$

To get an idea of the operation of the **while** loop, enter and run the following program:

```
program Test_While_Loop;

  const SPACE      = #32;

  var   character,
        first_chr,
        last_chr   : Char;

  begin
    ClrScr;
    Write('Press a key to indicate first character to display. ==>');
    Read(Kbd,first_chr); WriteLn(first_chr);
    character := first_chr;
    Write('Press a key to indicate last character to display.  ==>');
    Read(Kbd,last_chr); WriteLn(last_chr);
    while (character <= last_chr) do
      begin
        Write(character,SPACE);
        character := Succ(character);
      end;
    WriteLn; WriteLn('End of program');
  end. { Test_While_Loop }
```

The program asks you to enter a character from the keyboard and then to enter a second character that follows the first alphabetically. These two characters serve as the lower and upper bounds of a range of characters that will be printed with the while loop. The while loop must test before a character has been printed to ensure that the upper boundary has not been exceeded. This is done in (**character <= last_chr**) condition, where **last_chr** is the upper bound and **character** is the last character printed. The variable **character** is initially assigned to the first character entered, the lower bound, but with each printing is reassigned to the next character in order. If the first character you entered is alphabetically greater than the second, (**character <= last_chr**) evaluates to FALSE and the body of the loop is never executed. Be sure you understand why the program ends after the last character has been displayed. Try changing the condition tested to (**character < last_chr**) and compare the results.

The Repeat-Until Loop   There are often situations when you need a loop that will always execute at least once. The repeat-until loop can be used in such cases because its condition test is not performed until the statement part has executed. The form of the repeat-until loop is

> **repeat**
>   *statement₁*;
>   *statement₂*;
>   .
>
>   .
>
>   .
>
> **until** *condition*;

It may appear that there are several statements between repeat and until; however, they are considered to make up a single compound statement even though the traditional begin and end markers are not required. To experiment with the following program, just modify the code you entered to test the while loop. Try the same experiments you did using the original version and notice the difference in the results.

```
program Test_Repeat_Until_Loop;

  const SPACE       = #32;

  var    character,
         first_chr,
         last_chr   : Char;
  begin
    ClrScr;
    Write('Press a key to indicate first character to display. ==>');
    Read(Kbd,first_chr); WriteLn(first_chr);
    character := first_chr;
    Write('Press a key to indicate last character to display.  ==>');
    Read(Kbd,last_chr); WriteLn(last_chr);
    repeat
      Write(character,SPACE);
      character := Succ(character);
    until (character > last_chr);
    WriteLn; WriteLn('End of program');
  end. { Test_Repeat_Until_Loop }
```

The For-Do Loop   The following program represents a third version of the loop test program using the for-do loop. The for-do loop is ideal for cases where the number of times the statement will execute is predetermined. The form of the for-do loop is

$$\textbf{for } counter := exp_1 \textbf{ to } exp_2 \textbf{ do } statement_1;$$

The form of a for-do loop with compound statement is

> **for** *counter* := *exp₁* **to** *exp₂* **do**
> **begin**
>   *statement₁*;
>   *statement₂*;
>   .
>   .
>   .
>   **end;**

exp_1 is the lower bound and exp_2 is the upper bound of the range for counting. *Counter*, which serves as a counter for the loop and is a variable that must be declared, is assigned to exp_1 when the loop is encountered and is then automatically incremented each time the loop is executed until *counter* equals exp_2, after which execution of the for-do loop halts.

A Pascal for-do loop counter variable may be of any scalar type except Real. The loop limits must be of a compatible type. You can, however, force the counter variable to be decremented by substituting **downto** for **to** when setting up the loop. You also need to be aware that you cannot force an early exit from the loop by modifying the counter variable. If you need to do that, a while or repeat-until loop should be used. The following listing represents a third version of the character print program. It is superior to the others since the program knows exactly the number of letters to print before executing the loop.

```
program Test_For_Do_Loop;

  const SPACE     = #32;

  var    character,
         first_chr,
         last_chr  : Char;

  begin
    ClrScr;
    Write('Press a key to indicate first character to display. ==>');
    Read(Kbd,first_chr); WriteLn(first_chr);
    Write('Press a key to indicate last character to display.  ==>');
    Read(Kbd,last_chr); WriteLn(last_chr);
    for character := first_chr to last_chr do
      Write(character,SPACE);
    WriteLn;
    WriteLn('End of program');
  end. { Test_For_Do_Loop }
```

If-Then-Else   The if-then-else statement executes one, many, or no state-ments, depending upon the evaluation of the stated *condition*. The general form of the if statement is

if *condition* **then** *statement*₁ **[else** *statement*₂**]**

If *condition* is true, *statement*₁ is executed, otherwise *statement*₂ is executed. The **else** *statement*₂ part is optional, and if it is not included, control passes to the next program statement if *condition* is false. (In this book, optional parts of a statement will be surrounded by the left ([) and right (]) brackets — do *not* enter them with the statement.) The statement parts can be simple, com-pound, logic control, or subprogram statements. The following program illustrates some of these options:

```
program Test_If_Then_Else;

   const SPACE        = #32;
         TILDE        = #126;
         ESC          = #27;

         DIM          = 'D';
         BRIGHT       = 'B';

   var   character,
         attribute  : Char;

   begin
     ClrScr;
     WriteLn; WriteLn('Press <ESC> to Quit.');
     WriteLn('Press <B> to display bright characters.');
     WriteLn('Press <D> to display dim characters.');
     repeat
       NormVideo;
       WriteLn; Write('Enter your selection. ==> ');
       Read(Kbd,attribute);
       if (attribute = BRIGHT) or (attribute = DIM) then
         begin
           WriteLn(attribute);
           if (attribute = BRIGHT) then
             Normvideo
           else
             Lowvideo;
           for character := SPACE to TILDE do
             Write(character,SPACE);
           WriteLn;
         end;
     until (attribute = ESC);
     WriteLn('End of program');
   end. { Test_If_Then_Else Statement }
```

The first if statement does not have an optional else part. Its statement part is a compound statement. Within that compound statement is the second if statement, which does have an else part. Both statement parts of the second if statement use predefined Turbo Pascal procedures that control the video attributes.

Note that an if statement with an else is considered to be one statement. For that reason, it has only one semicolon as a statement separator. That is why there is no semicolon following the statement preceding the reserved word **else**. After entering and testing the code in the preceding program as shown, replace the Norm Video subprogram statement before the else with the following compound statement:

```
begin
    NormVideo;
    WriteLn;
end;
```

Don't include the last semicolon. If you do, you will get an error when you try to compile the code. The point is that regardless of the statement, a statement before **else** must not be followed by a semicolon.

You should also beware of situations involving nested if statements. That's where the statement part of an if statement is another if statement.

```
if some__condition then
if another__condition then
project1__cost
else
project2__cost;
```

A quick review of this code would lead you to believe that if **some__ condition** is FALSE, **project2__cost** statement will be executed. Actually **project2__cost** will execute if **some__condition** is TRUE and **another__ condition** is FALSE. This is because the else part of an if statement is always associated with the nearest **if**. The problem can be solved by inserting a dormant, or dummy, **else** to match the second **if**.

```
if some__condition then
    if another__condition then
        project1__cost
    else
else
    project2__cost;
```

Better yet, rearrange the logic to avoid the problem. For example,

```
if (not some__condition) then
    project2__cost
else
    if another__condition then
        project1__cost;
```

The Case Statement   The form of a case statement is

> **case**   *selector* **of**
>
>> *constant*$_1$: *statement*$_1$;
>>
>> *constant*$_2$: *statement*$_2$;
>>
>> .
>>
>> .
>>
>> .
>>
>> *constant*$_n$: *statement*$_n$;
>
> **else**
>
>> *statement*;

When a case statement is executed, the value of the *selector*, which is a variable and may be any scalar type except Real, is used to determine which, if any, of the case statements are executed. The constants associated with the statements must be of the same type as the *selector* variable. Did you notice that the last test program required you to enter an uppercase B or D to get past the first if test? The following program illustrates how a case statement can be used to permit both upper- and lowercase as valid entries.

```
program Test_Case_Statement;
  const ESC    = #27;
  var   menu,
        inchr  : Char;
  begin
    ClrScr;
    repeat
      WriteLn; WriteLn('Press <ESC> to Quit.'); WriteLn;
      WriteLn('Press <A> for Menu A, <B> for menu B or <C> for menu C.');
      WriteLn; Write('Enter your selection. ==> ');
      Read(Kbd,menu);
      if (menu = ESC) then
         WriteLn('End of program')
      else
        case menu of
          'A','a'  : begin
                       ClrScr;
                       WriteLn('Menu A - Press any key.');
                       Read(Kbd,inchr);
                     end;
          'B','b'  : begin;
                       ClrScr;
                       WriteLn('Menu B - Press any key');
                       Read(Kbd,inchr);
                     end;
          'C','c'  : begin;
                       ClrScr;
                       WriteLn('Menu C - Press any key');
                       Read(Kbd,inchr);
                     end;
          else       WriteLn(menu,' is not a valid menu. Try again.');
        end; {Case}
    until (menu = ESC);
  end. { Test_Case_Statement }
```

/ = OR

As illustrated in the example, these constants may be a list of constants, separated by commas. A range of values may be indicated by two constants separated by two periods. For example, 'A'..'Z' or '0..31' could be used to select any value in the indicated range.

If the value of the *selector* variable does not match any of the constants listed, the statement following the case statement is executed. If an optional **else** is included, the statement following else is executed when no match is found in the constant list. This differs significantly from standard Pascal. Standard Pascal does not provide an else option. In fact, if the value being evaluated doesn't match one of the listed constants, you get an error.

Occasionally you may hear the case statement maligned as inefficient compared to a series of if-then-else statements. In some versions of Pascal this may be true. The Turbo Pascal implementation of the case statement, however, is actually more efficient than if-then-else when selecting from more than two options. Even when the type of the selector variable is Integer and only eight random values are used as selectors, a case of selection will be measurably faster and generate no more code than an if-then-else selection. Feel free to use the case statement as often as needed to simplify or clarify your code.

The Goto Statement Unlike the other statements in this group, **goto** is not at all vital to Pascal programming. With good planning and design, a program should never use this statement. The only possible exception is when a goto statement is used to simplify the handling of an unusual situation (usually an error condition). Even in these cases the statement is not necessary, but it may simplify the logic enough to justify its use. If you do use a goto statement, its destination must be marked by a label that precedes the statement to be executed following the transfer of control. The following program provides an example:

```
program Test_GoTo_Statement;

  label start_loop, exit;

  const SPACE      = #32;
        TILDE      = #126;
        ESC        = #27;

        DIM        = 'D';
        BRIGHT     = 'B';

  var   character,
        attribute  : Char;

  begin
    ClrScr;
    WriteLn; WriteLn('Press <ESC> to Quit.');
    WriteLn('Press <B> to display bright characters.');
    WriteLn('Press <D> to display dim characters.');
    start_loop: NormVideo;
      WriteLn; Write('Enter your selection. ==> ');
      Read(Kbd,attribute);
```

```
      if (attribute = ESC) then
        goto exit;
      WriteLn(attribute);
      if (attribute = BRIGHT) then
        Normvideo
      else
        Lowvideo;
      if (attribute = BRIGHT) or (attribute = DIM) then
        for character := SPACE to TILDE do
          Write(character,SPACE);
      WriteLn;
    goto start_loop;
    exit: WriteLn('End of program');
end. { Test_GoTo_Statement }
```

Coding Conventions

The Pascal language definition does not specify a format for the source code. However, to make your source code readable and easy to maintain, you should use a format that emphasizes the block structure of the language and the logic flow within the statement part of a program or subprogram.

In this book, upper- and lowercase is used to help distinguish between the various Pascal identifiers. Notice that the underline character has been used freely to make the source code more readable.

- Constants are all uppercase.

- Type names will be initial uppercase. For example, Scrn, Str255, and Special _ Char.

- Variables and typed constants are all lowercase.

- Control statements are all lowercase.

- Operators are all lowercase (for example, **and, xor,** and **or**).

These same rules apply to all references in the text.

The apparent ambiguities are clarified by context and the way that the source code is indented. For example:

1. Type names always appear in the type definitions part or as part of a variable definition.

2. Operators are always part of an expression.

3. Control statements will be obvious due to the way that the code is formatted.

Indenting

A statement that is within a control statement will be placed on the line below the control statement and will be indented two spaces. If the control statement is begin-end or repeat-until, the last part of the control statement will be aligned with the first part. Because there are so many ways that control statements are used, the listings themselves make the best examples.

Multiple Statements per Line

Generally, the rule is one statement per line. An exception is made for simple and short statements that are logically related. For example,

GoToXY(1,23); ClrEol;

Those two statements clear line 23 by first moving the cursor to column 23, row 1, which is one logical function and may appear as shown.

Comments

Comments are used within a program to document the operation of the program, but they do not affect the operation. By including comments in your program, you or other programmers can read it months later and understand its operation. Use comments liberally.

Turbo Pascal provides two ways to include comments in source code files. Comments may be enclosed in braces { } or this pair of characters (* *). A comment marked using one method may be included within a comment marked using the other method. For example:

(* This is a comment. All text will be ignored until a matching end of comment mark is encountered.

{ This is also a comment that is contained within the larger comment. It terminates with a matching brace like this. } Comments may appear anywhere in your source code except inside quote marks or between the parts of an expression. Here is the end of this comment. *)

THREE

Turbo Pascal
Advanced Data Structures

It is possible to write Pascal programs using only predefined types. However, the power and elegance of the Turbo Pascal language cannot be exploited without using types, which you define to suit your applications.

User-Defined Types

Before defining data types, a review of the purpose of Pascal types is in order. Your objective, of course, is to make your programs easier to understand both for you and for other programmers that may have to maintain them. As you will see, the ability to describe the data to suit the program greatly simplifies the development of complex applications.

Remember that a type definition has no effect on a program until a variable (or function) is declared using the defined type. When such a variable is declared, the type definition is used by the compiler to determine how much memory space to reserve for that data item and to establish some limits for values that may be assigned to it. The compiler is in a position to detect errors in your program that could not otherwise be detected. To take full advantage of this assistance from the compiler, you must give serious consideration to data types during the design phase of program development.

For a simple example, let's say a furniture inventory program oversees the number of chairs in a warehouse. The variable **chairs** contains the number of chairs in stock, which is never to exceed 50. Normally **chairs** would be declared as type Integer, affording it the possibility of exceeding the limit. But in Pascal it is possible to define a type, name it Limited with a range from, say, 0 to 50, and then declare **chairs** to be of type Limited. If **chairs** should exceed 50, the compiler would give an error and the program would halt. Terminating program execution through type definitions may not be the best way to handle a simple overrun error; however, defining types allows you to place stricter controls over the range of values a variable can assume.

Simple Types

Types can be categorized as *simple* (also called *scalar*), *structured*, and *pointer*. The predefined types discussed in the last chapter were all simple types. There are two ways that you can define your own simple types. One way is to create a list of identifiers that will form the ordered set of values that make up the type being defined. Just as FALSE and TRUE compose the set of values that define Boolean type, you can define a type composed of values of your choice and then declare variables of that type as illustrated here:

```
type Month_Name = (JAN,FEB,MAR,APR,MAY,JUN,JUL,
                    AUG,SEP,OCT,NOV,DEC);

var month,
    birth_month : Month_Name;
```

The type definition part is introduced by the reserved word **type** followed by one or more type definitions. Each definition consists of an identifier, an equal sign, and a description of the type being defined. The format of the description depends on what kind of type you are defining. The Month_Name type is called an enumerated type. The format used to describe an enumerated type is a list of identifiers separated by commas and enclosed in parentheses. A semicolon terminates the definition. The list of identifiers becomes the list of literal constants for the newly defined enumerated type. When a type is defined in the type definition part as illustrated here, it is called a *named type*.

Types may also be defined at the time a variable is declared. When that is done, the type definition replaces the type identifier in the variable declaration. This example shows how it's done:

```
var month,
    birth_month : (JAN,FEB,MAR,APR,MAY,JUN,JUL,AUG,
                   SEP,OCT,NOV,DEC);
```

When you define a type this way, it is formally known as a *new type*. You may prefer to think of it as a *nameless* type. Using nameless types is convenient in many cases, but you pay for that convenience by limiting the things you can do with variables declared using nameless types. You will recall that one of the reasons variables have types is to prevent assignments involving mismatched types. The limitation of variables declared with nameless types is that they are only compatible with other variables defined in the same variable definition statement. For example, **month** and **birth_month** are

Table 3-1.   Predefined Ordinal Functions

Identifier	Function or Procedure	Standard	Turbo	Description
Chr	F	Y	Y	Converts Integer or Byte parameter to equivalent ASCII character
Odd	F	Y	Y	TRUE if ordinal value is odd
Ord	F	Y	Y	Returns ordinal value of parameter
Pred	F	Y	Y	Returns decremented value of parameter
Succ	F	Y	Y	Returns incremented value of parameter

compatible because they are defined together. However, if another variable were declared using an identical type description, it would not be compatible with them. At this point that may not seem to pose much of a problem, but when subprograms are discussed, you will find that it can be a serious limitation.

Like the predefined scalar types, enumerated types are *ordinal.* In other words, their literal constants form a series that can be referred to as the first value, the second value, and so forth. Pascal provides a set of predefined ordinal functions that are very useful in working with ordinal types. Table 3-1 outlines these functions and describes the result returned by each one. These functions will be used in the examples in this chapter.

Using enumerated types along with the ordinal functions permits you to include easy-to-read statements such as these in your programs:

```
if (month = APR) then
    Write('Tax time again???');
Write('It is month #',Ord(month) + 1);
if (month < DEC) then
    month := Succ(month)
else
    month := JAN;
```

Here are some things you need to be aware of when you use enumerated types.

- The ordinal value of the first literal constant of an enumerated type is 0. In other words, Ord(JAN) equals 0.

- Variables that have an enumerated type cannot be input or output using the predefined procedures Read and Write. If you use statements like

  Read(month);
  or
  Write('This month is ',month);

  you will be advised by the compiler that **I/O not allowed**.

- You may define a type that is a *subrange* of an enumerated type. For example, the following is a valid type definition, assuming the prior definition of a type like Month __Names:

  type Spring__Months = MAR..MAY;

Subrange Types

Defining a subrange is the second method of creating a simple type. A subrange begins with a literal constant from a previously defined scalar type followed by two periods and a second constant of the same type. To define Limited from the hypothetical warehouse, you could define it as a subrange of the Integer type like this:

type Limited = 0..50;

Structured Types

You can organize data of the simple types discussed so far into more complex types known in Pascal as *structured types*. Structured types, like simple types, provide information used by the compiler in allocating storage and catching errors. However, they play an even greater role in clarifying how the data they describe is used by your program. When you declare a variable as a structured type, you may manipulate the entire structure or you may work with the individual data items that make up the structure. This provides tremendous flexibility in working with groups of related data items. Turbo Pascal offers five basic structures—array, string, record, file, and set. In the following pages, each of these structures will be discussed and illustrated using code segments and short programs.

Arrays

The array is the best known of the type structures because it is widely used in other languages. An *array* is an assembled, fixed number of data items, each of the same type, which is known as the *base* type of the array. The individual data items that make up the structure are called *elements* of the array. You may also see the data items, referred to as *components*, and the base type as the *component* type. The terms are interchangeable. In this book, element and base type will be used consistently.

To define an array type structure, you must specify both the base type and the number of elements. The base type of an array may be any of the simple types as well as any of the structured types mentioned previously. That means you can define an array of arrays. The resulting structure is called a *multidimensional array*. The only limit imposed on the number dimensions permitted by Turbo Pascal is the amount of memory available for data. It's unlikely that an application will exceed a three-dimensional array. The number of elements in an array is determined by its *index* and must be specified when the array type is defined.

The array index, itself a type, must appear between brackets in the description part of the type definition following the reserved word array. An index may be any scalar type, including predefined, subrange, or enumerated types. The index may be a previously defined named type or it may be defined on the spot as a nameless type. Here is an example using named subrange types.

```
const   SCREEN_WIDTH      =  80;
        SCREEN_LENGTH     =  24;

type    Column_Range      =  1..SCREEN_WIDTH;
        Line_Range        =  1..SCREEN_LENGTH;
        Video_Line        =  array[Column_Range] of Char;
        Video_Buffer      =  array[Line_Range] of Video_Line;

var     vid_line,
        line_buf          :  Video_Line;
        vid_scrn,
        vid_buf           :  Video_Buffer;
        column            :  Column_Range;
        line              :  Line_Range;
```

This series of definitions and declarations defines two array type structures, Video_Line and Video_Buffer. In both cases, the named type that is used to define the index, Column_Range and Line_Range, is also used to declare the variables, **column** and **line**, that will be used to access individual elements of the array. This assures complete compatibility under all circumstances.

The type structures defined here could be used to store and manipulate information that is to appear on a video monitor capable of displaying 24 lines of 80 characters. There are three levels at which you can now easily access that information. At the most elementary level, your program can access individual characters using statements such as these:

```
column := 3;
vid_line[column] := 'A';
```

The variable **vid_line** is an array of 80 characters. The statement assigns the character A to the third element of **vid_line**. Note that the base type of array **vid_line** is Char, and only Char type values can be assigned to it. The index type of array **vid_line**, as well as the variable **column**, is Column_Range. This means that **column** must always contain an integer value in the range 1 to 80 or an error will result. Finally, note that the *index value*, which may be a variable, a constant, or an expression, appears between square brackets following the array type variable.

You can transfer information from an array to a variable like this:

line_buf := vid_scrn[line];

This statement assigns each of the 80 Char type elements of **vid_scrn[line]** to the **line_buf** array.

At the highest level you can copy a whole screen full of data at once by assigning the entire two-dimensional array **vid_buf** to the two-dimensional array **vid_scrn**:

vid_scrn := vid_buf;

With one simple statement, which will execute very quickly, you have transferred 1920 characters of information. Imagine how convenient it would be if **vid_scrn** could be located in the section of memory used to store the data that appears on the video screen. If you are using a system that uses addressable memory to store video images as text, Turbo Pascal makes it possible for you to use structures such as this to access the video screen.

You probably noticed that **vid_buf** is a two-dimensional array. That means that to access a specific character, you must specify two index values. Turbo Pascal allows you to do that two different ways with the same result. If **column** equals 14 and **line** equals 10, either of the following statements will display the fourteenth character from the tenth line of the **vid_buf** array:

Write(vid_buf[line][column]);
Write(vid_buf[line,column]);

Using either method, the sequence of the index values must match the sequence in which the dimensions were defined. In this example the first index references the line and the second denotes the column.

Because Pascal is so flexible as to the way types are defined and variables declared, it would be impossible to illustrate all of the combinations in the space available. There are many alternative ways to define the type structures and declare the variables used in the preceding example. You should do some experimenting and develop a style that suits you and then stick with it. However, avoid nameless types since they can cause type compatibility problems.

Strings

Using the **vid＿buf** variable as declared and assuming it has been initialized with data, you can output a full line of characters with the WriteLn statement.

WriteLn(vid＿buf[3]);

As a rule, array elements (and other data items that are part of type structures) must be input and output one at a time. The exception is made for arrays of type Char. This is as close as standard Pascal comes to admitting to the existence of character strings. While it is true that character strings are nothing more than character arrays, they are so common that it is desirable to work with a programming language that specifically provides for their processing. Fortunately Turbo Pascal allows for the definition of String types and provides a complete set of predefined subprograms to use when working with variables of those types. Those subprograms will be discussed individually in Chapter 4.

The reserved word String is used in Turbo Pascal to define structured types. Here, some String types are defined and variables declared using String types:

type	Short＿String	=	String[5];
	Long＿String	=	String[80];
	Any＿String	=	String[255];
	Str＿20	=	String[20];
var	title	:	Short＿String;
	first＿name,		
	last＿name	:	Str＿20;
	remark	:	Long＿String;
	description	:	Any＿String;

The integer constant enclosed in brackets is a required part of the String description. The value of that constant may range from 1 to 255. Its purpose is to define the maximum length of the string that determines how much storage is allocated for the variables. Turbo String type variables differ from standard array of Char type variables as follows:

- A standard array of Char type variables is only compatible with variables of the same type. On the other hand, Turbo String variables may be assigned to String types, regardless of their defined length or type identifier. When copying a string, if the source string is longer than the destination string, the destination string will contain a truncated version of the source after the assignment. When you output a Turbo string using Write, the number of characters output is determined by its current length, not the defined length.

    String arrays are flexible, and an array of Char type variables may be assigned to String type variables. That is to say, using variables declared earlier in the discussion.

    If the following statements are executed:

    ```
    remark := vid_line;
    title := line_buff;
    description := vid_scrn[line];
    first_name := vid_buf[line, column];
    ```

    remark will have a length of 80 and contain all 80 characters that compose the **vid_line** array;

    title will contain the first five characters of the **line_buf** array;

    description will contain the complete array **vid_scrn[line]**;

    first_name will contain the character in **vid_buf[line, column]**.

- The space allocated for a Turbo string type variable is one byte greater than the length indicated in its type definition. The additional byte is used to hold the current length of the string. This length byte is contained in element zero of the character array that holds a Turbo string. Using the string variable **remarks**, as declared previously, the following statements:

    ```
    remark := 'This is a remarkable concept ';
    Write(remark,Ord(remarks[0]));
    ```

    would produce the output

    This is a remarkable concept 29

    Another interesting feature is the Ord function, which is used to convert the Char type value at element zero of a Turbo string to an integer value. There is also a function that performs the opposite of Ord by converting an integer value to its corresponding ASCII character value. It is the Chr function. This opens up some interesting possibilities in the realm of string manipulation. For example,

```
        remark[0]:=Chr(17);
        Write(remark, Ord(remark[0]));
```

will produce the output

This is a remark 17

Records

The record type structure allows you to create a type that is composed of data items of various types, as opposed to the array, which is made up of elements of the same type. The individual data items in a record are known as fields and they are declared as variables when the record type is defined. Each field may be of any type except the file type, which will be discussed next. Here is a simple record definition:

```
type Name_Record =       record
                   surname        :    String[15];
                   first_name     :    String[15];
                   title          :    String[5];
                 end;
```

The description part of a record type definition begins with the reserved word **record**, which is followed by a series of field variable declarations such as **surname**, **first name**, and **title**. The reserved word **end** followed by a semicolon terminates the record definition. As with all type definitions, this one has no effect until a variable is declared to be of this type, so declare the variable **name** to be of record type Name_Record.

```
        var name : Name:_Record
```

When assigning or accessing a record variable, you must include the variable name followed by a period and then the field name. For example,

```
        name.first_name:='Bullwinkle':
```

will assign Bullwinkle to the field **first_name** in the record variable **name**.

If there is a series of fields from a record variable that will be repeatedly accessed, writing the record variable for each field can be tedious.

You can use the **with** statement to solve this problem. The form is

        with *variable_record* **do** *statement*₁;

The reserved word **with** followed by one or more record variables, the reserved word **do**, and one statement can reference a field without providing the variable record's name. To be of much use, statement₁ should be a compound statement, thus changing the form to

> **with** *record variable* **do**
> **begin**
>   *statement₁*;
>   *statement₂*;
>   **end**;

As an example, the **with** statement replaces the record variable in the following assignment statements:

> **with** name **do**
> **begin**
>   firstname := 'Bullwinkle';
>   surname := 'Moose';
>   **end**;

The following listing illustrates two ways that a field variable in a record variable may be accessed:

```
program Illustrate_Record_Type;

  const SPACE = #32;

  type Name_Record = record
                        surname    : string[15];
                        first_name : string[15];
                        title      : string[5];
                     end;

  var name      : Name_Record;
      full_name : string[35];

  begin
    name.surname := 'Moose';
    name.first_name := 'Bullwinkle';
    name.title := 'Sir';
    full_name := '';
    with name do
    begin
      if Length(title) > 0 then
        full_name := title + SPACE;
      full_name := full_name + first_name + SPACE
                   + surname;
      WriteLn(full_name);
      full_name := surname + ', ';
      if Length(title) > 0 then
        full_name := full_name + title + SPACE;
      full_name := full_name + first_name;
      WriteLn(full_name);
    end; {with}
  end. { Illustrate_Record_Type }
```

The with statement does not restrict you from referencing record fields from a different record variable (although you must include the record variable identifier), nor does it restrict you from using any other statements.

Variant Rules   The record types illustrated thus far have been *fixed* records, which is to say that the fields are fixed by the type definition. The alternative is called a *variant record*. Its purpose is to save storage by allowing different data to occupy the same area in memory at different times. If, for example, you needed to create a mailing list that includes both individuals and businesses, a variant record variable could be used.

```
program Illustrate_Variant_Record;

   const SPACE = #32;

   type Name_Record = record
                        surname    : string[15];
                        first_name : string[15];
                        title      : string[5];
                      end;
   type  Name_Address = record
                          address1 : string[40];
                          address2 : string[40];
                          city     : string[20];
                          state    : string[2];
                          zip      : record
                                       zip5 : string[5];
                                       zip4 : string[4];
                                     end;
               case business : Boolean of
                       TRUE  : (name     : Name_Record);
                       FALSE : (bus_name : string[40];
                                attn     : string[40]);
                      end;

   var list_data : Name_Address;
```

The record type defined here has both a fixed part and a variant part. The fixed part ends at the reserved word **case**. In this example, the identifier **business** is a Boolean type variable. It could, however, be a variable of any ordinal type. It is called the *tag field* variable. The tag field serves to indicate which data items are stored in the variant part of the record. In this example if **business** is TRUE, the variant part should contain the name of an individual stored in a Name—Record type structure. When **business** has a value of FALSE, you should find the name of a business and an attention line in that same area. The term should is used because it is up to the programmer to see that the tag field accurately reflects the contents of the variant part of the record. By using a variant record you avoid having to allocate storage for both an individual's name and the business information. Each record will contain one or the other as indicated by the tag field variable.

Since the type of the tag field is Boolean in this example, there are only two possible kinds of data that could be indicated. By using other ordinal types you may reuse the same storage for several different kinds of information; however, every value that makes up the type of the tag field must be included in the list of constants that follows the tag field declaration. As a result of this requirement, tag field variables are usually of subrange or enumerated types. The field variable declarations following each constant must be enclosed in parentheses as illustrated.

Note that the semicolon following the last field declaration for each constant must be placed after the closing parenthesis. Finally, it is permissible to indicate that the value represented by a constant will not be used by replacing its field declarations with a pair of empty parentheses.

There are two kinds of variant record types. One contains both a fixed part and a variant part and is called a *discriminated union*. The other contains only a variant part and is called a *free union*. Here is an example of a free union variant record type definition:

```
type Item_Ordered=(SPECIAL,BURGER_PLATE,FISH_PLATE,CHILDS_PLATE);


    Order_Record = record
            case Item_Ordered of
            SPECIAL          :    (chicken,
                                   fries1,
                                   drink1    :    Real
                                   discount  :    Real);
            BURGER_PLATE  :       (burger,
                                   fries2,
                                   drink2    :    Real);
            FISH_PLATE    :       ( );
            CHILDS_PLATE  :       (nuggets,
                                   chips,
                                   drink3    :    Real;
                                   age       :    Byte);

            end;
    var    order : Order_Record;
```

Besides not having a fixed part, a free union is different in that the case selection is no longer controlled by a tag field variable. It is controlled by a type definition. How then, you may wonder, can you tell what kind of data is in the record. In theory it is determined by the most recent assignment statement affecting the record. For example, following this statement:

```
order.nuggets := 1.39;
```

it is presumed that CHILDS_PLATE data occupies the record. That is why the field identifiers following each constant must be unique (**fries1** and **fries2**). Turbo Pascal and many other Pascal compilers do not support this theory, however. Therefore, it is up to you, as the programmer, to keep track of what kind of data occupies the record at a given time.

If you are new to Pascal and this seems a bit confusing, don't be too concerned. One of the primary uses of free unions in standard Pascal is to circumvent its strict typing restrictions by overlaying one type of data with another. As you will see in Chapter 7, the absolute directive offers an easier way to accomplish the same objective.

Before ending the discussion of records, here is a review of the things you should be aware of when using them.

1. A record variable is composed of a group of field variables that must be declared when the record type is defined.

2. The field variables may be of any type except file.

3. Field identifiers are unique from other identical identifiers that appear outside the record definition. Field identifiers within a record may not be identical, including those in the variant part, if any.

4. Field variables may be accessed by using a combination of the record variable identifier and the field identifier, or by using the with statement.

5. A record may contain just a fixed part, a fixed part and a variant part, or just a variant part. If both parts are present, the fixed part must precede the variant part.

6. When a variable is declared as a variant record type, storage will be allocated to store the field variables for the variant field list requiring the most space. For example, a variable of the Name—Address type would be allotted 82 bytes of storage for its variant part. That is the space required to store the field list consisting of **bus—name** and **attn**. The field list for the FALSE case requires only 38 bytes for its single Name—Record type field. In this example, the space saved by using variant records is 38 bytes per record, assuming that the information stored in the tag field would be needed in either case.

7. It is up to you to see that the values present in the variant part agree with value of the tag field. For example, if the tag field **business** has a value of FALSE, the field variables **bus—name** and **attn** should contain the name of a business and an attention line. Under those circumstances, if you try to access the variable **list—data.name.last—name**, you will be accessing the first part of the business name. This will produce unpredictable results because of the different string lengths involved. Incidentally, doing things like that on purpose is how standard Pascal programmers get around some of the typing restrictions on systems that don't check for such mischief.

8. The case structure defining the variant part of a record must include field variable declarations (a field list) for every constant of the tag type. The definition may indicate an unused value by declaring an empty field list, which is denoted by a pair of parentheses with nothing between them.

9. If a record has both a fixed part and a variant part, the variant tag type is determined by the type of a field variable called the tag field. Such a record is called a discriminated union. If a record has only a variant part, the tag type is specified by a type identifier and the record is known as a free union.

Files

The file type represents an area where Turbo Pascal goes far beyond standard Pascal and even discards some of the less efficient procedures. The power and flexibility of the Turbo implementation will become apparent during the following examination of this unique structure.

Programming applications often need to store large volumes of related data. Loan records for an amortization program or patients' transaction records in a medical billing system are examples of such data. It is easy to see that information pertaining to an individual borrower or to one patient's visit could be defined using the record type structure discussed earlier. The problem is that a record type variable ceases to exist when the program is terminated.

What is needed is a data type that exists independently of any particular program and that may be accessed by other programs as needed. The *file type* does just that. In addition, the size of a file type variable doesn't have to be declared in advance. In other words you don't have to tell the compiler how many borrowers there will be or how many patients' transactions to make room for. Actually, your programs will probably have to address these matters because of the limitations imposed by the amount of external storage space available, but there is no limitation imposed by the type itself.

Using the Name—Address type, here are two ways to declare a file type variable. Using a named type:

> **type** Name—File = **file of** Name—Address;
> **var** name—list : Name—File;

or using a nameless or new-type:

> **var** name—list : **file of** Name—Address;

In either case you've advised the compiler that you'll be accessing some external data that is composed of one or more data items of the Name—Address type. File type variables are often composed of record type data items, but they do not have to be. The data items that make up a file are known as components. They may be of any type except file type. Therefore, you are free to make declarations such as

> **var** annuity—data : **file of array**[0..75] of Real;

In this example each component of the file variable **annuity—data** will be an array of 76 Real numbers.

One of the primary uses for file variables is to permit data to be transferred to and from disk files. As will be demonstrated, this is done using the same Read and Write procedures you have used to get data from the keyboard and display it on the video monitor. However, before a file variable can be used at all there is some housekeeping along with some terminology that must be taken care of.

External Devices

What is an external device? Usually the device is a magnetic disk, but it could be any device that has been *interfaced* to your computer system, which includes the printer and console. The term interface refers to the hardware and software that make it possible for your programs to exchange data with an external device. The device itself is then physically connected to the computer with wires, cables, or other connectors. Once the external device is connected to the computer, special software is used to arrange proper communications between the two.

One reason for programming in a high-level language like Pascal is to avoid worrying about the system on which the program will run. The reason you are spared this concern is that the developers of the language have taken care of these details for you. As a result you can concentrate on your program and let the programming language control the system. You have probably heard the term *application program* associated with accounting systems, mailing list programs, and so forth; programs that directly control the hardware (I/O drivers and operating systems, for example) are called *system programs*. Turbo Pascal provides a number of predefined procedures and functions that you may use to allow your application program to communicate with external files and devices without being concerned with the details of the system interface. These subprograms are outlined in Table 3-2. Some of them will be used in the file-related examples to follow.

The following statements are needed to create a new disk file containing Name—Address type data items as defined earlier:

Assign (list—file, 'LIST.DAT');

Using the predefined Assign procedure links the file variable **list—file** to a physical disk file named LIST.DAT. Naming conventions are determined by your operating system, and you should consult your operating system manual for details. After this Assign statement executes, any reference to **list—file** is actually a reference to the LIST.DAT disk file. Note that while this procedure is commonly available, it is not required in standard Pascal.

A call to the Rewrite procedure creates a new disk file that has the name that is now associated with its file variable parameter. For example,

Table 3-2.   File and Device I/O Subprograms

Identifier	Function or Procedure	Standard	Turbo	Description
Assign	P	N	Y	Associate file name with file variable
BlockRead	P	N	Y	Untyped transfer from disk to memory
BlockWrite	P	N	Y	Untyped transfer from memory to disk
Chain	P	N	Y	Load and execute Turbo .CHN file
Close	P	N	Y	Exit housekeeping on external file
Eof	F	Y	Y	TRUE if file pointer at end of file
EoLn	F	Y	Y	TRUE if Text file at end of line
Erase	P	N	Y	Remove external file from directory
Execute	P	N	Y	Load and execute a .COM file
FilePos	F	N	Y	Returns position of file pointer
FileSize	F	N	Y	Returns size of non-Text file
Flush	P	N	Y	Forces sector buffer out to disk
Get	P	Y	N	Low level input; not needed in Turbo
LongFilePos	F	N	Y	Returns file pointer positions > 32K
LongFileSize	F	N	Y	Returns non-Text file size > 32K
LongSeek	P	N	Y	Positions file pointer in files > 32K
Put	P	Y	N	Low-level output; not needed in Turbo

Table 3-2. File and Device I/O Subprograms (*continued*)

Identifier	Function or Procedure	Standard	Turbo	Description
Read *and* Read	Ln P	Y	Y	Input data from external file or device
Rename	P	N	Y	Change filespec of external disk file
Reset	P	Y	Y	Open existing external disk file
Rewrite	P	Y	Y	Create and open new external disk file
Seek	P	N	Y	Position file pointer in non-Text file
Write *and* Write Ln	P	Y	Y	Output data to external file or device

> Rewrite(list_file);

In this case the new file will be on the currently logged drive and will be named LIST.DAT. Note that if a drive specifier, directory path, or both are included in the file name string, the file will be created on the drive and in the directory indicated. (Directory paths are supported only on systems running MS-DOS 2.0 or later.) In any case, the newly created file will be empty and accessible.

Warning: If you use this procedure to create a file with the name of a file that already exists, the old file will be lost.

After a Rewrite call, the file pointer will point to file component 0 (the first component), and the Eof(**list_file**) function, which indicates when a pointer is at the end of a file, will return TRUE. You can request the value of the pointer using the FilePos function and reposition it using the Seek procedure. Keep in mind that the first component of a file is 0.

If the file to be accessed already exists and you do not want to lose its contents, the Reset procedure should be used in place of the Rewrite procedure. Here is an example:

Reset(list—file);

When Reset is used to prepare a disk file for access, it is assumed that the file already exists. If not, an I/O error will result; otherwise the file is made ready for access and the file pointer is set to 0. Since it is possible for a disk file to exist and yet contain no data, the Eof(**list—file**) function may return TRUE or FALSE.

Now you know everything necessary to gain access to an external file. The listing that follows presents a complete program that

1. Creates a name and address file on disk.

2. Initializes a file variable with appropriate information.

3. Writes that variable to the disk file.

4. Closes the disk file.

5. Reopens the file using the Reset procedure.

6. Reads the information from the disk file.

7. Displays the information on the video monitor.

8. Closes the disk file and erases it.

```
program Illustrate_File_Handling;

  const SPACE    = #32;

  type Name_Record = record
                       surname    : string[15];
                       first_name : string[15];
                       title      : string[5];
                     end;

  type  Name_Address = record
                         address1 : string[40];
                         address2 : string[40];
                         city     : string[20];
                         state    : string[2];
                         zip      : record
                                      zip5 : string[5];
                                      zip4 : string[4];
                                    end;
                       case business : Boolean of
                            TRUE   : (name     : Name_Record);
                            FALSE  : (bus_name : string[40];
                                      attn     : string[40]);
                       end;

  var list_data : Name_Address;
      list_file : file of Name_Address;
      inchr     : Char;

  begin { Illustrate_File_Handling }
    ClrScr; WriteLn('One moment please...');
    Assign(list_file,'LIST.DAT');
    Rewrite(list_file);
```

```
with list_data, list_data.zip, list_data.name do
begin
   address1 := '123 Main Street';
   address2 := 'P.O. Drawer DISNEY';
   city := 'Middleton';
   state := 'CA';
   zip5 := '91005';
   zip4 := '3476';
   business := FALSE;
   surname := 'Duck';
   first_name := 'Donald';
   title := 'Mr.';
end;
Write(list_file,list_data);
Close(list_file);
Write('File created. Press ANY KEY ==> ');
Read(Kbd,inchr);
Reset(list_file);
Read(list_file,list_data);
WriteLn; WriteLn;
with list_data, list_data.zip, list_data.name do
begin
   WriteLn(title,SPACE,first_name,SPACE,surname);
   WriteLn(address1); WriteLn(address2);
   WriteLn(city,', ',state,SPACE,zip5,'-',zip4);
end; {with}
Close(list_file);
Erase(list_file);
end. { Illustrate_File_Handling }
```

In the preceding lines, the standard procedures Write and Read are used to move data to and from the disk file. The file variable preceding the data item to be transferred tells the compiler that the standard *input* and *output* devices (the keyboard and screen) are not to be used; instead, the data is transferred to or from the physical file that is associated with the file variable used. The base type of the file variable must match the type of the data items being transferred. In this example both are of the Name—Address type. Although it is of no consequence in this example, you should know that each time a file component is transferred using Read or Write, the file pointer is automatically incremented by 1.

This program also provides additional examples showing how record type structures are created and used. Notice how the with statement is used to gain direct access to the field variables at each level. If you would like to see what happens when you disregard the value of the tag field when accessing the variant part of a record, change the Write statement that displays the name as follows:

WriteLn(bus—name);

and rerun the program. Based on what you know about String types, can you explain the results? Try changing the value of **business** to TRUE and assign valid values to **bus—name** and **attn**, replacing the **surname, first—name**, and **title** assignments. Then compile and run the program with the original WriteLn statements that display the information on the video monitor. Can you change the output section so that the values displayed make sense?

Using Text Files and Devices

Text is the only predefined structured type. It is the required identifier for a file type structure that is an extension of this type definition:

type Text = **file of** Char;

As you might guess, each component of a Text type file variable is a character. This type has been predefined to allow the inclusion of predefined text processing procedures such as ReadLn and WriteLn using the predeclared Text type file variables **input** and **output**.

Standard Pascal requires that **input** and **output** be predeclared to serve as the default source and destination of data processed by the predefined I/O procedures Read and ReadLn and Write and WriteLn. When you use those procedures without specifying a file variable, **input** and **output** are assumed to be the source and destination, respectively. In earlier examples, these procedures have been used to accept characters from the keyboard and to display characters on the video monitor. Based on those clues, you might correctly deduce that Pascal treats those devices (the keyboard and monitor) as if they were Text files. Turbo Pascal takes that concept further and predefines some additional Text file variables that allow you to treat printers and communications devices as Text files. Chapter 8 will go into more detail as to how these variables are used.

The predefined type, Text, is different from any other file type. For one thing you can read from or write to a Text file, but you can't do both without closing the file first and reopening it. Also Text files do not have file pointers like other file types. When you process a Text file you must begin at the start and process its contents sequentially. The only exception is that, beginning with version 3.0, Turbo Pascal provides an Append procedure, which opens a Text file for output in such a way that subsequent Write statements will add data to the end of the file. The unique feature of Text files is the use of end-of-line and end-of-file markers. As indicated in Table 3-2, there are some predefined functions that permit you to determine when you have reached the end of a line or the end of the file. When reading a Text file with ReadLn, Turbo Pascal interprets a carriage return character (#13 or ^M) as the end of a line and CTRL-Z (ASCII character #26) as the end of the file. When WriteLn is used to output a line, a line feed character (#10 or ^J) is added following the carriage return character. When Read (instead of ReadLn) is used to input data from a Text file, the number of characters input is determined by the declared length of the String type variable or variables that the text is read into. When Write is used to output data to a Text file, the number of characters output is determined by the actual length of the String type variables that the text is written from.

The following program illustrates the use of Text files. The program reads a character from the keyboard and then writes it to a file named TEXT.DAT. The process continues until you press CTRL-Z, after which the program closes the file, reopens it, and reads it for display on the terminal.

```
program Illustrate_Text_Files;

  const ENTER     = #13;
        LINE_FEED = #10;

  var inchr     : Char;
      text_file : Text;
      inp_str   : string[255];

  begin
    ClrScr;
    WriteLn('Enter text. Press <CTRL><Z> when finished.');
    WriteLn;
    Assign(text_file,'TEXT.DAT');
    Rewrite(text_file);
    repeat
      Read(Kbd,inchr);
      if (inchr <> ^Z) then
        Write(inchr);
      if (inchr = ENTER) then   { Delete this statement if echoed input }
        Write(LINE_FEED);       { is double spaced on your system. }
      Write(text_file,inchr);
    until (inchr = ^Z);
    Close(text_file);
    WriteLn;
    Write('Press any key  to read and display text. ==> ');
    Read(Kbd,inchr); WriteLn;
    Reset(text_file);
    while (not Eof(text_file)) do
    begin
      ReadLn(text_file,inp_str);
      WriteLn(inp_str);
    end;
    Close(text_file);
    Erase(text_file);
  end. { Illustrate_Text_Files }
```

What is the purpose of the two if statements in the repeat statement? What happens on your system if you leave them out? What happens if you enter more than 255 characters before pressing RETURN for a single line?

Modify the section that redisplays the text so that it reads the file and displays the input one character at a time. On some systems the lines will overwrite one another. Why would that happen? *Hint:* Some display terminals automatically insert a line feed character following every carriage return character, which explains why the input echo appears to be double-spaced on those systems.

This exercise should have convinced you that file type variables are not all that mysterious. A lot of the confusion was eliminated when Borland International decided to discard the complicated standard Get and Put procedures and their associated buffer pointers.

Set Types

Set type variables take on properties that are difficult to duplicate in other languages with anything approaching the elegance of the Pascal concept. The structured types considered so far have been made up of data items of predefined types or types constructed from predefined types. For example, an array[1..10] of Integer is composed of Integer type data items; record type structures are composed of fields of a variety of types. The *set type* structure differs from these in that it is not composed of typed data items at all.

The purpose of the set type structure is to allow you to determine whether a particular value or group of values is included in another group of values of the same type. For example, say you are to divide a group of people based on hair color (BLACK, BLONDE, BROWN, GREY, and RED) and marital status (SINGLE, MARRIED, and DIVORCED). For example, one group will be single, blonde people and another will be married redheads. The following program will be responsible for reading in the list of people from the keyboard, segregating them into their respective hair color and marriage status groups, and then writing each group to a file named GUEST.DAT.

```
program Illustrate_Set_Types_Part1;

type   Characteristics = (BLACK,BLONDE,BROWN,GREY,RED,
                          DIVORCED,MARRIED,SINGLE);
       Hair_Color      = set of BLACK..RED;
       Marital_Status  = set of DIVORCED..SINGLE;
       Name_Str        = string[30];

       Guest_Record    = record
                           name   : Name_Str;
                           hair   : Hair_Color;
                           status : Marital_Status;
                         end;

var    guest      : Guest_Record;
       guest_list : file of Guest_Record;
       inchr      : Char;

begin
  Assign(guest_list,'GUEST.DAT');
  Rewrite(guest_list);
  repeat
    ClrScr;
    WriteLn('Enter guest list. Hair color codes are:');
    WriteLn('1 = Black, 2 = Blonde, 3 = Brown, 4 = Grey, 5 = Red');
    WriteLn; WriteLn('Marital Status codes are:');
    WriteLn('1 = Divorced, 2 = Married, 3 = Single, 4 = END LIST');
    WriteLn;
    Write('Enter guests name. Up to 30 characters.  ==> ');
    ReadLn(guest.name);
    Write('Press key (1-5) for hair color code.    ==> ');
    Read(Kbd,inchr); WriteLn(inchr);
    with guest do
      case inchr of
        '1'  : hair := [BLACK];
        '2'  : hair := [BLONDE];
        '3'  : hair := [BROWN];
        '4'  : hair := [GREY];
        else   hair := [RED];
```

```
        end; {case}
      Write('Press key (1-4) for marital status code. ==> ');
      Read(Kbd,inchr); WriteLn(inchr);
      with guest do
        case inchr of
          '1'  : status := [DIVORCED];
          '2'  : status := [MARRIED];
          '3'  : status := [SINGLE];
          else   status := [];
        end; {case}
      if guest.status <> [] then
        Write(guest_list,guest);
    until (guest.status = []);
    Close(guest_list);
  end. { Illustrate_Set_Types_Part1 }
```

The groups are then read from GUEST.DAT and those who are single or divorced with black or blond hair are printed on the screen. This is all done by the following program:

```
program Illustrate_Set_Types_Part2;

  type   Characteristics = (BLACK,BLONDE,BROWN,GREY,RED,
                            DIVORCED,MARRIED,SINGLE);
         Hair_Color      = set of BLACK..RED;
         Marital_Status  = set of DIVORCED..SINGLE;
         Name_Str        = string[30];

         Guest_Record    = record
                             name   : Name_Str;
                             hair   : Hair_Color;
                             status : Marital_Status;
                           end;

  var    guest       : Guest_Record;
         guest_list  : file of Guest_Record;
         select      : set of Characteristics;

  begin
    ClrScr;
    Assign(guest_list,'GUEST.DAT');
    Reset(guest_list);
    select := [DIVORCED,SINGLE,BLACK,BLONDE];
    WriteLn('Guests who are single or divorced with black or blonde hair:');
    WriteLn;
    while (not Eof(guest_list)) do
    begin
      Read(guest_list,guest);
      with guest do
        if ((hair + status) <= select) then
          WriteLn(guest.name);
    end; {while}
```

Of primary interest are the types Hair—Color and Marital—Status, as well as the variables declared to be of those types. Both types are subranges of the enumerated type Characteristics, which consists of eight values. Characteristics is said to be the *base* type of the two set types. The base type of a set type may not represent more than 256 values. For example, you may define a set type as a set of Char but not as a set of Integer. In general a set type definition is composed of the reserved words **set of** followed by a type identifier or nameless type definition, which represents 256 or fewer values.

Having defined a set type, the next step is to declare one or more variables of that type. In the first program, the field variables **hair** and **status** are declared as set types. Notice also the declaration of the **select** variable in the second program. It has a nameless set of Characteristics type. Values can be assigned to set type variables using any of the three methods used to assign values to other Pascal variables. Here's a quick review of assigning values to set variables.

1. Assign a constant to the variable. How are set constants represented? Set constants consist of a pair of square brackets (if your keyboard does not have square brackets, you can use (. .) as substitutes) enclosing zero or more constants of the set's base type. If more than one value appears, they may be separated by commas to indicate a series of values or by double periods (..) indicating a range. Examples are provided by the assignments to **hair** and **status** in the first listing and to **select** in the second listing. Notice the assignment that takes place if the marital status code entered is not 1 through 3. The empty brackets represent an *empty* set, which is compatible with sets of any base type.

Table 3-3.   Set Operators

Expression	Standard	Turbo	Description/ Result
*set1 * set2*	Y	Y	Set intersection. Result is a set containing only members common to *set1* and *set2*
set1 + set2	Y	Y	Set union. Result is a set containing combined members from *set1* and *set2*
set1 − set2	Y	Y	Set difference. Result is a set containing members of *set1* that are not members of *set2*
set1 = set2	Y	Y	TRUE if *set1* equals *set2*
set1 <> set2	Y	Y	TRUE if *set1* not equal to *set2*
set1 <= set2	Y	Y	TRUE if *set1* is a subset of *set2*
set1 >= set2	Y	Y	TRUE if *set2* is a subset of *set1*
set1 in set2	Y	Y	TRUE if *set1* is a subset of *set2*, except that *set1* may be a single data item of the *set2* base type

2. Assign the result of an expression to the variable. Pascal provides set operators that are used in expressions involving set type data. These operators are outlined in Table 3-3. As you see, the symbols are a mixture of the arithmetic and relational operators introduced earlier. Their meaning is determined by the type of the operands. The operators +, −, and * produce a set type result when the operands are set types. This result may be assigned to a set variable of the same base type. The following statement is a valid assignment statement:

select := select + hair;

If, prior to this statement, **select** had equaled [SINGLE,BROWN] and **hair** [RED], after the statement, **select** would equal [SINGLE, BROWN,RED]. Finally, note that set constants can be defined and used on the spot as needed. For example, this statement:

```
repeat
    Read(Kbd,inchr);
until (inchr in ['0'..'9','−','.']);
```

will screen keyboard input, permitting only those values indicated by the set constant to be accepted.

3. Assign the value of another set variable to the variable. For this to work both sets must be of the same type. The statement

hair := status;

would cause a type mismatch error.

Once values have been assigned to set type variables, you can then use the relational set operators (<, <=, >, >=, in) to perform comparisons. The power of the set type is evident in the simplicity of this selection process. How would this process be carried out using the languages you are currently familiar with? To become more familiar with the Pascal set type, you may want to experiment with these two example programs. What would it take to add another selection criteria? What changes would be needed to make the selection based on hair color only? For a more advanced project you may want to modify the programs so that the selection criteria is input by the user.

Before leaving the topic of sets you will find it useful to know how they are constructed. A set type structure is not made up of data items of a previously defined type; rather, it is composed of bits. One bit is used to represent each item in the base type of a set. Since the base type of the sets used in the example programs has eight values, each set variable in those programs needs only one byte of storage. On the other hand, a variable with a type, set of Char, would need 32 bytes or 256 bits to represent all possible values. The storage for set type variables is allocated in bytes, so if the base type of a variable contains 17 values, three bytes will be allocated. As you can see, sets not only help in creating simpler, easier to read programs, they also help conserve memory.

Pointer Types

So far you have examined the properties of simple types and structured types. There is one other type available in Pascal—the *pointer* type. All of the types discussed so far are used to provide the compiler with information about the size and structure of data items. Thus when a variable is declared to be of a certain type, enough is known to set aside sufficient storage for the variable and perform certain checks on operations using that variable. It is not uncommon, however, for a program to handle a group of related data items without knowing in advance how many items will be in the group. It is often necessary to access these items in a particular sequence. For example, assume you are writing an automatic phone dialer program. You plan to load the names and telephone numbers into memory from a disk file when the program starts, allowing the user to scan them in alphabetical order. There are two problems here. One, you don't know how many names and numbers there are. Two, they are not stored in alphabetical order. Both of these problems can be solved using pointers.

Pointers are used in Pascal to manage an area of memory known as the *heap*. You will also hear the heap referred to as *dynamic storage*. Figure 3-1 provides a general schematic of the way memory is allocated when a Turbo Pascal program is executing. The storage between the top of heap line and the top of stack line is unallocated and free for you to use as needed. The purpose of pointer type variables is to show you where to find data items you have stored in this area. In other words, they *point* to those items. When pointers are used you will often see them organized so a pointer points to a record type data item, which itself contains a pointer type field variable that points to the next item, and so forth. The result is a *linked list* or chain of related data items. The initial pointer, the one that points to the first item in the list, is called the *head* of the chain. The pointers within the records are known as links in the chain.

When a group of related data items is organized using pointers, they are said to form a *data structure*. There are several useful data structures that can be created using pointers. You will hear them referred to with terms like *list stack*, *queue*, and *tree*. If you are not already acquainted with these structures, you will find it helpful to review some of the texts available on the subject of data organization.

Building a Stack With Pointers   A commonly used analogy to describe a stack structure is a stack of plates on a spring-loaded plate holder at a cafeteria. When new plates are added, they are pushed onto the top of the stack. When items are removed, they are popped off the stack. The following program substitutes characters for plates. The objective is to accept charac-

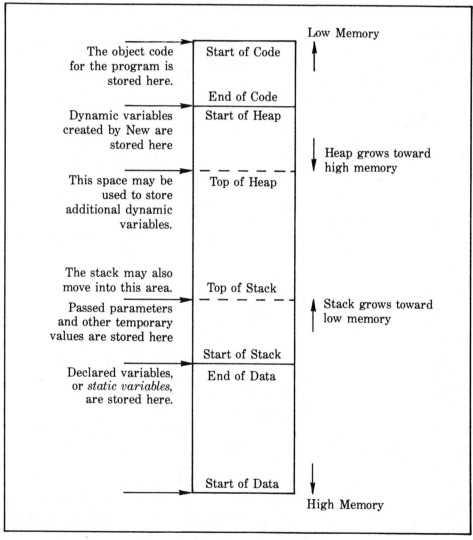

Figure 3-1. Simplified memory showing location of dynamic storage

ters from the keyboard, storing them in a stack structure, until the RETURN key is pressed. At that point the characters will be retrieved from the stack one at a time and displayed. Since the stack is a last-in first-out (LIFO) structure, what do you suppose the result will be?

```
program Illustrate_Pointer_Type_Prog1;

  const CR = #13;

  type Char_Ptr  = ^Char_List;
       Char_List = record
                     character : Char;
                     next_chr  : Char_Ptr;
                   end;

  var  chr_ptr,
       hold_ptr    : Char_Ptr;
       inchr       : Char;
       heap_marker : ^Char;

  begin
    ClrScr;
    WriteLn('Enter a line of text and press <CR>.'); WriteLn;
    Mark(heap_marker);
    chr_ptr := nil; hold_ptr := nil;
    repeat
      Read(Kbd,inchr); Write(inchr);
      if (chr_ptr = nil) then
        begin
          New(chr_ptr);
          chr_ptr^.next_chr := nil;
        end
      else
        begin
          hold_ptr := chr_ptr;
          New(chr_ptr);
          chr_ptr^.next_chr := hold_ptr;
        end;
      chr_ptr^.character := inchr;
    until (inchr = CR);
    WriteLn;
    while (hold_ptr <> nil) do
    begin
      Write(hold_ptr^.character);
      hold_ptr := hold_ptr^.next_chr;
    end; {while}
    Release(heap_marker);
  end. { Illustrate_Pointer_Type_Prog1 }
```

Before running the program, take a close look at the type and variable definitions. Char—Ptr is declared as a pointer of type Char—List. Pointer type *definitions* begin with a circumflex character (^), followed immediately by a type identifier. Char—Ptr is a pointer to a Char—List type, but notice the reference to Char—List precedes its definition. This is permitted only for pointer type definitions to overcome a deadlock, since Char—Ptr is used in the definition of Char—List.

In the variable declarations you will see that **chr—ptr** and **hold—ptr** are Char—Ptr type pointers. Since a stack structure is being built, the last item added to the stack will always be the first item to be removed and thus represents the head of the chain. The program is designed so that **chr—ptr** will always point to the most recently entered character. If no characters

Table 3-4. Predefined Dynamic Storage Subprograms

Identifier	Function or Procedure	Standard	Turbo	Description
Dispose	P	Y	Y	Free space previously allocated by New
FreeMem	P	N	Y	Free space allocated by GetMem
GetMem	P	N	Y	Allocates a specified amount of space
Mark	P	N	Y	Saves pointer to top of heap
MaxAvail	F	N	Y	Returns largest space open in the heap
MemAvail	F	N	Y	Returns space remaining on the heap
New	P	Y	Y	Allocates space based on pointer type
Pack	P	Y	N	Directs compiler to pack data item
Ptr	F	N	Y	Returns pointer to its dynamic parameter
Release	P	N	Y	Restores top of heap as saved by Mark

have been entered, it will point to **nil**. **Nil** is a reserved constant that represents a pointer to nowhere and is usually used to denote the end of a chain of pointers. You will note that both **chr‗ptr** and **hold‗ptr** are initialized to point to **nil**. The variable **hold‗ptr** is used to hold the old value of **chr‗ptr** when a new character is added to the stack.

Just how is a character added to the stack? Turbo Pascal provides predefined procedures that manage the dynamic storage area. Table 3-4 gives an overview of them. The three that are used in the stack program are New, Mark, and Release. New "creates" (actually reserves) space in the heap area for a pointer variable. Whenever you use the New procedure, you must follow it with a pointer type variable in parentheses. The type associated with the variable determines how much space to allocate for the new variable. In addition, the pointer variable is assigned a value that points to the newly created dynamic variable.

Following the statement New(**chr‗ptr**) in the stack program, **chr‗ptr** points to Char—List, which will be used to store the most recently entered character. The field variable where the character is to be stored is **character**. Accessing a field in a pointer variable is similar to accessing a field in a standard record variable; just include the circumflex to identify it as a pointer. For example, the statement

chr—ptr^.character := inchr;

results in the value of **inchr**, which accepted the character from the keyboard, being assigned to the **character** field.

When the New procedure is used to create variables in the heap, the space allocated will remain allocated until you deallocate it—even if you are not using it. Turbo Pascal provides the predefined procedures Mark and Release to allow you to deallocate dynamic variables in the heap. Notice the variable **heap—marker** in the stack program. It is declared as a pointer type variable. When the statement

Mark(heap—marker);

is executed, **heap—marker** will point to the current top of the heap. As subsequent New(**chr—ptr**); statements are executed, the top of heap will be adjusted to account for the allocated storage, but **heap—marker** will not move. When you are ready to deallocate that storage, this statement

Release(heap—marker);

has the effect of restoring the top of the heap to the location pointed to by **heap—marker**. This makes the previously allocated memory available again and effectively erases any variables that were stored in that memory.

Pointers are very useful although somewhat confusing at first. In an effort to clarify their use, a step-by-step explanation of the statement part of the stack program will follow.

1. First the screen is cleared and a prompt is displayed.
2. Mark is used to store the current top of heap address in **heap—marker**.
3. **chr—ptr** and **hold—ptr** are initialized to **nil**.
4. A repeat loop is set up that will continue until the user presses the RETURN key.
5. A character is read from the keyboard and temporarily stored in **inchr**.
6. If **chr—ptr** is **nil**, indicating that the stack is empty, the New procedure is used to allocate space for a Char—List type variable and make

chr—ptr point to that record. The **next—chr** field is set to point to **nil**, indicating that there are no more characters on the stack. Remember that the first item added to a stack is the last item removed.

If **chr—ptr** is not equal to **nil**, indicating that there are already characters on the stack, the current value of **chr—ptr**, which points to the last record added to the stack, is saved in **hold—ptr**. The New procedure allocates space for the next Char—List record and makes **chr—ptr** point to that record. The value stored in **hold—ptr**, which points to the last record added, is stored in the **next—chr** field of this record. This adds a link to the chain.

7. The character in **inchr** is stored in the **character** field of the record just added.

8. If the user presses a character other than RETURN, the steps beginning at step 5 are repeated. When the user presses RETURN, however, the repeat loop is terminated and a new line is started on the monitor using WriteLn.

9. A while loop is set up, based on the value of **hold—ptr**, to print the stack. Initially **hold—ptr** will point to the character that was entered just prior to the RETURN character, unless no characters were entered, in which case **hold—ptr** will point to **nil** and the statement part of the loop will be skipped.

10. As long as **hold—ptr** is not pointing to **nil**, the character in the **character** field will be displayed and **hold—ptr** will be updated to point to the next record in the chain.

11. The loop will end when the last character has been displayed, since the **next—ptr** field in the record that contains the last character points to **nil**.

12. The Release procedure is used to restore the top of heap to where it was to begin with, thus deallocating the storage used for the Char—List records.

The data structure illustrated here is not a stack in the true sense of the term because the program does not actually *pop* the characters from the structure. To do this, the pointers would have to be maintained so that if a character were removed and then another entered, the new character would replace the one removed. For example, if the BACKSPACE key is pressed, that is what should happen. To test yourself on pointers, you might want to modify the program so that it works like a real stack.

For those of you who would rather see another example, the following program uses pointers to create a sorted linked list. The program will permit you to enter any number of characters (until you run out of heap space, which is not likely), and then it will redisplay them in alphanumeric order. The interesting thing is how quickly the list is maintained and how sorted output is ready to display the instant you press RETURN. Even when maintaining a

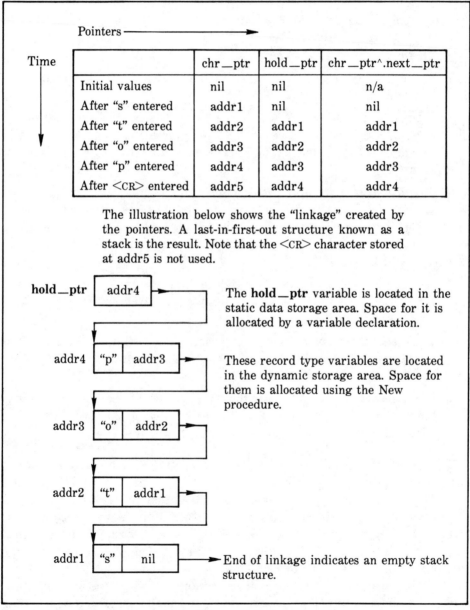

	chr_ptr	hold_ptr	chr_ptr^.next_ptr
Initial values	nil	nil	n/a
After "s" entered	addr1	nil	nil
After "t" entered	addr2	addr1	addr1
After "o" entered	addr3	addr2	addr2
After "p" entered	addr4	addr3	addr3
After <CR> entered	addr5	addr4	addr4

The illustration below shows the "linkage" created by the pointers. A last-in-first-out structure known as a stack is the result. Note that the <CR> character stored at addr5 is not used.

The **hold_ptr** variable is located in the static data storage area. Space for it is allocated by a variable declaration.

These record type variables are located in the dynamic storage area. Space for them is allocated using the New procedure.

End of linkage indicates an empty stack structure.

Figure 3-2. How a stack structure is built with pointers

list of over 1000 characters, the time to add and sort a character is negligible. Figure 3-2 illustrates the record and pointer values as the first four characters are entered into the stack structure. As a final review of pointers, see if you can illustrate the action of the sorted linked list program the same way.

```
}program Illustrate_Pointer_Type_Prog2;

 const CR = #13;

 type Char_Ptr  = ^Char_List;
      Char_List = record
                     character : Char;
                     next_chr  : Char_Ptr;
                  end;

 var  chr_ptr,
      hold_ptr,
      first_ptr,
      last_ptr  : Char_Ptr;
      heap_mark : ^Char;
      inchr     : Char;

 begin
   ClrScr;
   WriteLn('Enter a line of text and press <CR>.'); WriteLn;
   Mark(heap_mark);
   chr_ptr := nil; hold_ptr := nil;
   repeat
     Read(Kbd,inchr);
     if (chr_ptr = nil) then
       begin
         New(chr_ptr);
         chr_ptr^.next_chr := nil;
         first_ptr := chr_ptr;
         chr_ptr^.character := inchr;
       end
     else
       begin
         hold_ptr := first_ptr;
         last_ptr := first_ptr;
         New(chr_ptr);
         while (inchr >= hold_ptr^.character) and (hold_ptr <> nil) do
           begin
             last_ptr := hold_ptr;
             hold_ptr := hold_ptr^.next_chr;
           end;
         if (inchr < first_ptr^.character) then
           begin
             first_ptr := chr_ptr;
             chr_ptr^.next_chr := last_ptr;
           end
         else
           begin
             last_ptr^.next_chr := chr_ptr;
             chr_ptr^.next_chr := hold_ptr;
           end;
         chr_ptr^.character := inchr;
       end;
     Write(inchr);

   until (inchr = CR);
   WriteLn;
   while (hold_ptr <> nil) do
     begin
       Write(hold_ptr^.character);
       hold_ptr := hold_ptr^.next_chr;
     end; {while}
   Release(heap_mark);
 end. { Illustrate_Pointer_Type_Prog2 }
```

Before leaving the subject of pointers here are some rules you should be aware of:

- Pointer variables may only be assigned to other pointer variables that point to data items of the same named type.

- The predefined value **nil** can be assigned to any pointer variable.

- If a pointer variable points to **nil** or has not been initialized, it must not be used to reference a dynamic variable.

- Attempting to allocate more dynamic storage than is available will result in a heap/stack collision. The predefined MemAvail function can be used to determine the amount of unallocated space remaining.

- An alternative method of deallocating dynamic storage is provided to maintain compatibility with standard Pascal. It uses the Dispose procedure, which will be explained when the predefined subprograms are reviewed in Chapter 9. For most purposes, Turbo's nonstandard Mark and Release procedures are better.

In general you will find that pointer variables and their associated dynamic variables are powerful allies when you must deal with organized data structures such as trees, queues, and lists. As has been illustrated, it is much quicker to redirect pointers than to rearrange data items. The disadvantages are a certain amount of overhead inherent with pointers and the ever-present potential for confusing the pointer with the pointee. If this is your first exposure to these concepts and they seem a bit unclear, don't worry. You'll find that the first time you write a program that has a legitimate need for pointers everything will begin to fall into place. Some additional study of the data structures noted previously will also be helpful.

FOUR

Turbo Pascal Subprograms

Subprograms are like miniature programs within a program. They even resemble programs, beginning with a header and followed by an optional declaration and definition part and a statement part. Subprograms are located in the declaration part of the program; however, they operate in their own environment separate but not always isolated from the main program. A subprogram can declare variables that are accessible only to the subprogram, it can use variables from the main program, or it can use a mixture of the two.

Subprograms come in two versions: procedures and functions; for now let's concentrate on the more widely used procedures.

All procedures must begin with the reserve word **procedure** followed by an identifier and a semicolon. After the header comes the declaration part. When a procedure is executed, the variables and constants in the declaration part are created in memory, but after the procedure has terminated, they vanish. Variables, constants, and type definitions in a procedure exist only during the life of the procedure, making procedures economical since unused variables do not use memory.

Following the declaration part of the procedure is the statement part, which always begins with the reserve word **begin** and ends with the reserve word **end** and a semicolon. Procedures are activated, or *called*, in the main program by giving the name of the procedure as a single statement. The following program, which prints the phrase "I will not talk in class." ten times, shows how a procedure is declared and called:

```
program Homework;

  procedure Repeat_Phrase;
    var count: Integer;

    begin
      for count := 1 to 10 do
        WriteLn('I will not talk in class.');
    end; { Repeat_Phrase }

  begin { Homework }
    Repeat_Phrase;
  end. { Homework }
```

This program is a poor way to demonstrate procedures since Repeat‒Phrase is called once and could have easily been part of the program, but it shows how procedures are activated. In a sense, procedures are like defining your own keywords. Should the Homework program expand and require the services of Repeat‒Phrase, all that the program need do is add more Repeat‒Phrase statements.

There are no limits (discounting memory) to the number of procedures in a program. In fact, a procedure can call other procedures. For example, Repeat‒Phrase can delegate part of its job by having a procedure called Print‒Phrase print the phrase "I will not talk in class."

```
program Homework;
  procedure Print_Phrase;
    begin
      WriteLn('I will not talk in class.');
    end; { Print_Phrase }

  procedure Repeat_Phrase;
    var count: Integer;

    begin
      for count := 1 to 10 do
        Print_Phrase;
    end; { Repeat_Phrase }

  begin { Homework }
    Repeat_Phrase;
  end. { Homework }
```

Procedure Repeat‒Phrase can reference Print‒Phrase only if Print‒Phrase literally precedes procedure Repeat‒Phrase. This is a rule for all procedures; a procedure cannot call another procedure that is declared below it.

Procedures can also be *nested;* that is, a procedure can be defined in another procedure's declaration part, not unlike when a procedure is defined in a program. The following program shows Print—Phrase as a nested procedure to procedure Repeat—Phrase:

```
program Homework;

   procedure Repeat_Phrase;
     var count: Integer;

     procedure Print_Phrase;
       begin
         WriteLn('I will not talk in class.');
       end; { Print_Phrase }

     begin
       for count := 1 to 10 do
         Print_Phrase;
     end; { Repeat_Phrase }

   begin { Homework }
     Repeat_Phrase;
   end. { Homework }
```

Nested procedures can be limiting, since the only procedure that can reference Print—Phrase is Repeat—Phrase. Even the program can't call Print—Phrase. A nested procedure can be called only by the procedure that stores it. The advantage of a nested procedure is that the procedure exists only when the "mother" procedure, the one that contains the nested procedure, is executing, which means a savings in space.

Parameters

Many of the predefined subprograms used earlier required you to supply one or more values. The file-handling Assign procedure, which opens a file buffer and links a file to it, requested two values: a file variable and a file name. For example,

Assign(list—file,'LIST.DAT');
ClrScr;

The variable **list—file** and the constant LIST.DAT are parameters. The file variable **list—file** creates a data buffer, used for transferring information to and from a disk file, and the string constant LIST.DAT links the file to the buffer. The Assign procedure can be used to assign any file type variable associated with any string type constant or variable. In other words, Assign is a *general-purpose routine* that performs a specific task based on the parameters it receives. Procedure ClrScr, on the other hand, is a *single-purpose routine* that does not require any outside information to perform its task. When you write your own subprograms, you will need to determine whether or not they will need parameters.

When you write subprograms that require parameters, information about those parameters is included in the header. They must be declared within parentheses following the identifier. Parameter declarations are much like variable declarations both in form and purpose. Each identifier is separated by a semicolon, and each must be declared as a *named* type. Thus, variables with nameless types are not available to subprograms as parameters.

The parameters declared in the header are known as the *formal* parameters. The identifiers of formal procedures take on the values passed by the calling routine and are then used in the statement part of the procedure.

Repeat—Char is a simple procedure with parameters that display a character by a factor indicated in **count**.

```
procedure Repeat_Char(character: Char; count: Integer);
    var i : Integer;
    begin
            for i := 1 to count do

                Write(character);

    end;   { Repeat_Char }
```

When a program calls Repeat—Char, it passes a character and a number. For example,

Repeat—Char('a',80)

would print "a" 80 times. The letter "a" would be handed to the **character** parameter, and 80 would be handed to the **count** parameter.

Parameter calls are not limited to constants; variables, expressions, and even functions can be passed as well. The following series of procedure calls are equivalent to Repeat—Char('a',80):

- out—chr := 'a';
  chr—cnt := 80;
  Repeat—Char(out—chr,chr—cnt);

- out—chr := 'a';
  chr—cht := 20;
  Repeat—Char(out—chr,(chr—cnt * 4));

- out—chr := 'A';
  chr—cht := 80;
  Repeat—Char(LowerCase(out—chr),chr—cnt);

In each Repeat—Char statement, the values between parentheses are known as the *actual* parameters. Actual parameters must match the formal parameters both in sequence and type and are separated by commas. When constants, functions, or expressions are used as actual parameters, they must be of the same type or result in a value of the same type as the formal parameter. Actual parameter identifiers need not match the formal identifiers in name. Repeat—Char does not require the actual parameters to be **character** and **count**.

Parameter Passing by Value or Reference

There are two methods used to pass parameters to a subprogram: by value or by reference. When a parameter is passed by *value*, a copy of the actual parameter value is passed to the procedure. The procedure does not have access to the actual variable and therefore cannot modify it.

A procedure can change the value of a value parameter, but upon returning to the program, the original value of the actual parameter is unchanged. A rather simple demonstration of passing parameters by value is procedure Increment:

```
procedure Increment (plus_one:Integer);
    begin
        plus_one := plus_one + 1;
        Writeln (plus_one);
    end;
```

When the following statements are executed:

```
advance := 1;
Increment (advance);
Writeln(advance);
```

The output, on separate lines, will be **2** and **1**. The variable **advance**, which is declared in the main program, is assigned to 1 and a copy is delivered to Increment in the form of **plus—one** when the procedure is called. Increment immediately changes the value of **plus—one** to 2 and then prints it to confirm that the value has been changed. The change is not permanent; only a change to the copy has been made, and when Increment is finished operating and control returns to the program, **plus—one** does not hand the new value to **advance**, it just dies.

After the procedure call, **advance** is printed, which is 1. Both parameters in Repeat—Char are value parameters, but the procedure's purpose was not to change the value of the parameters.

If parameters could be passed by value only, the purpose of a procedure would be limited to not much more than printing messages. Calculations and string manipulation would be impossible, since any work would be wiped clean when control returned to the program. Of course, a procedure could settle on global variables to modify values and ignore parameters altogether, but then a procedure would never qualify as a general-purpose routine. It would not be able to accept different variables or values and would be bound to global variables. Fortunately, a procedure can modify any parameter variable permanently.

If you want a procedure to have direct access to an actual parameter, precede the declaration of the formal parameter with the reserved word **var**. When you do, the formal parameter is known as a *variable parameter* or *var parameter* for short, and the process is known as passing a parameter by *reference*. When this method is used, the address of the actual parameter is passed rather than a copy of its value. The procedure then uses the address to access and modify the value of the actual parameter.

When passing parameters by reference, the actual parameter must be a variable or a typed constant. Regular constants or expressions cannot be passed by reference since their values cannot be altered. Keeping in mind that variable parameters are passed as an address, can you think of another reason that constants and expressions couldn't be passed by reference?

Modifying Increment to permanently increment the parameter **plus―one** means converting **plus―one** into a variable parameter.

```
Increment (var plus―one: Integer);
   begin
      plus―one := plus―one + 1;
      Writeln (plus―one);
   end;
```

Now the statements

```
advance := 1;
Increment (advance);
Writeln(advance);
```

will output **2** and **2**. The operation of Increment remains the same; however, the value of **plus―one** will be returned to **advance**. This is reflected when advance is printed in the next statement.

The formal declaration can consist of both value and variable parameters.

    procedure Mitigate(**var** help,me:Real; **var** out:Boolean; there:Char);

Here **help** and **me** are both variable parameters of Real types; **out** is also a variable parameter but of type Boolean; and **there** is a character and a value parameter.

Functions

The difference between a procedure and a function is that the identifier of a function assumes a value when the function has terminated and returns this value to the calling routine in the guise of the function name. In a very large sense, the function name is also a variable.

Everything mentioned about defining procedures also applies to defining functions. Here is a function that converts its Char type parameter to lower-case if the parameter is in the range "A" through "Z":

```
function LoCase(character: Char): Char;
  begin
    if (character in ['A'..'Z']) then
        LoCase := Chr(Ord(character) + 32)
    else
        LoCase := character;
  end; { LoCase }
```

Since the function assumes a value, the function itself must have a type. Following the parameter declaration part of the header there is a colon and a type identifier.

A function may be of any scalar type, string type, or pointer type. The type of a function must be indicated by a type identifier; nameless type definitions are not permitted.

Another requirement for functions is that an assignment must be made to the function identifier at some point in the statement part. The value assigned to the function name will be returned to the calling routine. In more complex functions, where several assignments may be made, the last assignment before returning to the calling routine determines the value of the function.

Referencing a function is quite simple. Treat the function name in a statement or expression as if it were a variable with parameters (or without parameters if the function has none). Thus, the following statements are legal, assuming **temp** is of Char type:

```
Writeln (LoCase('A'));
temp := LoCase ('B');
```

Sort list procedure.

parameters: An array of values to be sorted. Passed by reference.
An integer indicating the first array element to be
processed.
An integer indicating the last array element to be
processed.

- If the difference between the first and last elements is less than 1, then no action is required and return to the calling routine.

- If the difference between the first and last elements equals 1 and if the first element is greater than the last element, then swap the first and last elements and return to the calling routine.

- If the difference between the first and last elements is greater than 1, then begin the following eight statements.

  - Determine the value of the center element.

  - Initialize the values of a new first and last element to be equal to the current first and last elements.

  - While the new first element is less than or equal to the new last element, repeat the following three sequences.

  - While the value of the new first element is less than the value of the center element, then increment the new first element.

  - While the value of the new last element is greater than the value of the center element, then decrement the new last element.

  - If the new first element is less than or equal to the new last element, swap the values stored at the new first and last elements; increment the new first element; and decrement the new last element.

- Execute this entire procedure again using the old first element and the new last element as parameters marking the partition to be processed.

- Execute this entire procedure again using the new first element and the old last element as parameters marking the partition to be processed.

- Return to the calling routine.

Figure 4-1.   Pseudo-code for the Sort—List procedure

Recursive Subprograms

As was mentioned earlier, a subprogram is activated by using its identifier as a statement in the statement part. In fact, a subprogram may call itself from within its own statement part. When this is done, the subprogram is said to be *recursive*. Recursive routines can provide elegant solutions to certain types of problems. They are particularly valuable when the divide and conquer strategy is used to process a large volume of information by successively dividing the information into smaller pieces. For example, processing data organized in a *tree* structure is ideally suited to recursive routines. Explaining the intricacies of such structures is beyond the scope of this book, but you are encouraged to pursue the subject further if your programs involve processing large quantities of information.

The following program uses recursion to sort an array of items using the quicksort method. Quicksort uses a divide-and-conquer approach to sorting. Figure 4-1 uses pseudo-code to describe the design logic of the Sort—List procedure. Each time the array is divided, each part is then divided again until there's nothing left to divide. Then the parts are sorted and combined to form larger parts; the process repeats until the array has been sorted. The quicksort algorithm is generally acknowledged as one of the fastest for sorting large quantities of data.

```
(* Include the following directive if code is being compiled on
   an 8 bit CP/M system.
{$A-}
*)
  procedure Sort_List(var values: Word_Array; lo, hi: Integer);
    var  new_lo,
         new_hi    : Integer; { Used to divide the array of values.}
         center_value,
         hold_value : Word_Str;   { Used when values are swapped.}

    begin
      if ((hi - lo) > 1) then
        begin
          center_value := values[(hi + lo) div 2];
          new_lo := lo; new_hi := hi;
          while (new_lo <= new_hi) do
          begin
            while(values[new_lo] < center_value) do
              new_lo := Succ(new_lo);
            while(values[new_hi] > center_value) do
              new_hi := Pred(new_hi);
            if (new_lo <= new_hi) then
              begin
                hold_value := values[new_lo];
                values[new_lo] := values[new_hi];
                values[new_hi] := hold_value;
                new_lo := Succ(new_lo);
                new_hi := Pred(new_hi);
              end; {if}
          end; {while}
          Sort_List(values,lo,new_hi);
```

```
            Sort_List(values,new_lo,hi);
        end
      else
        if ((hi - lo) = 1) then
          if (values[hi] < values[lo]) then
            begin
              hold_value := values[hi];
              values[hi] := values[lo];
              values[lo] := hold_value;
            end;
  end; { Sort_List }

(* Include the following directive if code is being compiled on
   an 8 bit CP/M system.
{$A+}
*)
```

If you are using an 8-bit CP/M implementation of Turbo, you will need to use the {$A−} compiler directive preceding the definition of Sort_List so that the compiler will permit the recursion. An {$A+} directive should follow the definition.

The Sort_List procedure sorts the array of values and passes it as a variable parameter. Two value parameters indicate the first and last elements of the array to be sorted. If you want to see exactly how this process results in a sorted array, use a pencil and paper to draw an array of six or seven random values. Then trace the logic of the program, redrawing the array each time Sort_List calls itself, tracking the value of key variables.

The Sort_List procedure can be modified to sort any scalar data type by changing the type identifier of the values parameter so that it identifies an array of the desired type. In addition, the type identifier of the base type must be used to declare the variables **center_value** and **hold_value**.

Scope

To understand the concept of scope, you must first understand Pascal's block-within-a-block method of building programs. If you are familiar with a block structured language, this will seem natural. Figure 4-2 presents a do-nothing program that illustrates both block structure and the concept of scope. Boxes have been drawn to enclose the blocks created by the program itself and the subprograms nested within it. Notice the level numbers associated with each block. If you work on large projects, you may see the level of a subprogram indicated on some of the documentation. Level 0 refers to the main program block, while higher level numbers indicate how deep a subprogram is nested. Some systems limit this depth; however Turbo Pascal programs are limited only in that the object code may not exceed 64K bytes.

The program in Figure 4-2 can be entered and executed. You may find that experimenting with it will help to clarify the concept of scope. Before

```
program Illustrate_Scope;              {Level 0}

  var i : Byte;
  procedure Proc_A(i: Integer);        {Level 1}

    procedure Proc_B;                  {Level 2}

      var i : Real;
      begin {      }
        i := 2.0;
        WriteLn('Output from subprogram B = ',i);
      end;

    procedure Proc_C;                  {Level 2}

      procedure Proc_D;                {Level 3}

        var i : Boolean;
        procedure Proc_E;             {Level 4}

          begin { Proc_E }
            i := FALSE;
            WriteLn('Output from subprogram E = ',i);
          end; { Proc_E }

        begin { Proc_D }
          i := TRUE;
          WriteLn('Output from subprogram D = ',i);
          Proc_E;
        end; { Proc_D }

      begin { Proc_C }
        i := 3;
        WriteLn('Output from subprogram C = ',i);
        Proc_D;
      end; { Proc_C }

    begin { Proc_A }
      WriteLn('Output from subprogram A = ',i);
      Proc_B;
      Proc_C;
    end;

begin { program Illustrate_Scope }
  i := 1;
  Proc_A(2 * i);
  WriteLn('The final value of i = ',i);
end. { Illustrate_Scope }
```

Figure 4-2.   Block structure illustrating the effect of limited scope

reviewing the rules of scope, some terminology needs to be explained. As is often the case in the world of computers, the terminology relating to subprogram levels can be a bit confusing. For example, when it comes to levels, subprograms with high-level numbers are referred to as low-level routines and vice versa. So when you hear statements like "The objective is to push program detail into low-level routines so that the logic flow will be more apparent in the high-level subprograms," remember that the highest level, the program block itself, is level 0. With that in mind, here is a general description of the scope of an identifier:

- An identifier is accessible to the subprograms in which it is defined and all lower level subprograms, unless that identifier is redefined in a lower level. For example, i functions as a Real variable in level 2 but as a Byte variable in level 0. An identifier may not be redefined in the block that defines it.

- Identifiers defined in a subprogram do not exist prior to or following the activation of that subprogram and therefore may not be accessed by a subprogram at a higher level. Values may be transferred, however, by passing variable parameters.

- A subprogram is said to be active starting at the time it is activated (called or executed) and throughout the execution of its statement part, including other subprogram statements.

Advantages and Disadvantages

The benefit of limited scope means you can develop low-level routines using identifiers and not worry about altering a value of another identifier with the same name. The larger the project, the more important this is.

In most cases it is not practical to use parameter passing as the sole means of making outside information available to lower level routines. As a result, you will find that variables declared in higher level blocks are often treated as *global*. The term global, as used in some languages, does not apply in Pascal. For example, when a variable is created in BASIC, it is immediately available throughout the program and is truly global. Pascal variables, even when they are declared in the main program block, are only relatively global since a subprogram may or may not elect to use them. Unless you exercise caution, it is possible to reuse the identifier of such a supposedly global variable inadvertently, thus making it inaccessible. By being aware of scope and using parameters rather than relying on identifiers defined at a higher level, the benefits far outweigh the potential problems.

Sort text files program

Objective: Read the text from a user-selected text file as a series of
words. A word is defined as a series of one or more characters from the set of characters A-Z plus a-z plus the
underline. The words are then to be sorted in ascending
alphabetic sequence and optionally displayed. Each unique
word is to be displayed only once, preceded by a count
indicating the number of times it occurs in the text.

- Prompt the user to enter the name of a text file.

- Open the text file for processing.

- While there is text remaining in the file, read a line of text from the
file, or extract words from the line, storing them in an array and
keeping count of the total number of words.

- Close the text file.

- Display the number of words extracted and prompt the user to indicate when to start the sort.

- Sort the words using the **Sort__List** procedure.

- Prompt the user to indicate whether or not the sorted list should be
displayed.

- If the response is positive, then

  - Save the value of element 1 in the word array as the previous word.

  - Initialize the word count to 1.

  - Initialize the unique word count to 0.

  - For each word in the array beginning with element 2 do the
following

    - If the current word is equal to the previous word, then
    Increment the word count;
    Else

      - Display the count followed by the previous word.

      - Set the previous word equal to the current word.

      - Set the word count to 1.

      - Increment the unique word count.

Figure 4-3.   Pseudo-code for a program that sorts the words from a text file

- Display the count followed by the previous word.

- Increment the unique word count.

- Display the unique word count.

Note: The procedures for reading the text and displaying the sorted list should be coded as subprograms.

Figure 4-3.   Pseudo-code for a program that sorts the words from a text file (*continued*)

A Sort Program

The following program uses a variation of the Sort—List routine. The objective is to read data from a text file as a series of words, sort the list of words, and optionally display the list. Figure 4-3 outlines the program in pseudo-code. This version of the Sort—List procedure has been "modularized" by moving the sections that divide the array and swap array elements into lower level subprograms. This makes the statement part of the Sort—List procedure much clearer. The price you pay for this is a slight (four to five percent) loss in execution time. The main reason this was done is to illustrate that changes like this can be made without changing the higher level routines. As you will see when advanced features of Turbo Pascal are explained, you can even replace the Sort—List routine with one written in assembler if performance is of paramount importance and you have an assembler routine that is faster.

Users of 8-bit CP/M systems should include the {A+} compiler directive. The directive has been separated from the program by comments. If you get an **out-of-memory** error when compiling the program, reduce the value of MAX—SIZE. You shouldn't run out of memory unless you are working on a system with a very limited memory, say, a 48K system or less. In the next chapter you will find that there is a better way to solve the problem, but for now changing the constant will suffice.

```
program Illustrate_Recursive_QuickSort;
  const SPACE      = #32;
        MAX_SIZE  = 500;

  type Word_Str   = string[10];
       Word_Array = array[1..MAX_SIZE] of Word_Str;
```

```pascal
var   word_list  : Word_Array;
      i          : Integer;
      inchr      : Char;
      word_cnt   : Integer;

procedure Read_TextFile(var words: Word_Array; var count: Integer);
  var   text_file : Text;
        text_line : string[255];
        file_name : string[64];

  procedure Extract_Words;
    var line_chr,
        word_chr : Integer;
        word     : string[255];

    begin
      word_chr := 1; line_chr := 1;
      repeat
        word_chr := 1;
        while (text_line[line_chr] in ['A'..'Z','a'..'z','_']) and
              (line_chr <= Length(text_line)) do
          begin
            word[word_chr] := text_line[line_chr];
            word_chr := Succ(word_chr);
            line_chr := Succ(line_chr);
          end; {while}
        if (word_chr > 1) then
          begin
            word[0] := Chr(word_chr - 1);
            count := Succ(count);
            words[count] := word;
          end; {if}
        line_chr := Succ(line_chr);
      until (line_chr > Length(text_line)) or (count = MAX_SIZE);
    end; { Extract_Words }

  begin { Read_Text_File }
    ClrScr;
    Write('Enter name of file containing text to be sorted. ==> ');
    ReadLn(file_name);
    WriteLn('Loading words from ',file_name);
    count := 0;
    Assign(text_file,file_name);
    Reset(text_file);
    while (not eof(text_file)) and (count < MAX_SIZE) do
      begin
        ReadLn(text_file,text_line);
        WriteLn(text_line);
        Extract_Words;
      end; {while}
    Close(text_file);
  end; { Read_TextFile }

(* Include the following directive if code is being compiled on
   an 8 bit CP/M system.
{$A-}
*)
  procedure Sort_List(var values: Word_Array; lo, hi: Integer);
    var new_lo,
        new_hi   : Integer;

    procedure Swap_Values(low, high: Integer);
      var hold_value : Word_Str;

      begin
        hold_value := values[low];
        values[low] := values[high];
        values[high] := hold_value;
      end; { Swap_Values }

    procedure Divide_Array(left, right: Integer);
      var center_value,
          hold_value : Word_Str;
```

```
      begin
        center_value := values[(hi + lo) div 2];
        left := lo; right := hi;
        while (left <= right) do
        begin
          while(values[left] < center_value) do
            left := Succ(left);
          while(values[right] > center_value) do
            right := Pred(right);
          if (left <= right) then
            begin
              Swap_Values(left,right);
              left := Succ(left);
              right := Pred(right);
            end; {if}
        end; {while}
        new_lo := left;
        new_hi := right;
      end; { Divide_Array }

    begin { Sort_List }
      if ((hi - lo) > 1) then
        begin
          Divide_Array(lo,hi);
          Sort_List(values,lo,new_hi);
          Sort_List(values,new_lo,hi);
        end
      else
          if ((hi - lo) = 1) then
            if (values[hi] < values[lo]) then
              Swap_Values(lo,hi);
      end; { Sort_List }

  (* Include the following directive if code is being compiled on
     an 8 bit CP/M system.
  {$A+}
  *)
    procedure Display_List;
      var prev_word : Word_Str;
          i, count,
          unique     : Integer;

      begin
        prev_word := word_list[1]; count := 1; unique := 0;
        for i := 2 to word_cnt do
          begin
            if (word_list[i] = prev_word) then
              count := Succ(count)
            else
              begin
                WriteLn(count:3,' ',prev_word);
                prev_word := word_list[i];
                count := 1; unique := Succ(unique);
              end; {else}
          end; {for}
          WriteLn(count:3,' ',prev_word); unique := Succ(unique);
        WriteLn; WriteLn(unique:5,' Unique words');
      end; { Display_List }

  begin { Illustrate_Recursive_Quicksort }
    Read_TextFile(word_list,word_cnt);
    WriteLn(word_cnt,' words.');
    Write('Press ANY KEY to start sort. ==> ');
    Read(Kbd,inchr); WriteLn;
    Sort_List(word_list,1,word_cnt);
    Write('List sorted. Do you want to see it? (Y/N) ==> ');
    repeat
      Read(Kbd,inchr); inchr := UpCase(inchr);
    until (inchr in ['Y','N']);
    WriteLn(inchr);
    if (inchr = 'Y') then
      Display_List;
  end. { Illustrate_Recursive_QuickSort }
```

After you have entered, successfully compiled, and saved the source code, give the program a test run. When prompted for a file name, enter the name that you used for the source code, including the .PAS extension. MS-DOS users with hard disks should include a path name if the file is in a subdirectory. To keep things simple, no error trapping is performed. If you enter a bad file name the program will abort, returning you to the editor when you press ESC. If that happens, just exit the editor and run the program again; no harm will be done.

When a valid file name is entered, you will see the source code displayed as the file is read from disk. You will then be notified as to the total number of words in the file and asked to press a key when you're ready to sort. You can clock the sort from the time you press a key until the next message is displayed. The message asks if you want to display the sorted list. When you press Y, each unique word will be displayed in sorted order preceded by a number indicating how many times that word appears in the text. At the end of the list the number of unique words will be shown. Remember that you may use CTRL-S to pause the scrolling and CTRL-Q to start it again. That is a built-in feature of all Turbo Pascal programs unless you use a compiler directive to disable it.

This program illustrates most of the things that have been covered to this point. You might find it helpful to list the source code on your printer and draw blocks around the code and add level numbers to indicate the scope of the identifiers in each routine. You might also consider how the program could be expanded to analyze the readability of a text file, or how it could be used as the basis for a cross-reference utility. As written, the program considers two words connected by an underline to be a single word. What change would you make so that it treats them as separate words?

When you've finished experimenting, prepare to get better acquainted with the more advanced features of the Turbo Pascal development environment. They will be the subject of Chapter 5.

FIVE

A Closer Look at
The Turbo Environment

One feature that increases Turbo Pascal's productivity is its unique, all-in-one program development system. In this chapter, the advanced features of the Turbo environment will be reviewed by having you type in a sample program and describing the editing and composing processes.

Using Turbo's Development System

The following program determines prime numbers between 1 and 16,384, using the sieve of Erastosthenes algorithm. The outer loop in the program causes the sequence to be repeated ten times to make the time easier to measure on faster systems.

```
program Primes; { Count prime numbers from 3 through (SIZE * 2 + 3) }

{$R+}              { Turn on run time range checking }

const   SIZE    = 8190;
                                { Note that the array is too small }
var     flags                 : array[0..8180] of Boolean;
        i, j, k, prime, count  : Integer;

begin { primes }
  ClrScr GoToXY(1,12);         { Video housekeeping. Note missing semicolon  }
  WriteLn('10 iterations');
     for i := 1 to 10 do       { Set up main loop for 10 iterations }
        begin
          count := 0;                         { Initialize counter }
          FillChar(flags,SizeOf(flags),TRUE); { Initialize all flags to True }
          for j := 0 to SIZE do               { note use of FillChar here    }
            begin
              if flags[j] then                { Next prime base found }
                begin
                  prime := j + j + 3;         { Calculate next prime }
                  k := j + prime;
```

```
        {       WriteLn(prime);  }           { Un-comment to see primes }
                While (k <= SIZE) do
                   begin
                      flags[k] := FALSE;      { Mark multiples as not primes }
                      k := k + prime;
                   end;
                count := Succ(count);         { Increment count }
            end; { if }
         end; { for j }
      end; { for i }
   WriteLn(count,' primes.');                 { Output number of primes found }
end. { Primes }
```

To begin, start your computer and load Turbo Pascal. Figure 5-1 illustrates the Turbo main menu as it appears on the CP/M and MS-DOS systems. In addition to examining Turbo's built-in debugging tools, you will see how some of these menu selections are used as you enter and debug the Primes program. Follow the steps outlined here.

1. Edit the source code. Since you will be working on the Primes program, press W to select Work file from the menu and enter PRIMES when prompted for a file name. Next, press E to select Edit and the screen will clear as you enter the Turbo editor. You should enter the source code as shown in the listing, except you may leave out the comments. The WriteLn statement that is isolated by comments should, however, remain isolated for timing purposes. You may activate the statement by removing the comments if you would like to print the prime numbers as they are identified. As noted in the comments, a couple of errors have been purposely planted in the source code to illustrate Turbo's built-in debugging aids.

2. Now compile the source code by pressing CTRL-KD to exit the editor and return to the Turbo Pascal menu. Unless you want to abandon the changes you made while editing, you should press S to save your work after exiting the editor. Now press C to compile the source code. Almost instantly the compiler advises you that there is a problem with the source code in the form of a missing semicolon. Here is the actual message:

```
Compiling
   9 Lines
Error 1: ';' expected. Press <ESC>
```

Press ESC and you will find yourself back in the editor with the cursor positioned at the error. Then it's a matter of a few keystrokes to correct the problem and you are ready to try compiling it again. Exit the editor and press C to compile the source code once again. A second or so will pass as it successfully compiles into ready-to-run machine code or object code.

3. After the program has successfully compiled and you are in the main menu, run the machine code by pressing R.

4. You will be surprised to see that your efforts have failed again.

Although syntactical errors can be detected during the compiler phase, logic errors aren't detected until run-time. Since the program was compiled in memory, you will see this error message after the program failed:

```
Run-time error 90, PC=28E3
Program aborted

Searching
  22 Lines

Run-time error position found. Press <ESC>
```

What you see here is an error number and a 4-digit hex value representing the PC, or *program counter*. A quick check of the Turbo reference manual indicates that run-time error 90 is an **Index out of range** error. With a short program like Primes, you could probably find the error without too much difficulty, but in a large and complex program, the error message wouldn't give you much to go on. The second value in the error message, the PC value, is the key to finding exactly where the problem occurred. As a matter of fact, since this program was compiled in memory, the compiler is now eager to show you the statement that was executing at the time of the error. Just press ESC.

The culprit would appear to be the loop counter **k**, which is used as an index into the **flags** array. A quick check of the loop-limit constant SIZE and the array definition of **flags** and the problem is obvious. Change the upper limit of the **flags** array to 8190.

As this experiment has shown, the combined editor and compiler development system allow you to spend your time coding and testing as opposed to waiting while the system juggles disk files, which is too often the case with

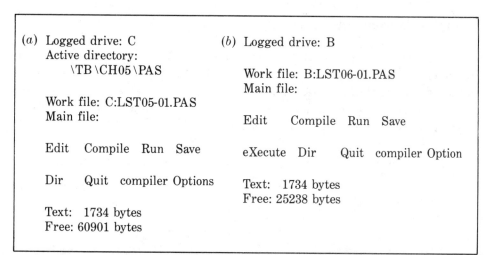

(*a*) Logged drive: C
Active directory:
    \TB\CH05\PAS

Work file: C:LST05-01.PAS
Main file:

Edit   Compile   Run   Save

Dir   Quit   compiler Options

Text: 1734 bytes
Free: 60901 bytes

(*b*) Logged drive: B

Work file: B:LST06-01.PAS
Main file:

Edit   Compile   Run   Save

eXecute   Dir   Quit   compiler Option

Text: 1734 bytes
Free: 25238 bytes

Figure 5-1.   The Turbo Pascal main menu for (*a*) MS-DOS and (*b*) CP/M versions

traditional compilers. However, what good is this time saved if the result is not efficient? Now that you've successfully compiled the corrected version of the Primes program, run it again and check the timing. On a standard IBM PC system, it runs in about 17 seconds. That's a respectable time; however, it could be better. The {$R+} compiler directive located after the program declaration switches on Turbo's range-checking option (discussed in Chapter 7). Range checking will help find index errors, but once the program is error-free range checking serves no purpose except to slow execution of the program.

On some Pascal compilers, range checking is not optional; you get it whether you want it or not. Turbo Pascal allows you to decide whether the additional overhead is worth the help in locating errors. By either eliminating the directive from the program or deactivating it by changing the + to a −, you can turn off Turbo's run-time range checking. Just for fun, do that and then recompile and time the program again. You will find that Turbo's object code for this program is just as fast and efficient as that produced by any other compiler.

Compiler Options

Turbo Pascal offers three ways to compile a program. As you will see, each one has its benefits and limitations. Depending on the method selected, there may be additional options that allow you to control certain aspects of the compilation. These additional options will be covered briefly here and in depth in Chapter 7 when chain files are discussed.

To select a compiler option just press O while at the Turbo menu screen. The Options menu in Figure 5-2 will be displayed. Each of the three methods of compilation as well as the find-error selection will be discussed.

Compile to Memory

The Compile to Memory option is the default selection that is in effect when Turbo is loaded. As long as you are working on small programs, this method is the best. Compilation is fast, and test runs are as easy as pressing R. Run-time errors are detected automatically. There are some limitations though.

The primary limit is the amount of memory available. Even using *include*

```
compile → Memory
          Com-file
          cHn-file

command line Parameters:

Find run-time error   Quit
```

Figure 5-2.   The compiler Options menu

files to save memory (explained in Chapter 7) is not an adequate solution because a large program will produce a large object program, which must remain in memory. Eight-bit CP/M implementations will reach this point much sooner than the 16-bit versions, since everything has to fit into 64K of memory under CP/M-80.

Compile to a .COM File

When a program is copied to memory, no permanent record is made of the object code. This is fine during the development and testing phases; however, you will eventually want to store the object code in a disk file. The Com option will save the executable object code in a .COM file. To execute the file, simply type the file name from the operating system from the Turbo main menu. You can see this is much simpler than compiling the program every time you want to execute it.

To save the executable object code, select O for the compiler Options menu. Then press C to indicate that you want to save the object code in a .COM file. Now press Q to leave the Options menu and return to the main menu. Press C to start the compilation process.

If the program has been compiled to memory and no changes have been made to the program prior to issuing this command sequence, the object code is immediately saved to disk as a .COM file. Otherwise, when you enter C to compile the program, the object code is transferred to disk as it is generated. Because the object code is compiled directly to disk, much larger source files may be compiled using the Com option as compared to the Memory option, where the source and object code must reside in memory at the same time.

When you press C to select Com from the compiler Options menu, you will notice that some additional selections are added to the menu. These selections are different depending on whether you are using a CP/M or an MS-DOS version of Turbo Pascal. The significance of these choices will be covered in Chapter 7 as the Chain procedure is discussed.

Compile to a Chain File

When you compile a program using the Chain option, the object code is saved to a file with an extension of .CHN. While this .CHN file is not directly executable from the operating system, it is executable from another Turbo Pascal .COM or .CHN program. It is this facility that makes it possible to write applications that are theoretically unlimited in size.

To better understand the benefits of .CHN files, you should see how a .CHN file compares to a .COM file. Whenever you compile a program to a .COM file, the object code for the predefined Turbo subprograms, such as the WriteLn and Assign procedures, is saved to the .COM file first. This code is called the *nucleus*. Depending on the version of Turbo you are using, the smallest programs will create a .COM file of about 9 or 10K.

If you were to examine the program's object code that follows the nucleus, you would find that much of it consists of calls to routines to the nucleus. When you use the Chain compiler option, all that is saved is the program's object code, *not* the nucleus. As a result, .CHN files will always be 9 or 10K smaller than a comparable .COM file.

Chain files are executed by other programs using the Chain procedure. This procedure is included in the program and names the chain file that it wants to execute. When the Chain procedure is used to execute a program compiled to a .CHN file, it assumes that the nucleus code has already been loaded via the prior execution of a Turbo .COM file. Chapter 7 will explain chain files in detail, but the benefits of using them are twofold: first, it means large applications can be divided into chain programs to run on systems with limited memory; second, time and disk space are saved by not duplicating the nucleus in each program segment.

Command Line Parameters

Beginning with version 3.0, Turbo Pascal supports *command line parameters*. Command line parameters are entered following a program name when the program is executed from the operating system. For example when you issue the operating system command

TYPE MYFILE.TXT

MYFILE.TXT is a parameter that is passed to the operating system TYPE command. Suppose that you want to write a Pascal program like TYPE that formats its output. You might call it FTYPE, and the user would use it by entering

FTYPE MYFILE.TXT

from the operating system command line. The problem is that once your program starts executing, how can it determine what the command line parameter was? Before the release of version 3.0 it could be done, but you had to make your program system-dependent to do so. As the advanced predefined subprograms are outlined in Chapter 7, you will find routines named ParamCount and ParamStr that let the .COM file know how many parameters were entered on the command line and what each one was.

The purpose of the parameters selection from the compiler Options menu is to simulate the passing of command line parameters. This is only needed when you are developing an application using the Compile to Memory option. When you select P, for Parameters, you are prompted to enter the parameters you want to test. After doing so you can run the program compiled in memory, and ParamCount and ParamStr will perform as if the program had been executed as a .COM file from the operating system command line. This permits you to test your program without the inconvenience of exiting to the operating system to perform the test.

Finding Run-Time Errors

When you were debugging the Primes program and had the **Index out of Range** problem, the compiler was right there to point out the location of the error. This is because the program had been compiled to memory. Suppose, however, that in a burst of overconfidence you had assumed all was well after the successful compilation. To recreate that set of events, follow these steps:

1. Enter the Turbo editor and load the working version of the Primes program. Be sure it includes the {$R+} directive.

2. Reintroduce the range error by changing the **flags** array declaration back to 8180.

3. Exit the editor and press O for Options, C for Com, Q for Quit, and C for Compile. This will compile Primes into a file called PRIMES.COM.

4. After the program successfully compiles, press Q for Quit to leave Turbo and return to the operating system. Upon doing so you will be asked if you want to save the modified .PAS version of Primes. Press N unless you want to save this broken version.

5. Now execute the program by entering PRIMES.

You will get the same error message (with a different PC value) that appeared when it was tested in memory. But this time the compiler is not here to come to the rescue by showing you where the problem occurred. If you will make a note of the four-digit hexadecimal value of the program counter, you can still use the Turbo compiler to find the problem.

6. Restart Turbo and press Y for messages. Then press O to get to the Options menu. Now press F for Find. The Find option searches for run-time errors by asking for the program counter and the name of the program.

7. Enter the program counter by giving the hexadecimal value. Next you will be prompted for the name of the source file. After you identify the file, it will be loaded and searched until the offending statement is located and displayed for you to examine.

As you become familiar with this process and use it more and more, you'll see that the Find option is indispensable when you're working with large programs.

Changing the Logged Drive and Directory

When you enter TURBO to load Turbo Pascal, the disk drive containing the Turbo disk will be the logged drive when the main menu is first displayed. Let's say that the file you want to work with is on a disk in drive B and you are currently logged on to drive A.

Press L to indicate that you wish to change drives, and then press B RETURN or press B: to specify drive B.

After changing the logged drive, the menu screen still shows the logged drive as A:. The menu is not automatically refreshed. You must press a key that is not a command key to update the menu. The Turbo reference manual suggests using the SPACEBAR without explaining why the update isn't done automatically. One suggestion is that it saves time for those who are using Turbo on a system with a terminal that has a slow video refresh.

If you try to select a drive that doesn't exist, nothing happens. If you select a drive that exists but is not ready — the drive door is open, for example — the result will depend on your operating system and computer. If your system is running under CP/M, you will return to the CP/M system prompt or wait until the not ready condition is corrected. MS-DOS users are given the options to retry, abort, or ignore the problem.

Changing the Active Directory

This option appears only on the MS-DOS version of Turbo Pascal and is used primarily by those with hard disk systems.

The command is initiated by pressing A. You will then be prompted to enter the *path name* of the directory you want to access. For an in-depth description of paths and their uses, see your MS-DOS manual. The purpose of this command is to permit free access to files in any directory. This facility has been greatly enhanced in MS-DOS Turbo version 3.0, in that any time a file name is required, a path and drive specification may be included. If you try to move to a nonexistent directory, the system will beep and nothing happens.

If you are using Turbo Pascal on an MS-DOS hard disk system and will be working on more than one project, you may want to place the TURBO.COM file in a subdirectory with the .COM, .EXE, and .BAT files that you commonly use. You should include the MS-DOS PATH command in the AUTO-EXEC.BAT file that takes control when you start up the system. The PATH command tells the operating system where to look for executable files if they can't be found in the currently active directory. This eliminates the need to copy TURBO.COM files in every subdirectory for which you will be working with Turbo. Unfortunately, PATH doesn't work with non-executable files. So in order to access the Turbo message file, TURBO.MSG, it will have to be present in the directory where you are working, unless you are using Turbo 3.0 or later.

Moving Files Between Drives

Turbo does not offer a command in the main menu to copy a file directly from one drive or directory to another. At first glance you might think you could log on to the source drive, load a file into the editor using the work file selection, change the logged drive (or directory) to the destination drive, and save the file by selecting Save. Actually, nothing will be accomplished by these maneuvers. Turbo always saves a file back to the name and drive it was loaded from. You can copy a file by changing the active drive, but there is a little trick to it.

1. Use the Logged drive selection to log on to the drive that will be the final destination of the file to be copied.

2. Use the Work file selection to indicate the destination file name.

3. Press E to activate the Turbo editor.

4. Import the source file with the Block Read command by pressing CTRL-KR, followed by the name of the source file, preceded by a drive specifier. For example, B:TESTFILE.PAS.

5. Exit the editor and press S to save the file on the destination drive.

An alternative version of this same idea uses the editor's Block Write command. It is especially useful when you need to transfer a chunk of code from another file.

The DIR Menu Selection

Pressing D at the main menu gives you access to the operating system's DIR command without leaving the Turbo environment. The command functions exactly like the operating system's directory command, including the use of wild cards and drive identifiers. MS-DOS path names are not supported in versions of Turbo Pascal prior to 3.0, so you will have to use the Active directory command to indicate the subdirectory.

When you press D you will be prompted to enter a directory *mask*. If you want to see the complete directory, just press RETURN. The space remaining in bytes per thousand on the active drive is also indicated. To display only the Pascal source files, you could enter a mask of *.PAS, just as you would at the operating system level. MS-DOS users will note that the directory is presented in the wide format without date and time information.

The Work File and the Main File

The Work file may be used to specify the file you will be working with. If you press E, C, R, or S prior to assigning a file to the work space, you will be prompted for a file name. In the case of C and R (Compile and Run), you must enter an existing Pascal source file. If your choice was E (for Edit), the file specified may be an existing file, which will be loaded into the editor, or a new file, which will be created by the editor. A file in the work space saves you from entering a file name every time you use a Turbo command; it becomes the default file used by the Edit, Compile, Run, and Save commands.

One advantage of a work file is when you are working with one file and need to change to a different file. This will happen frequently as you work on applications involving include files.

The selection of a main file provides convenience when working with include files. While an in-depth discussion must wait until Chapter 7, a brief explanation of include files seems to be in order.

One reason Turbo Pascal compiles programs quickly is because it is able to do most of its work in memory, which means there is a minimum of disk activity. This is possible because the compiler is small enough to reside in memory along with the source code it is compiling. Of course this imposes a limitation on the amount of source code that can be available for compilation at any one time. The way around this limitation is the use of include files. The program may be divided into groups of subprograms with each saved as a separate file. The number of divisions depends on the memory available and the size of the program. The main program file then references or calls these files by using the {$I *filename*} include directive, where *filename* represents a file containing a section of source code. The end result is a small main program file consisting of a series of include directives. As the main program is compiled and an include directive is encountered, the source code from the include file is read and compiled.

As long as the source code in the include file compiles without error, the main program file remains resident in memory and is the current work file. However, when the compiler detects an error in the include file, the include file is automatically loaded and becomes the current work file so that you may easily fix the problem. Once that's done, you want to try to compile again. However, if you try to compile the include file, which is *not* a complete program, it will be rejected; the compiler must start with the main program. One solution is to save the corrected include file, then reset the work file to indicate the main program file, and then restart the compilation.

This process can be extremely time-consuming and inconvenient if you are compiling a program with many include files. If you have used Main to indicate the main program file, the steps outlined here will be taken care of automatically. Specifying a main file for compilation solves the problem by having the main program immediately available for compilation. Once a file is set to the main file, the compiler always begins with the main file. Then if an error occurs in an include file, it is loaded into the work file for the editor, and when you press C to recompile, the include file is saved and the main file reloaded before compilation begins.

The Execute Command *(CP/M-80 Only)*

The Execute command allows you to run any .COM program and return to the Turbo system automatically. When you press X, for Execute, you will be prompted to enter the file name of an executable program. It can be a Turbo .COM program, an operating system utility, or what have you. When program execution ends, you will find yourself back in Turbo.

This is possible because of a Turbo loader routine residing directly below CP/M in high memory. Turbo causes the loader routine to be executed upon termination of the system program. Unfortunately for MS-DOS and CP/M-86 users, this scheme doesn't work.

SIX

Predefined Subprograms

In this chapter you will examine procedures and functions that are predefined in Turbo Pascal. This chapter will provide both an introduction to the subprograms and a quick reference source.

Procedures and functions have been grouped together by category. Within each group, subprograms will be presented in alphabetic order. Table 6-1 summarizes the I/O-related subprograms. Unless otherwise noted, when a variable is used to illustrate a parameter, it may be replaced by a constant or an expression of the same data type. A general exception is file type parameters, which are never represented by constants or expressions.

Predefined Video and Keyboard Procedures and Functions

As you will notice in Table 6-1, I/O has been subdivided into video and keyboard sections and an external device and file section. The video control procedures together with Borland's Terminal Installation Program go a long way toward solving the terminal incompatibility problems that plague developers trying to serve a broad market. The problem exists because there is no accepted, standard set of control codes for manipulation, as in positioning the cursor or clearing the line from the current cursor position to the end of the line.

When you install Turbo Pascal for your terminal, you are modifying the compiler so that it will issue control codes to your video. Because the code for these routines is hardware-dependent, the actual result will depend on your terminal type. For example, if your terminal does not support highlighting, the HighVideo and LowVideo procedures won't have any effect.

Table 6-1. Predefined I/O Procedures and Functions

Identifier	Function or Procedure	Standard	Turbo	Description
Video and Keyboard I/O				
ClrEol	P	N	Y	Clear from cursor to end of line
ClrScr	P	N	Y	Clear video screen and position cursor at home
CrtExit	P	N	Y	Output terminal reset control string
CrtInit	P	N	Y	Output terminal initialization string
DelLine	P	N	Y	Delete line at cursor position
GoToXY	P	N	Y	Position cursor at coordinates indicated in parameter
HighVideo	P	N	Y	Output in high intensity
InsLine	P	N	Y	Insert line at cursor position
IOresult	F	N	Y	Returns I/O status for error trapping
KeyPressed	F	N	Y	TRUE if character waiting in keyboard buffer
LowVideo	P	N	Y	Output in low intensity
NormVideo	P	N	Y	Same as HighVideo
Page	P	Y	N	Clear video or top of form
External Device and File I/O				
Append	P	N	Y	Open Text file for appended output
Assign	P	N	Y	Associate file name with file variable
BlockRead	P	N	Y	Untyped transfer from disk to memory
BlockWrite	P	N	Y	Untyped transfer from memory to disk
Chain	P	N	Y	Load and execute Turbo .CHN file
Close	P	N	Y	Exit housekeeping on external file

(continued)

Table 6-1. Predefined I/O Procedures and Functions (*continued*)

Identifier	Function or Procedure	Standard	Turbo	Description
External Device and File I/O				
Eof	F	Y	Y	TRUE if file pointer at end of file
EoLn	F	Y	Y	TRUE if Text file at end of line
Erase	P	N	Y	Remove external file from directory
Execute	P	N	Y	Load and execute a .COM file
FilePos	F	N	Y	Returns position of file pointer
FileSize	F	N	Y	Returns size of non-Text file
Flush	P	N	Y	Forces sector buffer out to disk
Get	P	Y	N	Low-level input—not needed in Turbo
LongFilePos	F	N	Y	Returns file pointer positions for files greater than 32K
LongFileSize	F	N	Y	Returns non-Text file size for files greater than 32K
LongSeek	P	N	Y	Positions file pointer in files for files greater than 32K
Put	P	Y	N	Low-level output—not needed in Turbo
Read	P	Y	Y	Input data from file or device
ReadLn	P	Y	Y	ReadLn skips to end of line
Rename	P	N	Y	Change file name of external disk file
Reset	P	Y	Y	Open disk file
Rewrite	P	Y	Y	Create and open new disk file
Seek	P	N	Y	Position file pointer in non-Text file
Truncate	P	N	Y	Mark end of non-Text file at file pointer
Write	P	Y	Y	Output data to a file or device
WriteLn	P	Y	Y	WriteLn adds end of line

ClrEol

The ClrEol procedure clears the line from the cursor position to the end of the line without moving the cursor. The syntax is

ClrEol;

ClrScr

The ClrScr procedure clears the video screen and positions the cursor in the upper-left corner, which is column 1, row 1. The syntax is

ClrScr;

CrtExit and CrtInit

These two procedures output user-definable terminal control strings to the terminal. Some terminals permit you to define programmable function keys by sending control codes followed by the codes to be produced when a selected function key is pressed. When you install Turbo Pascal, you may specify both an initialization and an exit-control string that define the function keys upon entering a program and reset them to a default value as the program terminates. The CrtInit procedure sends the terminal-initialization string, while CrtExit sends the exit-control string. Both of these strings may be defined when Turbo Pascal is installed. The syntaxes are

CrtInit;

and

CrtExit;

DelLine

The DelLine procedure deletes a line of text at the cursor position and shifts all text below up one line. The syntax is

DelLine;

GoToXY

The syntax is

$$GoToXY(x\_col, y\_row);$$

The parameters x_col, which indicates the column, and y_row, which indicates the row, must be integer values. The upper-left corner is column 1, row 1. An error will occur if the parameters are out of range.

HighVideo or NormVideo

Subsequent output to the screen will be highlighted if your terminal or system monitor supports dual-intensity output. The two procedures are equivalent. The syntax is

$$HighVideo;$$

or

$$NormVideo;$$

InsLine

The InsLine procedure inserts a blank line at the current cursor position and shifts all lines below it down one line; the last line is lost from the screen. The syntax is

$$InsLine;$$

IOresult

The IOresult function, which returns an integer value, must be called following any I/O activity if you are doing your own I/O error trapping. This is determined by the setting of the {$I—} compiler directive, which will be discussed in Chapter 7. If an error occurs, IOresult returns an error number corresponding to those listed in the Turbo reference manual under "I/O Error Messages." If there is no error, zero is returned. The syntax for IOresult is

$$IOresult;$$

KeyPressed

The Boolean function KeyPressed returns a value of TRUE if a key has been pressed at the keyboard. The syntax is

> KeyPressed;

This function is dependent on the operating system console status routine. Therefore, depending on the system, keyboard input may be stored in a buffer capable of holding more than one character. Here is an example of how KeyPressed halts your program until the user presses a key:

> **repeat**
> **until** KeyPressed;

Keep in mind that KeyPressed does not do anything with the character after it has been entered on the keyboard. Instead the character will appear when input is requested with the Read procedure.

LowVideo

The LowVideo procedure displays output to the video monitor in low intensity if the terminal supports dual-intensity output. The syntax is

> LowVideo;

Page

The Page procedure sends a top-of-form character to an output device, usually the printer. The Page procedure is defined in standard Pascal but not in Turbo Pascal. The reason is that CP/M does not define a form feed character. You can implement the Page procedure yourself.

```
procedure Page(var output_device: Text);

{requires that global constant FF be set to the system
form feed character, which is #12 for most printers.}

begin
Write(output_device,FF);
end; {Page}
```

This procedure will work with any Text type device or file, but normally it forces a page eject on a printer. On some systems, an ASCII #12 will cause a form feed when sent to the printer and clear the video when output to the console device. Even if you're not that fortunate, it will still work in almost every case if **output_device** represents a printer. If you are using a serial printer, pass Aux as the output device; otherwise, use Lst. The syntax is

Page(*output_device*);

External and Disk File Procedures and Functions

The following subprograms are concerned with moving data to and from external devices and disk files. The Get and Put procedures are listed in this section, though they are not used by Turbo Pascal.

Append

Append was added to Turbo Pascal with the release of version 3.0. It is not available on the CP/M versions. Append may be used in place of Reset to open an existing Text type file and position the file pointer at the end of the file. The file is opened for output; therefore, any attempt to read from it will cause an I/O error. The syntax is

Append(*text_file*);

where *text_file* is the name of an existing file and is of type Text.

Assign

The Assign procedure links a file variable to a file name on disk. The syntax is

Assign (*file_var, file_name*);

file_var may be any Text file or user-defined file of type variable, except the predefined variables Con, Lst, Aux, and so on. *file_name* must be a valid file name.

On MS-DOS systems, *file_name* may include a path name. Following the activation of Assign, a disk file specified by *file_name* is associated with *file_var* until *file_var* is used as the parameter for the Close procedure.

BlockRead

The BlockRead procedure reads in 128-byte blocks from an untyped disk file into a buffer variable, which may be of any type. BlockRead is a useful procedure for processing an external file when you are uncertain of the type of the data stored in the file. BlockRead is helpful for converting data from one system to another, copying data from one file to another, or trying to determine the content and structure of data items created by another system. An I/O error is generated if you attempt to read past the end of the disk file. Note that the subprograms Eof, FileSize, FilePos, and Seek, as described later in this chapter, can be used with untyped files. The syntax is

BlockRead(*untyped,any__var,rec__cnt*);

or for version 3.0

BlockRead(*untyped,any__var,rec__cnt,count*);

untyped is an untyped file variable that has been assigned to a disk file and opened with Reset or Rewrite. *any__var* represents any variable that is large enough to hold the transferred data. The space may be calculated as *rec__cnt* * 128, where *rec__cnt* indicates the number of 128-byte blocks to be read from disk into memory starting at the address of *any__var*. *count* is an optional variable parameter, available beginning with Turbo version 3.0, that returns the number of 128-byte blocks actually read by the BlockRead procedure. *count* may not be replaced by a constant or an expression.

BlockWrite

BlockWrite, the complementary procedure of BlockRead, writes data in 128-byte blocks from memory to a disk file. The syntax is

BlockWrite(*untyped,any__var,rec__cnt*);

or for version 3.0

BlockWrite(*untyped,any__var,rec__cnt,count*);

Upon activation, BlockWrite will transfer 128 * *rec__cnt* bytes from memory, starting with the first byte of *any__var*, to the disk file indicated by *untyped*. If you have a memory-mapped system on your computer, you will find that this is a great way to store and retrieve video images with amazing speed.

The optional fourth parameter returns the number of records actually written.

Chain

The Chain procedure is used to load and transfer control to a .CHN file, which is created by the Turbo Pascal compiler using the Chain option. The purpose of .CHN files will be covered in Chapter 7. The syntax is

$$\text{Chain}(chn\_file);$$

where *chn*—*file* is assigned to a .CHN file, with the Assign function, prior to activating the Chain procedure. *chn*—*file* can be declared as any file type.

Close

The Close procedure closes an open file and writes any information in the file buffer to the disk file. The Close procedure should be called prior to terminating a program; failure to do so will very likely result in lost data. It is a good practice to close all files that have been opened (see Reset and Rewrite) even if you haven't modified the data. If you are using Turbo version 3.0 or later on an MS-DOS system, you must close any file that has been opened. Because these systems access files via MS-DOS *file handles*, if you don't use Close to release the file handles, DOS will issue an **out of handles** error when the maximum number of handles has been allocated. For more information on file handles see your MS-DOS technical reference manual. The syntax for Close is

$$\text{Close}(file\_var);$$

where *file*—*var* is a file variable of any file type.

Eof and SeekEof

The syntax for Eof is

$$\text{Eof}(file\_var);$$

The file variable *file*—*var* can be of any file type. Eof returns a value of TRUE if the file pointer for *file*—*var* is positioned at the end of the file.

SeekEof was added to Turbo when version 3.0 was issued. It works like Eof except that tabs (#9) and blanks (#32) are skipped prior to testing for the end-of-file character.

EoLn and SeekEoLn

Use EoLn with Text type file only. If *text—file* represents a disk file, EoLn will return TRUE if the next character is an end-of-line or end-of-file character. Where *text—file* represents a logical device, EoLn will return TRUE if the last character read was an end-of-line or end-of-file character. The following example reads characters from the file variable **cashe** until an end-of-line marker is encountered.

> **while not** (EoLn (cashe)) **do**
> Read (cashe,chrl);

SeekEoLn was added to Turbo when version 3.0 was issued. It works like EoLn except that tabs (#9) and blanks (#32) are skipped prior to testing for the end-of-line sequence, which is a carriage return and line feed character.

Erase

The syntax for Erase is

> Erase (*file—var*);

Use Erase to delete the file indicated by *file—var*, which can be any file type. Unless you own a good file recovery utility, the results of Erase are final. You should always be sure a file is closed before you erase it. Erasing an open file may confuse the file directories if you later try to close the same file.

Execute

The syntax for Execute is

> Execute(*exec—file*);

Execute loads and transfers control to the disk file indicated by *exec—file*. *exec—file* may be any valid .COM program file if you are using a CP/M-80 version of Turbo Pascal. The MS-DOS and CP/M-86 versions are restricted to .COM programs created by the Turbo compiler.

FilePos

The syntax for this Integer function is

> FilePos(*file—var*);

FilePos returns the value of the file pointer for *file_var*, thus indicating which data item will be read from or written to. The first item in a file is numbered 0, and the file must be open. The parameter *file_var* may be any untyped file or user-defined file of type variable, but may not be of the Text type.

FileSize

The syntax for FileSize is

$$FileSize(file\_var);$$

The Integer function FileSize returns the size of *file_var*, a non-text file. The size is expressed as a number of data items based on the component type of *file_var*. If *file_var* represents an untyped file, the component size is 128 bytes.

Flush

On CP/M systems the Flush procedure forces data from the buffer file interface block (FIB) to the disk file without closing the file. It has no effect on MS-DOS systems and is not valid for Text type files. The syntax is

$$Flush(file\_var);$$

Get and Put

Get and Put, which are not implemented in Turbo Pascal, are low-level I/O procedures in standard Pascal that manipulate buffer variables. Buffer variables allocate storage for a single data item from the base type of the file. The buffer variable is accessed using the file identifier plus a circumflex character, in much the same way a dynamic variable is accessed. Get transfers a data item from a file to its buffer variable. In standard Pascal all files are sequential, and Put can only be used to add items to the end of the file. Fortunately Turbo Pascal offers a rich set of file manipulation routines that eliminates the two-stage process of Get and Put.

LongFilePos

This version of FilePos is for files with more than 32K records. It returns the position of the file pointer as a Real value. LongFilePos is not available on

CP/M systems. The syntax for LongFilePos is

$$\text{LongFilePos}(\textit{file\_var});$$

LongFileSize

LongFileSize returns the size of a non-text file as a Real value. The syntax for LongFileSize is

$$\text{LongFileSize}(\textit{file\_var});$$

If *file_var* represents an untyped file, each component item is 128 bytes long. Because LongFileSize returns a Real value, it may be used to determine the size of very large files. It is not available on CP/M systems.

LongSeek

Function LongSeek, coupled with the LongFilePos and LongFileSize functions, accommodates the extended file sizes for MS-DOS-based systems. The syntax for LongSeek is

$$\text{LongSeek}(\textit{file\_var,rec\_ptr});$$

LongSeek positions the file pointer so that the next record accessed will be indicated by *rec_ptr*. Since *rec_ptr* is a Real value, the size of a file is limited only by disk storage capacity.

Read

The format for Read is

$$\text{Read}([\textit{file\_var}_1]);$$

If the first parameter is *not* a file type variable, the predefined Text file is assumed and data is accepted from the keyboard. A number of variables may follow a file of Text. They may be a mixture of Real, String, Integer, Byte, or Char. For example, if **str1** is a String variable, **int1** an Integer type variable, **fp** a Real type variable, and **chr1** a Char variable, then

$$\text{Read}(\text{text\_file, str1, int1, fp, chr1});$$

will read a String, an Integer, a Real number, and a Char from **text__file**. The Read procedure assumes that the four data items in **text__file** will match the variable types; if not, an error will occur. If all goes well, the Text file pointer will advance so that the next call to Read will input the data item following **chr1**.

If the data source is a user-defined type, the variable must be a component type of the file. For example, if **pmt__file** and **payment** are both declared to be of user-defined type **Payment__Rec,**

> **var** pmt__file : file f Payment__Rec;
> payment : Payment__Rec;

then the following Read statement will input one **Payment__Rec** type data item from **pmt__file** into **payment:**

> Read (pmt__file,payment);

This assumes that **pmt__file** has been assigned to a disk file containing data items of the Payment__Rec type.

ReadLn

ReadLn reads data from Text files, just like the Read procedure, except that all characters including the next end-of-line indicator will be skipped. The end-of-line indicator in Turbo Pascal is the ASCII two-character sequence #13 #10, usually called the carriage return and line feed sequence and abbreviated CR LF.

The format for ReadLn is

> ReadLn ([*file__var*], *variable*₁)

If *file__var* is included, it must be assigned to a Text file; otherwise, ReadLn will read the keyboard. The variable *variable*₁ may be any string type. ReadLn may be called without any parameters or with only the **text__file** parameter. For example,

> ReadLn;
> ReadLn(text__file);

causes ReadLn to skip an entire line. Attempting to use Read or ReadLn past the end of a file will result in an I/O error.

Rename

Rename changes the file name of an external disk file. The format for Rename is

Rename*(file—var,'newname');*

where *file—var* is a file variable assigned to a file and *'newname'* is a string constant or string variable of the new file name. For example, if the file variable **acorn** has been assigned to an external file named 'TEXT.DAT', the statement

Rename(**acorn**,'PAYMENT.DAT');

will rename the file PAYMENT.DAT. Rename does *not* check to see if a file named PAYMENT.DAT already exists. If such a file does exist, serious problems can result. Never use Rename if the disk file indicated by *file—var* is open.

Reset

Reset opens a file and sets the file pointer to the beginning of the file. The syntax is

Reset*(file—var)*;

where *file—var* is a file variable assigned to a file. If the external file indicated by *file—var* does not exist, an I/O error occurs. If *file—var* is a Text type variable, the file is opened for input only. Attempting to write to Text file opened with Reset will generate an I/O error. Read or ReadLn will read data items from the file sequentially. After the last data item is read, the end-of-file condition will become TRUE.

Rewrite

Rewrite creates a file with a file specification according to the file variable. If a file already exists with that specification, then its contents are lost. Don't use Rewrite when you intended to use Reset. The syntax for Rewrite is

Rewrite*(file—var)*;

where *file—var* is a file variable that has been assigned to a file name.

If *file—var* is a Text type variable, the file is opened for output only. Attempting to read the file will generate an I/O error. Write or WriteLn will add data items to the end of the file. When the file is closed, the end-of-file indicator is added automatically.

Following the use of either Reset or Rewrite on a non-text file, the file pointer will reference the first data item in the file, which is element 0. When used with Text files, Reset and Rewrite set the file pointer at the beginning of the file, ready to begin sequential processing.

Seek

Use Seek to move the file pointer in a file. The syntax is

$$\text{Seek}(\mathit{file\_var,rec\_ptr});$$

where *file_var* has been assigned to the file and *rec_ptr*, an integer variable or constant, is the number of positions to move the file pointer. If *file_var* has not been opened or *rec_ptr* is greater than the size of the file or less than zero, an I/O error will be generated. Don't forget that the first data item in *file_var* is zero.

Truncate

The Truncate procedure was added to Turbo with the release of version 3.0. Its purpose is to mark the end of the file at the current file pointer position, which effectively truncates the file. The syntax for Truncate is

$$\text{Truncate }(\mathit{file\_var});$$

where *file_var* is a file variable of any file type.

Write

The Write procedure outputs data items to an external file or device. The format for Write is

$$\text{Write}([\mathit{file\_var1}]\dots);$$

If the first parameter is *not* a user-defined file variable, the predefined Text file output is assumed, which is the video monitor. When the first parameter is a Text type variable, a list of parameters may follow. Those parameters may be any mixture of the predefined types Real, String, Integer, Byte,

Char, or Boolean. For example, if **str1** is of type String, **int1** of type Integer, **fp** of type Real, and **bool** of type Boolean, then

> Write(text—file,str1,int1,fp,chr1,bool);

will output a String, an Integer, a Real number, a Char, and a Boolean value. Note that Boolean is an exception to the rule that you cannot use Write to output variables or literal constants of enumerated types. For example, assuming you have defined an enumerated type called Measure and declared a variable of type Measure

> **type** Measure = (TSP,TBS,CUP,PINT,QUART);
> **var** amount : Measure;

the following statement will result in an error:

> Write('Current quantity = ',amount,' Maximum = ',QUART);

Finally, remember that all output to Text type files is appended to the end of the file.

Write also outputs data to non-Text files. For example, **pmt—file** and **payment** are both declared to be of user-defined type Payment—Rec. The statement

> Write(pmt—file,payment);

will result in the data stored in **payment** being transferred to the disk file represented by **pmt—file**. The position at which the data item is stored is determined by the location of the file pointer. After the data transfer, the file pointer is advanced to the next data item.

Write parameters are used to format data items as they are output to a Text type file or device. For example, you might use the Real type variable **price** to store the price of an inventory item. Assuming the value stored in **price** is $33.60, the statement

> Write(price);

will produce the output

> **3.3600000000E+01**

Unless you use write parameters to specify otherwise, Real values are output in scientific notation. Using write parameters to format the output, the statement

> Write(price:8:2);

will produce

33.60

which is much more appropriate for an inventory report. The first number, 8, indicates how many digits are printed to the left of the decimal point, and 2 indicates how many digits are printed to the right of the decimal point. See Appendix B, Table B-8, for more examples of write parameters.

A write parameter consists of a colon (:) and an integer value. As illustrated here, Real values can have two write parameters. The other types may only use one. The range of values for write parameters is 0 to 255, except that the second write parameter for a Real value must be in the range 0 to 24.

WriteLn

Like ReadLn, WriteLn is limited to Text files. It performs the same function that Write does on Text type files except that an end-of-line indicator is added to the file following the last value in the parameter list. WriteLn may be called without a parameter list or with just a file parameter. For example,

```
WriteLn;
WriteLn(text_file);
```

In the first example, an empty line (CR LF) is output to the terminal, and in the second example, an empty line is sent to the Text file **text_file**.

String-Handling Procedures and Functions

The following procedures and functions provide Turbo Pascal with string-handling capabilities. Those of you who are familiar with BASIC may find that the methods employed take a bit of getting used to. You may rest assured, however, that these tools get the job done very efficiently. Table 6-2 provides a reference.

Concat

The Concat function will accept any number of string type parameters as long as the combined length of the parameters does not exceed 255 charac-

Table 6-2.   String-Handling Procedures and Functions

Identifier	Function or Procedure	Standard	Turbo	Description
Concat	F	N	Y	Concatenate two or more strings
Copy	F	N	Y	Extract a substring from a string
Insert	P	N	Y	Insert object string into a target string
Length	F	N	Y	Returns current length of a string
Pos	F	N	Y	Returns position of object in target
Str	P	N	Y	Convert numeric type to string type
UpCase	F	N	Y	Returns uppercase of its Char parameter
Val	P	N	Y	Convert string type to numeric type

ters. The purpose of Concat is to combine or concatenate its string parameters, returning a single string. The syntax of Concat is

$$\text{Concat}(string_1, string_2, \ldots);$$

where $string_1$ and $string_2$ can be a constant or variable string. Turbo Pascal offers the string + operator, which is generally a more convenient way to combine strings. Here's an example illustrating both methods:

```
str4 := Concat(str1,str2,str3);
str4 := str1 + str2 + str3;
```

The string operator + has the same effect and the same limitations as the Concat function. Concat provides compatibility with Pascal/MT+86 by Digital Research.

Copy

The syntax of the Copy command is

Copy(*string,start,count*);

where *string* is a string variable or constant, *start* is the starting position in the string, and *count* is the number of characters to copy.

If *start* + *count* is greater than the length of *string*, the length of the returned string will be the length of *string* minus *start*. In other words, you'll get the last part of *string* beginning at *start*. If *start* is greater than the length of *string*, a null string will be returned. If *start* is greater than 255, an error will result. The following statements illustrate the Copy function, assuming **work__string** is a String variable:

```
work__string := 'Que sera';
Write(work__string, Copy(workstring,4,5));
```

The Write statement will output

Que sera sera

Delete

The syntax for Delete is

Delete (*string,position,count*);

This procedure removes *count* characters beginning at *position* in *string* and closes up the gap. To change "Turbo is incredible" to "Turbo is inedible"

```
work__string := 'Turbo is incredible';
Delete(work__string,12,2);
```

As usual, *position* must be less than 256. If *position* + *count* is greater than the length of *string*, *string* will be effectively truncated to a length of *position* minus 1. Note that *string* must be a variable; it cannot be a string constant or expression. The variables *count* and *position* may be any integer variable, constant, or expression.

Insert

The syntax for Insert is

Insert(*ins＿string,string,position*);

When you call Insert, *ins＿string* is inserted in *string* at *position*. Here again, *string* must be a variable while the others may be constants or expressions. Thus, to undo the damage of Delete,

Insert('cr',work＿string,12);

If *position* is greater than the length of *string, ins＿string* is effectively con-catenated with *string. Position* must be less than 256 or an error will result.

Length

The syntax for Length is

Length(*string*);

The value returned by Length is the length *string*, as opposed to the maxi-mum declared length of *string*, which depends upon its defined type. You may use the SizeOf function to determine the maximum length of a string variable.

Pos

The syntax for Pos is

Pos(*string, search＿string*);

This function searches the string variable *string* for the first occurrence of *search＿string*. If it finds a match, the position of the first character of *search＿string* in *string* is returned. If no match is found, zero is returned. String variables are indexed from position 1; that is, the position of the first character in a string variable is 1, not 0.

Str

The Str procedure converts an integer or real value into a string. The for-mat is

Str(*number,work＿string*)

After calling the Str procedure, *work—string* will contain a formatted string representation of *number*, which can be an integer or real value. The format is indicated by appending a write parameter to *number*. Therefore, if the Real variable **con** equals 388.4, then

Str(con:8:2,new—string);

will result in **new—string** containing '   388.40'. In all cases, write parameters are optional.

UpCase

The syntax for the UpCase function is

UpCase(*char*);

where *char* is a variable or constant of type Char. If *char* is a lowercase character, UpCase will return its uppercase equivalent; otherwise, *char* is unchanged.

Val

The syntax for Val is

Val(*string,number,status*);

The Val procedure converts a character *string* to an integer or real value and returns it in *number. status* is a variable parameter used to indicate the success or failure of the conversion. It is set to zero if the conversion was successful; otherwise, its value indicates the position of the character in *string* that caused the problem. *status* or *number* may not be a constant or an expression. Note that *string* must not contain any blanks or other non-numeric characters. Scientific notation is permitted.

Dynamic Memory Allocation

The predefined functions and procedures outlined in Table 6-3 provide some useful tools for managing the storage resources of your system. These routines are divided into two categories. The first manages the heap. You may recall that the heap is a dedicated part of memory where dynamic variables are stored. The second group of subprograms permits you to access specific memory locations and to determine the location of data items and subprograms.

Table 6-3. Memory Allocation and Manipulation

Identifier	Function or Procedure	Standard	Turbo	Description
Dynamic Memory Allocation				
Dispose	P	Y	Y	Free space previously allocated by New
FreeMem	P	N	Y	Free space allocated by GetMem
GetMem	P	N	Y	Allocate a specified amount of space
Mark	P	N	Y	Save pointer to top of heap
MaxAvail	F	N	Y	Returns largest space open in the heap
MemAvail	F	N	Y	Returns space remaining on the heap
New	P	Y	Y	Allocates space based on pointer type
Pack	P	Y	N	Directs compiler to pack data item
Ptr	F	N	Y	Returns pointer to its dynamic parameter
Release	P	N	Y	Restore top of heap as saved by Mark
Memory Manipulation				
Addr	F	N	Y	Returns address of its parameter
Cseg	F	N	Y	Returns code segment address divided by 16
Dseg	F	N	Y	Returns data segment address divided by 16
FillChar	P	N	Y	Fills memory with specified value
Hi	F	N	Y	Returns value of high-order byte
Lo	F	N	Y	Returns value of low-order byte
Move	P	N	Y	Block move of specified memory area

(continued)

Table 6-3. Memory Allocation and Manipulation *(continued)*

Identifier	Function or Procedure	Standard	Turbo	Description
		Memory Manipulation		
Ofs	F	N	Y	Returns offset address of its parameter
Seg	F	N	Y	Returns segment address of its parameter
SizeOf	F	N	Y	Returns storage requirement of parameter
Sseg	F	N	Y	Returns stack segment address divided by 16
Swap	F	N	Y	Exchange high- and low-order bytes

Dispose

The Dispose procedure was added to Turbo Pascal with the release of version 2.0 to provide compatibility with standard Pascal's Dispose procedure. If you don't need that compatibility, you will find that Turbo's Mark and Release procedures, covered later in this section, provide a more efficient means of managing the heap. The syntax for Dispose is

Dispose (*pointer___var*);

where *pointer___var* is of a pointer variable.

The New procedure allocates storage from the heap. The purpose of Dispose is to deallocate that storage. When Dispose deallocates a dynamic variable, it may leave a "hole" in the heap, and New must determine if the variable it is creating will fit into an existing hole. If your application does a lot of dynamic variable juggling, Dispose and New can lead to a fair amount of overhead as well as an accumulation of *garbage*—little chunks of unused memory that aren't large enough to be allocated. Some Pascal systems provide routines for *garbage collection;* that is, from time to time chunks of memory are gathered together to make a usable hole. Since Turbo Pascal does not do garbage collection, you may find that you lose some heap capacity to garbage if you use Dispose instead of Mark and Release to manage the heap.

FreeMem and GetMem

GetMem allows you to allocate bytes from the heap. The syntax for GetMem is

GetMem(*pointer__var,size*);

where *pointer__var* is a dynamic variable to type pointer and *size* is an integer value indicating the amount of memory to allocate. After a call to Get-Mem, *pointer__var* will contain the address of the first byte allocated in memory.

FreeMem reclaims (deallocates) storage allocated by GetMem. The syntax for FreeMem is

FreeMem(*pointer__var,size*);

Note that FreeMem is not compatible with Mark or Release, while GetMem may be used with either method.

Mark and Release

The Mark procedure is used to record the address of the top of the heap and then at some later point, after the ceiling of the heap has fluctuated, you can restore that address with the Release procedure, thus effectively and efficiently recovering any storage allocated by New or GetMem in the meantime.

The syntax for Mark is

Mark(*var__pointer*);

and for Release

Release(*var__pointer*);

Since Mark stores the top of the heap internally, you only need to supply a dummy pointer parameter to trigger the procedure. These statements illustrate their use:

```
Mark(dummy__ptr);              {Mark top of heap.}
GetMem(pointer__var,$800);     {Allocate 2K bytes of storage.}

{Routines that use storage at
pointer__var go here.}

Release (dummy__ptr);          {Release the allocated storage.}
```

MaxAvail

The Integer function MaxAvail returns the size of the largest contiguous space available in the heap. The syntax is simply

MaxAvail;

Its use is not compatible with Mark and Release. On 16-bit systems the value returned is expressed in *paragraphs*, each of which represents 16 bytes of storage. While the value returned by MaxAvail will always be less than 64K, it may exceed MAXINT. You will recall that when a value greater than MAXINT and less than 64K is stored in an Integer variable, it appears as a negative value. When processing the result of MaxAvail, you will need to check for a negative value and convert it to a Real value. The following statement illustrates the use of MaxAvail, converting its result to a Real value by storing in **fp**:

```
if MaxAvail > 0 then
     fp := MaxAvail
else
     fp := MaxAvail + $10000;
```

If you are using Mark and Release to manage the heap, you should use Mem-Avail to determine the amount of free space available.

MemAvail

A call to MemAvail returns the amount of free space available on the heap when you are using Mark and Release. The same rules that applied to Max-Avail apply to MemAvail. Keep in mind that when you use Mark and Release to manage the heap, available heap space is always contiguous and may be determined by MemAvail. When Dispose is used, the heap may become fragmented and MaxAvail determines the largest available fragment. The Dispose and Mark and Release methods are mutually exclusive. The syntax is simply

MemAvail;

New

The New procedure allocates memory from the heap for pointer variables. The syntax of the command is

New(*ptr__var*);

where *ptr — var* is a pointer variable. For example, assume the following declarations and definitions:

```
type    Text—Ptr  =   ^Text—Rec;
        Text—Rec  =   record
                          character  : Char;
                          next—chr  : Text—Ptr;
                      end;
var     start—txt : Text—Ptr;
```

When the statement

New(start—txt);

is executed, enough space will be allocated from the heap to store Text—Rec, which is pointed to by **start—txt**. Record Text—Rec consists of two data items, a Char type (one byte) and a Text—Ptr type (two or four bytes depending on the system). Three bytes are allocated for CP/M-80 systems and five bytes are allocated for 16-bit systems.

Pack and UnPack

Like Get and Put, these procedures are a part of standard Pascal that is not needed nor implemented in Turbo Pascal. In standard Pascal, if you don't explicitly indicate that an array, record, set, or file is to be packed, Char type elements or components will be stored in a word, which is two bytes on microcomputer systems. The Turbo compiler is more than capable of determining which data items would benefit from being packed. That's one less thing for you to worry about.

Memory Manipulation

The following subprograms are used to locate and relocate items stored in your computer's memory. They are particularly useful if you are using Turbo Pascal to do system-level programming.

Addr

When you need to know where a variable is stored or where the start of a subprogram is located (CP/M-80 only), the Addr function will provide the address. The syntax for the statement is

Addr(any__var);

where any__var can be a variable, array, record, and subprogram. If any__var is an array or record type, you can indicate which element or field you are interested in. The type of the value returned by Addr depends on your implementation of Turbo. For CP/M-80 systems it is an integer and for 16-bit systems it is a 32-bit value that represents the address in segment:offset form. Since this is also the format used by pointer variables, you may store the result of Addr in a pointer variable of the same base type as the variable being located. For example the following declarations and assignment will work on either 8- or 16-bit systems:

```
var int__addr : ^Integer;
    int__val : Integer;

int__addr := Addr(int__val);
```

Following the assignment statement the address stored in the pointer variable **int__addr** may be assigned to any other Integer type variable. CP/M-80 users can convert the address to an integer using the Ord function. For example:

```
int1 := Ord(int__addr);
```

Keep in mind that an address greater than MAXINT will appear as a negative value. Those using 16-bit systems must rely on the Seg and Ofs functions, described later in this section, to convert **int__addr** into two integers representing the segment:offset form of the address returned by Addr.

The following statement illustrates the CP/M-80 option that permits you to pass a subprogram identifier as the parameter:

```
int__addr := Addr(Test__Proc);
```

The value assigned to int__addr is the entry address of the Test__Proc procedure.

Cseg (16-Bit Systems Only)

The Cseg function returns an Integer value indicating the starting address of the Code segment. The value returned is in paragraphs. The actual address may be calculated as 16 * Cseg, which covers a 640K byte range. The syntax for Cseg is

Cseg;

Dseg *(16-Bit Systems Only)*

The syntax for Dseg is

Dseg;

which is the same as Cseg, except it returns the starting address of the Data segment.

FillChar

FillChar is useful for initializing large data structures. The syntax of the command is

FillChar(*any__var,count,fill*);

FillChar causes the memory beginning at the first byte occupied by *any__ var* and continuing for *count* bytes to be filled with *fill*, which can be of type Byte or Char. For example:

var big__array : array[1..5000] of Real;

FillChar(big__array,SizeOf(big__array),0);

Following the FillChar statement, all 5,000 elements of **big__array** will be set to 0.

Hi

The Integer function Hi provides an easy way to determine the value of a high-order byte of an Integer variable. The syntax of the command is

Hi(*int__var*);

The value returned will be in the range 0 to 255. The high-order byte is then moved to the low-order byte and the high-order byte of the result is set to zero. For example,

int2 := Hi(int1);

If **int1** contains a value of $4F3F, **int2** will have a value of $004F following the statement.

Lo

The Integer function Lo returns the low-order value of an Integer variable with the high-order byte set to zero. The syntax is

$$\text{Lo}(int\_var);$$

In the following example,

$$\text{int2} := \text{Lo(int1)};$$

if **int1** contains a value of $4F3F, **int2** will have a value of $003F.

Move

The Move procedure literally moves the components of memory from one location to another. The syntax is

$$\text{Move}(any\_var1, any\_var2, count);$$

count bytes beginning at the address of *any_var1* are moved to the address of *any_var2*. The destination is moved before the source, so overlapping is not a problem, and the move is made very quickly.

Ofs and Seg (*16-Bit Systems Only*)

The Integer function Ofs returns the offset address of data or subprogram code. The format for Ofs is

$$\text{Ofs}(code);$$

and for Seg

$$\text{Seg}(code);$$

code is the name of a variable or subprogram. The offset value combined with the value returned by Seg provides the *segment:offset* address of the data or procedure. For example, to find the location of function Cube,

```
function Cube(fp: Real): Real;
    begin
        Cube := Sqr(fp) * fp;
    end;
```

The functions Seg and Ofs pass Cube as their parameters:

```
var seg_addr;
    ofs_addr : Integer;
begin
    seg_addr := Seg(Cube);
    ofs_addr := Ofs(Cube);
end;
```

Following these assignments, **seg_addr** is combined with **ofs_addr** to specify the location of the entry point to the Cube function.

SizeOf

The Integer function SizeOf provides an easy way to determine the amount of storage required for complex data types or any specific variable. The syntax is

SizeOf(*any_type*);

any_type can be a variable of any type or any type identifier.

Sseg *(16-bit Systems Only)*

The Integer function Sseg is the same as Cseg except it returns the starting address of the Stack segment. The syntax for Sseg is

Sseg;

Swap

The value returned by Swap is *int_var* with its high- and low-order bytes exchanged. The Swap function accepts an Integer variable, swaps its low- and high-order bytes, and returns the value as an integer. The syntax for Swap is

Swap(*int_var*);

For example, if **int—var** equals $3CC3 hexadecimal or 0011110011000011 binary, then

Swap(int1);

will return 1100001100111100 or $C33C. Swap will probably not be one of your most used functions, but it has its place.

Type Conversion and Scalar Functions

This group of functions is used to convert data items from one type to another and to manipulate scalar data items. Refer to Table 6-4 for a quick preview.

Chr

Chr is a useful character function that converts an integer value to its ASCII character equivalent. The syntax for Chr is

chr(*int*);

If *int* is passed with a value exceeding 255, it is treated as *int* mod 256. That is the remainder of *int* divided by 256. Values of *int* less than 128 are defined by the ASCII standard. Values from 128 through 255 are implementation-dependent.

Table 6-4. Conversion and Scalar Functions

Identifier	Standard	Turbo	Description
Chr	Y	Y	Converts integer or Byte to Char
Odd	Y	Y	TRUE if parameter is odd
Ord	Y	Y	Returns ordinal value of scalar parameter
Pred	Y	Y	Returns decremented value of parameter
Succ	Y	Y	Returns incremented value of parameter

Odd

The Boolean function Odd returns TRUE if its parameter is an odd number. The syntax of Odd is

Odd(*int_var*);

where *int_var* is an Integer variable. The following example prints the value of the parameter along with a statement if the parameter is odd:

```
if Odd(int1) then
    Write(int1, ' is an odd number.');
```

Ord

Ord is an especially useful Integer function when working with enumerated types. It returns the ordinal value of a variable declared as a scalar type. The syntax of the Ord is

Ord(*scalar_var*);

where *scalar_var* is a variable declared to be of a scalar type. A common use is to convert Char values to Integer values. For example

Ord('A');

will return 65. As illustrated earlier, on CP/M-80 systems Ord can be used to convert pointer type values to Integer values.

Pred

The Pred function decrements the value of a scalar variable. The type of the returned value is the same as that of the parameter. For example:

```
type Week_Days = (MON,TUE,WED,THU,FRI);
var day : Week_Days;
day := WED;
chr1 := Pred('B');        {chr1 will have a value of A.}
byt := Pred(1);           {byt will have a value of 0.}
day := Pred(day);         {day will have a value of TUE.}
```

Unusual problems will occur if you attempt to decrement a scalar variable below its lowest valid value. For example,

    byt := Pred(byt);
    day := Pred(MON);

Both of these statements are illegal, even though no error message will be printed, and will cause unpredictable results.

Ptr

The Ptr function requires one integer parameter for CP/M-80 implementations and two integer parameters for 16-bit systems. The syntax for CP/M-80 is

    Ptr(*pointer__var*);

where *pointer__var* is an Integer variable.

The Ptr function returns a pointer type variable that is compatible with all pointer types. It permits clandestine pointer juggling that is best avoided unless you are very certain what you are juggling and why. For example, the following segments will display the CP/M operating system command line buffer, assuming the following definition and declaration:

    type Cmd__Line : string[128];
    var cmd__ptr : ^Cmd__Line;

    cmd__ptr := Ptr($80);
    Write(cmd__ptr^);

Change the first statement as follows to produce the same result on 16-bit systems:

    cmd__ptr := Ptr(Cseg,$80);

Notice that the command line buffer is where the operating system stores any parameters you enter following a command name. For example, if you type the operating system command

                    TYPE FILE2.TXT

at the operating system level, the command line will contain the string "FILE2.TXT". The Turbo Ptr procedure offers one method of accessing this string as illustrated here.

Succ

The Succ function increments the value of a scalar variable. The value returned by Succ is the same type as the parameter. The syntax for Succ is

Succ(scalar_var);

where *scalar_var* is a variable declared of scalar type. If you increment *scalar_var* beyond its defined upper limit, the results will be unpredictable.

Scalar Type Conversion

Turbo Pascal can convert a scalar value to an ordinal value of a different scalar type. This is done by using a type identifier as a function identifier. A type conversion function can accept a single parameter of any scalar type. The result returned by the function is the same type as the function identifier, and its ordinal value matches that of the parameter. Here are some examples:

```
type    Days = (MON,TUE,WED,THU,FRI,SAT,SUN);
        Work_Period = (DAY,SWING,NIGHT);
var     today: Days;
        shift: Work_Period;
        int1: Integer;
        chr1: Char;
```

int1: = Integer(WED);	{**int1** will have a value of 2.}
today: = Days(5);	{**today** will have a value of SAT.}
chr1: = Char($41);	{**chr1** will have a value of 'A'.}
shift: = Work_Period(TUE);	{**shift** will have a value of SWING.}

Arithmetic Functions

The 16 arithmetic functions provide Turbo Pascal with more than ample number-crunching capabilities for most applications. Table 6-5 will serve as a quick reference to these functions. If your applications require more power in this area, you may want to consider the MS-DOS version of Turbo that supports the 8087 math coprocessor or the BCD option available starting with Turbo version 3.0.

Table 6-5. Arithmetic Functions

Identifier	Standard	Turbo	Description
Abs	Y	Y	Returns absolute value of Parameter
ArcTan	Y	Y	Returns angle based on tangent parameter
Cos	N	Y	Returns cosine of its angle parameter
Exp	Y	Y	Returns exponential of its parameter
Frac	N	Y	Returns the fractional part of parameter
Int	N	Y	Returns the integer part of parameter
Ln	Y	Y	Returns the natural log of parameter
Random	N	Y	Returns a pseudo-random value
Sin	Y	Y	Returns sine of its angle parameter
Sqr	Y	Y	Returns its parameter squared
Sqrt	Y	Y	Returns the square root of parameter
Trunc	N	Y	Returns truncated integer part of parameter

Abs

Depending on the type of the parameter, the Abs function will return the integer or real absolute value of a number. The syntax is

$$Abs(num\_var);$$

where *num_var* is either of type Real or Integer. For example, in the following statement:

$$fp := Abs(-12.89);$$

The Real variable **fp** will have a value of 12.89.

ArcTan

The syntax for ArcTan is

$$ArcTan(angle);$$

where *angle* is of type Real or Integer. The ArcTan function returns the arctangent in radians based on *angle*. The result is always a real number.

Cos

The Cos function returns the cosine of *angle* in radians. The syntax is

$$\text{Cos}(angle);$$

angle must be expressed in radians and can be either a Real or Integer type. The result of Cos is a real number.

Exp

The Exp function returns the exponential of *num*, which is e^{num}, where e equals approximately 2.718282. The syntax is

$$\text{Exp}(num);$$

where *num* is either of type Real or Integer. Exp always returns a real value.

Frac

The Real function Frac returns the fractional part of the parameter as a Real number. If the parameter is an integer, the result will always be 0.0. The syntax is

$$\text{Frac}(real\_num);$$

Int

The Int function returns the integer part of the parameter expressed as a real number. The syntax is

$$\text{Int}(num\_var);$$

When the parameter is an Integer type value, the result is a Real type value of the same magnitude. When the parameter is a real value, the result is equivalent to *num_var* minus Frac(*num_var*).

Ln

Ln returns the natural log of the parameter as a real number. The parameter must be greater than 0. The syntax is

Ln(*num__var*);

where *num__var* can be of type Integer or Real. The result of Ln is always real.

Random

The Random function generates a random number. The syntax is

Random;

or

Random(*int__var*);

If no parameter is passed, Random returns a pseudo-random value from 0 up to, but not including, 1. When an integer parameter is provided, a pseudo-random integer value from 0 up to, but not including, *int__var* is returned.

Round

The Integer function Round requires one parameter. For example:

Round (fp);

Round returns the Real parameter **fp** as an integer. The result is rounded toward zero. That is, 0.5 is added to values of **fp** equal to or greater than zero, while -0.5 is added to values less than zero. The integer part of the result is returned by Round.

Sin

The Sin function requires one parameter, which may be either an integer or a real number. For example,

fp := Sin(angle);

returns the sine of **angle** or **fp__angle**, which must be expressed in radians. The result is a real number.

Sqr

The Sqr function requires one parameter, which may be either an integer or a real number. For example,

$$\textbf{var} \quad \text{int1} \quad : \quad \text{Integer;}$$
$$\text{fp} \qquad : \quad \text{Real;}$$

The value returned by Sqr is equivalent to the parameter multiplied by itself. The type of the result is the same as the type of the parameter. The syntax is

$$\text{fp} := \text{Sqr(fp)}$$

or

$$\text{int1} := \text{Sqr(int1);}$$

Sqrt

The Sqrt function requires one parameter, which may be either an Integer or a real number. For example,

$$\textbf{var} \quad \text{int1} \quad : \quad \text{Integer;}$$
$$\text{fp} \qquad : \quad \text{Real;}$$

The square root of **int1** or **fp** is returned as a real number. The syntax is

$$\text{fp} := \text{Sqrt(int1);}$$

Trunc

The Integer function Trunc returns the integer part of a real number and discards the fractional part. The syntax is

$$\text{Trunc}(\textit{realnum});$$

where *realnum* is a real number.

SEVEN

System-Level Tools: Compiler Directives and Specialized Subprograms

This chapter examines some of the more advanced system-level tools of Turbo Pascal. For the most part these tools are used to develop programs that are too large to fit into memory with the Turbo compiler.

For those of you who are beginning Pascal or system-level programming, some of the material may seem very complex. Do not be too concerned. Except for some compiler directives and the Chain and Execute procedures, you *can* write major application-level programs without using any of the features explained in this chapter. If your goal is to write programs that will run on a wide variety of machines, you should avoid using most of the system-level tools that will be discussed.

Turbo Pascal will likely become a major standard as a portable development language for microcomputers. Unlike Cobol and Fortran, which were standardized by committee, Turbo Pascal has been standardized by its vendor. With the release of version 3.0, Borland International is committed to maintaining their standard while offering system-level enhancements as hardware technology advances. Except for these enhancements, which can be easily avoided when developing portable programs, Turbo source code is compatible across a full range of systems. Turbo Pascal may well unlock the door to portable application development.

Compiler Directives

Compiler directives are placed in the program to modify the activities of the compiler, which modifies the object code. Turbo Pascal offers numerous compiler directives. Table 7-1 provides a quick reference to these directives.

Table 7-1. Turbo Pascal Compiler Directives

Directive plus Default	Name	Version	Description
{A+}	Absolute	CP/M-80	If +, recursion not permitted; if −, recursion is permitted
{B+}	Buffered I/O	All	If +, buffered I/O to CON: device; if −, unbuffered I/O to TRM: device
{C+}	User break and scroll control	All	If +, CTRL-C and CTRL-S trapped during Read and Write; if −, CTRL-C and CTRL-S ignored. See {$U−}
{D+}	Disable buffering	MS-DOS	If +, disable buffering of I/O to devices; if−, all device I/O operations are buffered
{$F*n*}	Open file	MS-DOS	*n* defines the number of files that may be open simultaneously
{$G*n*}	Input buffer for I/O redirection	MS-DOS	If 0, standard input via CON: or TRM: per {$B+}; if greater than 0, standard input via current standard input device
{$I+}	I/O error trapping	All	If +, I/O errors trapped by system; if −, I/O errors passed to program via IOresult
{$I *filespec*}	Include file	All	Source code in *filespec* will be included for compilation
{$K+}	Stack overflow	16-bit systems	If +, verifies that stack space is available for subprogram local variables; if −, no check on availability of stack space for local variables

Table 7-1. Turbo Pascal Compiler Directives (*continued*)

Directive plus Default	Name	Version	Description
{$O@}	Locating overlay files		If the character @ is specified, overlay files are on the logged drive; otherwise, the letters A-P will indicate the drive
{$P*n*}	Output buffer for I/O redirection	MS-DOS	If 0, standard output via CON: or TRM: as per {$B+}; if greater than 0, standard output via current standard output device
{$R−}	Run-time index range checking	All	If +, run-time index range checking enabled; if −, no run-time index range checking
{$V+}	Parameter string length checking	All	If +, **var** parameter string lengths must match; if −, **var** parameter string lengths need not match
{$U−}	User abort control	All	If +, user may abort using CTRL-C at any time; if −, effect of CTRL-C governed by {$C+} directive
{W*n*}	Maximum **with** statement nesting	CP/M-80	*n* specifies the maximum depth for which the **with** statement may be nested
{$X+}	Array optimization	CP/M-80	If +, array processing optimized for speed; if −, array processing optimized for code size

Most directives have only two states, active and deactive, but some take on values. In the following sections, which discuss each directive, the heading will give the format, the directive's name, and its system dependencies, if any.

All compiler directives are surrounded by curly brackets. A dollar sign begins the directive, followed by the directive and a sign or value to indicate its status. Blank spaces are not allowed between the curly brackets and the directive. For example:

{$A+}

The letter A indicates the absolute-code directive and the plus sign (+) indicates that the directive is active. A directive is deactivated by using a minus sign (−) in place of the plus sign. The sign in the heading indicates the compiler's default setting. If a given directive does not appear in the source code, its default setting is assumed. Thus, the absolute-code directive is active if it does appear in a program.

{$A+} Absolute Code (*CP/M-80 Only*)

If your CP/M-80 implementation contains recursive procedures or functions, the absolute directive should appear just before and just after each recursive subprogram. The term *absolute* in this context refers to non-recursive code. The default setting for the absolute-code directive is active. In order to generate code for a recursive subprogram, you should turn off the directive {$A−} before the subprogram and turn it on {$A+} following it. The code generated when this directive is off will be bulkier and run slower. You might do better by using a non-recursive algorithm to solve the problem.

{$B+} Buffered I/O

The purpose of the buffered I/O directive is to offer some degree of control over keyboard input. In the default state, this directive stores keyboard input and offers rudimentary editing capabilities. While a noble gesture, it is inadequate for most interactive programs.

If you are developing a program that must conform to the requirements of standard Pascal, you should deactivate buffered I/O with a {$B−} directive. This will cause standard I/O to be handled by the unbuffered TRM: (terminal) device. Keep in mind that the buffered I/O directive is global to the entire program and must appear prior to any other part of the program block.

{$C+} User Break and Scroll Control

The state of this directive determines whether the user can terminate the program by pressing CTRL-C or start and stop video scrolling by pressing CTRL-S. In the default state, both of these capabilities are activated.

These capabilities apply only to the Read and Write procedures; CTRL-C won't interrupt a program if the Read and Write procedures aren't used. In fact, on some CP/M-80 systems CTRL-C is only detected by the Read procedure. See the user abort control directive {$U−} if this presents a problem.

The {$C−} state disables both the break and the scroll control. The {$C+} directive is global to the entire program and must appear before any program declarations and definitions.

{$D+} Disable Buffering (*MS-DOS Only*)

This directive is not available in Turbo Pascal versions prior to 3.0 and does not apply to MS-DOS versions prior to 2.0. For those that remain, here's what it does. When active, the {$D+} directive checks a Text file each time it is opened to see if the file is actually a device (for example, CON: or AUX:). If so, I/O buffering is disabled and I/O operations are performed one character at a time. When the directive is deactivated {$D−}, no such check takes place and I/O is buffered as usual.

The purpose of this directive is to control the I/O redirection facilities of MS-DOS. See the discussion of the {$Gn} and {$Pn} directives, which establish buffers for I/O redirection. Because {$Gn} and {$Pn} are global directives, the disable buffering directive {$D−} is provided to control their effect on selected files or devices.

{$Fn} Open Files (*MS-DOS Only*)

Users of Turbo Pascal 3.0 with MS-DOS 2.0 and later may use this directive to indicate how many files may be open simultaneously. The default is 16. The number of open files you may have in no way limits the number of file type variables that may be declared in a program; it only specifies the maximum number of files that may be open at any given time.

You should also be aware that this directive does not supersede the number of buffers allocated at the system level. The MS-DOS operating system checks for a file named CONFIG.SYS when it is initializing. If you don't have a statement in the CONFIG.SYS file to the contrary, you may not open more than five files simultaneously in addition to the standard I/O device files (the keyboard, the video monitor, and the error output device, which also uses the video monitor). If your program will need to access more than five files at the same time, you will have to place the following command in the operating system CONFIG.SYS file, which is used to boot your system:

FILES=*nn*

where *nn* is the maximum number of files opened simultaneously plus three for the standard I/O devices. See the FILES command in your MS-DOS manual for more details. Note that your Turbo editor can be used to edit the CONFIG.SYS file as well as any other ASCII text files.

{$G*n*} Input Buffer for I/O Redirection (*MS-DOS Only*)

The {$G*n*} directive is another new directive in Turbo Pascal version 3.0 that is concerned with the I/O redirection of MS-DOS. Since it is global, it must appear before any of the program declarations and definitions. In the default state, when *n* equals 0, input redirection is disabled and the standard input device will be CON: (the console) or TRM: (the terminal), depending on the status of the buffered I/O directive {$B+}. The maximum of *n* is limited by memory. If a buffer size is included with the directive (for example, {$G512}), the standard input device will be indicated by the MS-DOS standard input handle. See your MS-DOS reference manual for information about file handles and I/O redirection.

If you are writing an application and expect to benefit from I/O redirection, you must determine whether the I/O should be buffered if it is redirected to a device, as opposed to a text file. If you do want device I/O buffering, you must use the {$D−} directive to see that buffering is not disabled. Remember that the disable-buffering directive may be used as needed to control buffering of individual files or devices as they are opened.

{$I+} I/O Error Trapping

I/O error trapping is one of the more commonly used directives only because I/O errors are so common. In the default state (I/O error trapping enabled), any time an I/O error is encountered, your program will die an ungraceful death by immediately terminating with a standard run-time abort message. Since such behavior is frowned upon by users of commercial application software, you will probably want to develop your own I/O error-trapping routines. The Loan Amortization program, which will be developed in Part II, will illustrate how the I/O error trap directive is used to implement your own user-friendly error traps.

{ $I *filename*} Include File

This directive permits you to include source code from an external disk file. The object code of the program will be the same as if the included code were physically present in the source code being compiled. If an error is encountered in the include file, the file automatically becomes the current work file. Include directives may appear anywhere in the main program except in subprogram definitions or in the program statement block. Include files may not be nested: that is, an include file may not contain include directives. Later in this chapter include files will be examined in detail.

{ $K+} Stack Overflow (*16-Bit Systems Only*)

When active (the default state) the Stack Overflow directive checks available stack space each time a subprogram is invoked. Its purpose is to make certain that there is enough room for any local variables declared by the routine being activated.

Because 16-bit systems have additional storage capacity, there are many cases when a Stack Overflow check is unnecessary. If speed is top priority and you are absolutely certain that there is no chance of a collision between the stack and the heap, you can use { $K−} to disable this test. If you are compiling to a .COM file, you can control the amount of stack and heap space available using the compiler Options selection from the Turbo menu.

{ $O@} Locating Overlay Files (*Turbo Pascal 2.0 Only*)

Turbo's overlay capability was introduced with version 2.0. This capability will be examined later in this chapter. The { $O@} directive was added as a means of specifying the drive identification (A through P, or @, which signifies the default drive) of the disk containing the program overlay files at run-time. The default { $O@} indicates that the files should be on the currently logged drive. To specify a particular drive, the @ is replaced by the appropriate drive ID identification letter.

An improvement in version 3.0 are the procedures Overdrive for CP/M and Overpath for MS-DOS, which identify the location of overlay files. The problem with compiler directives is that you must know the drive specifications at compile time. The procedure method allows this determination to be made at run-time, which is certainly preferable.

{$P*n*} Output Buffer for I/O Redirection (*MS-DOS Only*)

Output buffer is the counterpart to the establish input buffer directive {$G*n*}. {$P*n*} works with output devices, while {$G*n*} works with input devices. In the default state, when *n* equals 0, output redirection is disabled and the standard output device will be CON: or TRM:, depending on the status of the standard I/O mode directive {$B+}. If a buffer size is included (for example, {$P512}), the output device will be as indicated by the MS-DOS standard output handle. See your MS-DOS technical reference manual for information on file handles and I/O redirection. If you are sending output to a device with buffering enabled, you must close the device so all data in the buffer is actually output to the device.

{$R−} Run-Time Index Range Checking

With range checking off, the default setting, no code prevents you from assigning a value to element 50 of a five-element array; however, the effects are unpredictable and rarely desirable.

Once testing is complete and there is no chance that such an assignment could be made, you should remove range checking to increase the program's speed. An example is the Primes program in the last chapter. In that case 30 percent was cut from the execution time by leaving range checking off. However, if had it been left off during the development stage, the erroneous array definition would not have been caught when the program was executed.

As a general rule this directive should be active {$R+} during the development phase of any program block that uses arrays. If an index selector value comes from user input, the program itself should check the value, and if it is out of range, require the user to input a new value.

{$V+} Parameter String Length Checking

When active, the parameter string directive verifies that strings passed to procedures are equal in length and type. This directive only applies to string variables passed by reference; that is, those declared following a **var** parameter in the formal parameter list.

There are times when string parameter protection is not required. The following procedure, called Uppercase, converts all lowercase character strings to uppercase. The parameter for Uppercase is defined as type Str−255:

```
type Str_255 = string[255];
procedure Uppercase(var inp_str: Str_255);
  var i : Integer;
  begin
    for i := 1 to Length(inp_str) do
    if (inp_str[i] in ['a'..'z']) then
      inp_str[i] := UpCase(inp_str[i]);
  end; { Uppercase }
```

Unless parameter-string checking is disabled {$V−} when Uppercase is called, Uppercase can only be used on strings with a declared length of 255 characters. The Get_Key procedure defined next uses Uppercase to convert any string entered by the user to all uppercase letters.

```
{$V−}
  procedure Get_Key;
    var key_str : string[8];
    begin
      BufLen := 8; ReadLn(key_str);
      Uppercase(key_str);
    end; { Get_Key }
{$V+}
```

Without the {$V} compiler directives before and after Get_Key, you would get a **type mismatch** error when compiling this section of code.

{$U−} User Abort Control

At the expense of slowing program execution, you can enable the user abort directive {$U+}, thus allowing the user to terminate a program any time by pressing CTRL-C. This directive extends the limited terminating capabilities of the user break directive {$C+}. While {$C+} is only effective if the I/O procedures Read and Write are activated, the {$U+} directive checks constantly for CTRL-C. The User Abort directive is used primarily during development, allowing you to exit a routine that inadvertently goes into an endless loop.

{Wn$} Maximum with Statement Nesting (*CP/M-80 Only*)

The {Wn$} directive specifies the maximum number (up to nine levels) a **with** statement can be nested. The default of n is 2. Increasing this value by one level will increase the storage requirements of each subsequent **with** statement by two bytes. Depending upon the application, this could be of considerable consequence.

{**$X+**} Array Optimization *(CP/M-80 Only)*

By default CP/M-80 arrays are optimized for speed at the expense of additional storage. The alternative {$X−} reverses the priority.

Using Include Files

Of all the compiler directives the include directive proves to be the most useful since it allows you to create libraries of reusable functions and procedures. The include directive is also useful when you need to reduce the size of the main program source code file so that your program can be compiled with the Memory compiler option.

The following steps performed by the editor isolate a subprogram and move it to a separate include file. Since the process deletes a section of code, you should be sure you have a backup copy of the source file.

1. Once the program is in the Turbo editor, mark a subprogram for removal by using the block mark facilities of the editor. Press CTRL-KB to mark the beginning and CTRL-KB to mark the end of the subprogram.

2. Use the block write editor command (CTRL-KW) to write the subprogram to an external disk file. The file you create in this step is an include file. This emphasizes the fact that there is nothing mysterious about include files; they are nothing more than chunks of source code. You may find it helpful to establish a naming convention that will enable you to identify a file as an include file. For example, append the .INC extension to all include file names.

3. Use the block delete editor command (CTRL-KY) to remove the code from the main source file.

4. Before leaving the editor, place an Include compiler directive, such as the following, in the main program:

{$I MYPROG1.INC}

Even on 16-bit systems, include files will only take you so far; eventually, the larger projects will reach a point where you can no longer compile to memory, even using include files. Your next recourse will be to compile the code to a .COM file by selecting the Com compiler option. Since this causes the object code to be compiled directly to disk, it no longer consumes memory resources. This greatly reduces, but does not eliminate, the possibility of an out of memory condition.

You can monitor available memory before compilation by checking the Turbo main menu screen. The free space listed on the screen, however, is not totally free. When the compiler is at work, the symbol table starts eating away at this space. Should it nibble into the area occupied by your source code, you will be greeted by **compiler overflow**, error 99.

If the project is very large and the object code approaches the 64K limit, you may want to use overlay or chain procedures. Both of these options will be explained in this chapter.

Using Include Files to Build Libraries

One of the complaints leveled against Turbo Pascal is that it doesn't produce object code files, often referred to as .OBJ (dot-oh-bee-jay) files, as do many traditional compilers and assemblers. Object code files are made up of modules that can be linked to an executable program. The purpose of .OBJ files is to assemble libraries of precompiled procedures and functions, which are then linked to a program without having to be coded and compiled. The other purported benefit is that .OBJ files produced by different compilers or assemblers may be linked together. However, because of problems of parameter passing, this advantage disappears for all but very simple linkages.

Turbo include files may be used to approximate .OBJ files. Admittedly an include file is not the same as a .OBJ file, since it consists of source code that must be recompiled each time it is used. The end result is the same, however, and the Turbo compiler is so fast that the time required to recompile may be less than a traditional compiler takes to link object code modules from a .OBJ file.

The main benefit of both include files and .OBJ files is that you may develop or purchase libraries of subprograms for your applications. A prime example is the Turbo Toolbox, offered by Borland International. It includes several outstanding library routines that index, access, and sort files.

A real advantage of using include files, as opposed to .OBJ files, in commercially distributed library routines, is that you get the source code. Many of the traditional libraries are delivered without the source code. All you get are the executable .OBJ files. If you want to modify a library subprogram, you either rewrite the subprogram completely, or you can possibly buy the source code for an additional fee.

Another difference between .OBJ files and Turbo include files is the way that the code is made a part of the executable program. The .OBJ files require an extra step called *linking* or *binding*. The advantage is that the linker can be selective: only those routines used by the main program will appear in the executable object code. When an include file is used, all of the routines in the include file, whether they are used or not, will be compiled into the program object code. Of course, no link or bind step is needed.

When using include files as libraries, there are a few things you can do to make them more effective. Here are some tips:

- Rather than storing each subprogram in a separate include file, create libraries of related procedures and functions.

- When you are developing a program that will use one or more subprograms in an include file, copy the file to the disk (or subdirectory) containing the program; then delete the subprograms that aren't needed. If a subprogram needs to be customized or optimized, you can easily make the changes without disturbing the original version.

- Establish your own conventions for program global constants, types, and variables. Then insert them in an include file, which is always referenced in the main program file. This saves you from having to declare variables and constants that reappear in program after program. This will be done in the Loan Amortization program.

Using Chain and Execute for Program Expansion

Even when you compile to a .COM file you may reach a point where the program outgrows the resources. When this happens your only alternative is to break the program into smaller pieces. With Pascal's modular structure and tools like the Chain procedure, this does not pose much of a problem.

The purpose of the Chain procedure is to transfer control to a separate program, which is stored in a .CHN file, and has been compiled using the Chain compiler option. When a program is compiled using the Chain option, the object code goes directly to the disk file without Turbo's nucleus run-time code. Thus you can't execute a .CHN file directly from the operating system; instead, a .CHN file must be executed from a Turbo Pascal program, which has loaded the required nucleus run-time code. The advantage of using .CHN program files to subdivide a large program is that they are smaller than .COM program files and, consequently, they load faster and save disk space.

If you decide to use .CHN programs, you should review the application at the design level. When a program calls a .CHN program, there will be a pause as the .CHN program is loaded into memory and executed. Naturally you should avoid excessive chaining. In many applications designed with menus, the main menu program is compiled as a .COM file, and it executes the user's selection by calling a chain program.

The following three programs demonstrate how control is transferred from a main program to a Chain program:

```
{CHAIN.PAS
   Enter this source code in a separate file to be compiled as
   a .COM program which will chain to the first .CHN program. }

program Chain_Test;

   type File_ID = string[64];

   var  inp_str  : string[80];
        out_text : Text;

   procedure Chain_To(file_name: File_ID);

     var chain_file : File;

     begin
       Assign(chian_file,file_name);
       Chain(chain_file);
     end;  {Chain_To}

   begin
     ClrScr;
     Assign(out_text,'CHN-TEST.TXT');
     Rewrite(out_text);
     WriteLn('Enter a line of text and press <CR>.');
     WriteLn; BufLen := 80;
     ReadLn(inp_str);
     WriteLn(out_text,inp_str);
     Chain_To('GETLINE2.CHN');
   end. { Chain_Test }
```

{ This is the main program and should be compiled using the <C>om compiler option. If you are using a 16 bit system, set the minimum Code size to 10 and the minimum Data size to 20 before compiling the program. }

Here is the next Chain program:

```
{ GETLINE2.PAS

   Enter this source code in a separate file to be compiled as
   a .CHN program which will be chained to by the CHAIN.COM program. }

program Get_Line2;

type File_ID = string[64];

var  inp_str  : string[80];
     out_test : Text;

procedure Chain_To(file_name: File_ID);

     var chain_file : File;

     begin
       Assign(chain_file,file_name);
       Chain(chain_file);
     end; {Chain_To}

   begin
     ClrScr;
     WriteLn('Enter a second line of text and press <CR>.');
     WriteLn; BufLen := 80;
     ReadLn(inp_str);
     WriteLn(out_text,inp_str);
     Chain_To('DISPTEXT.CHN');
   end. { Get_Line2 }
```

{ This is the first .CHN program and should be compiled as the c<H>n compiler option. }

Notice that in the last Chain program, as well as in the first two programs, the type definitions and the local procedure Chain—To have been repeated. This repetition can be eliminated with include files, which will be discussed shortly.

```
{ DISPTEXT.PAS

  Enter this source code in a separate file to be compiled as
  a .CHN program which will be chained to by the GETLINE2.CHN program. }

program Display_Text;

type File_ID = string[64];

var inp_str  : string[80];
    out_text : Text;

procedure Chain_To(file_name: File_ID);

  var chain_file : File;

  begin
    Assign(chain_file,file_name);
    Chain(chain_file);
  end; {Chain_To}

begin
  ClrScr;
  Reset(out_text);
  While (not Eof(out_text)) do
    begin
      ReadLn(out_Text,inp_str);
      WriteLn(inp_str);
    end;
  Close(out_text);
end. { Display_Text }

{ This is the second .CHN program and should be compiled using the c<H>n
  compiler option. }
```

As you review the program you will notice that the Chain procedure does not close any files and you must be responsible for closing them.

MS-DOS and CP/M-86 Memory Allocation Options

Whenever a .CHN program or a .COM program that calls a .CHN program is compiled, the following screen appears:

Code:	002B paragraphs (688 bytes),	0D09 paragraphs free
Data:	0013 paragraphs (304 bytes),	0FC9 paragraphs free
Stack/Heap:	0400 paragraphs (16834 bytes)	(minimum)
	A000 paragraphs (655360 bytes)	(maximum)

The minimum code segment and minimum data segment must be defined to provide space for the largest .CHN program. Unless you define the code segment, the data segment will be defined immediately following the code segment. If a larger .CHN program is then loaded, it will overwrite part of the data area. If you are unfamiliar with memory segmentation for the code, data, and stack under MS-DOS and CP/M-86, you may find it helpful to review the technical reference manuals for CP/M-86 and MS-DOS and any other aspects of the 8086 processors.

One way to determine the maximum code and data segments for a .CHN program is to compile it and make a note of the largest requirements indicated by the compiler statistics. If you are going to add more chain programs later and are uncertain of their size, another solution is to specify relatively large code and data segment sizes. D00 for code and F00 for data are adequate, since they are close to the maximum and are easy to remember. It is important that all .COM and .CHN programs be compiled with the same code and data segment values.

If your application requires more than 16K of dynamic storage, you will also have to modify the values that limit the minimum and maximum free dynamic storage.

When your project is near completion, recompile each .CHN program and note the code, data, and dynamic storage requirements, indicated by the compiler statistics. Finally, recompile the .COM program and specify values that will accommodate the largest code and data segment. It's a good idea to pad these values to allow for the last-minute changes that may expand a chain program.

The other memory management option is the allocation of heap and stack space. If you don't reserve memory for the heap and stack, all available memory above the code and data segments will be allocated to dynamic storage.

CP/M-80 Memory Allocation Options

When you select the .COM or .CHN compiler options for a CP/M-80 system, the additional options become available:

        Start address: 1FC0 (min 1FC0)
        End address: EA80 (max ED80)

The actual memory addresses will probably be different depending on how CP/M-80 is configured for your system. These values may be altered to reserve space outside of the code, data, heap, and stack areas.

The start address references the first byte after the Turbo Pascal run-time library. If you want to reserve and manage memory as you see fit, move the start address higher in memory. Then you may access memory between the end of the Turbo run-time code and the new start address.

Overlay Files

Turbo Pascal offers an alternative to using chain programs. With a minimum of fuss, a group of subprograms can share the same memory area at different execution times during the execution of the program. These subprograms are compiled into *overlay files* separate from the .COM file that contains the main program code. All overlay files are given a numeric extension, indicating the sequence in which they were created. This suggests you may have more than one set of overlay subprograms; in fact, an overlay subprogram may itself contain overlays, which are called *nested overlays*.

To declare an overlay procedure or function, simply precede it with the reserved word **overlay**. To be of any value, at least two and preferably more subprograms must be declared as overlays without any intervening declarations or definitions. The amount of memory reserved for the entire group of subprograms in an overlay file is determined by the largest subprogram.

To make optimum use of overlays, there are a number of factors to be considered. Here is a list of things to be aware of:

- Since only one subprogram from an overlay file may be resident in memory at any time, subprograms from the same overlay file cannot reference one another.

- Avoid calling two subprograms from the same overlay file in a repetitive structure like a **while-do** or a **repeat-until** loop. The constant swapping of the subprograms, as one subprogram replaces the other in memory, will slow the execution of the program. Place the two subprograms into separate overlay files, if possible.

- Overlay declarations, except for users of 16-bit systems with Turbo version 3.0 or later, may not appear in programs compiled using the Memory option. Note that this limitation has been removed with version 3.0.

- Forward declarations may not refer to subprograms that have been declared to be part of an overlay file. An overlay subprogram may, however, be activated from a forward declared routine. This offers a way around the limitation.

- A similar situation exists with recursive routines. While a recursive subprogram can't be part of an overlay file, it may call a subprogram that is part of such a file. As discussed previously, you wouldn't want to call two subprograms from the same overlay file in such a repetitive situation.

Unless you indicate otherwise, the program will search for overlay files on the currently logged drive. With version 3.0, Turbo introduced the OvrDrive procedure for CP/M systems and the OvrPath procedure for MS-DOS systems. These procedures allow you to specify where the overlay file may be found. Versions prior to version 3.0 can use the { $O @ } compiler directive. The advantage of the new procedures is that you can locate the files at run-time.

I/O Error Trapping

There are two ways to handle I/O errors with the { $I+ } directive: you can let code generated by the compiler catch the error { $I+ }, or you can do it yourself { $I- }. In practice a mixture of the two proves to be the most efficient.

When the compiler detects an I/O error, the program halts and an error message is displayed. The error message may be helpful to the programmer, but it is likely to frustrate the operator of the program. Thus, the directive should only be active during the program's development. After the program is in operation, I/O errors should not terminate the program and leave the operator hanging. The program should treat each error individually and instruct the operator how to correct it. No program should terminate because an operator entered an incorrect file name, which produced an error when the program searched the directory.

Detecting I/O errors individually is done by deactivating the { $I+ } compiler directive and then testing for an I/O error after every I/O subprogram with the IOresult function. The directive should be deactivated prior to any I/O subprogram, and IOresult is located directly after an I/O subprogram. The following list of I/O subprograms should be tested with IOresult:

Append (MS-DOS only)	Erase	Rename
Assign	Execute	Reset
BlockRead	Flush	Rewrite
BlockWrite	GetDir (MS-DOS only)	RmDir
Chain	LongSeek (MS-DOS only)	Seek
ChDir (MS-DOS only)	MkDir (MS-DOS only)	Write
Close	Read	WriteLn
	ReadLn	

After an I/O error, all I/O is suspended until IOresult has been executed. Thus, executing IOresult after each subprogram I/O is critical. IOresult returns a zero if the I/O subprogram executed successfully, or it returns an integer corresponding to the I/O error. The codes are presented in the Turbo reference manual. The program has no way of knowing what value IOresult returns unless you test it, so assign the result to a variable and test the variable.

The Boolean Exist function, which searches for a file and returns TRUE if found, demonstrates I/O error trapping.

```
function Exist(file_name : File_ID): Boolean;
  var test_file : File;

  begin
    Assign(test_file,file_name);
{$I-}  { Compiler I/O Error Trapping disabled. }
    Reset(test_file);
{$I+}  { Compiler I/O Error Trapping enabled. }
    if (IOresult = 0) then  { Return TRUE or FALSE based on the value }
      begin                 { returned by the IOresult function. }
        Exist := TRUE;
        Close(test_file);   { It is important to Close the file if you are }
      end                   { using Turbo version 3.0+ on an MS-DOS system. }
    else
      Exist := FALSE;
  end; { Exist }
```

Absolute Addressing

You can tell the compiler where in memory you want a variable to reside by appending the reserve word **absolute**, followed by a memory location, after the variable declaration. On 16-bit systems the memory location must be two integer constants, one for the segment in memory and the other the offset.

When the file name of a .COM program is entered at the operating system level, the parameters, if any, are stored in memory beginning at $80 for CP/M-80 systems and at the code segment plus $80 as an offset for CP/M-86 and MS-DOS systems. You can access and store the command-line parameter in a string by declaring a string beginning at the proper memory location.

> **var** cmd—str : String[128] **absolute** $80; {CP/M-80}
> **var** cmd—str : String{128} **absolute** Cseg:$80; {MS-DOS and CP/M-86}

You can make some tricky declarations with absolute declarations. For example, assuming a 16-bit system, in the declaration

> **var** real—ptr : $^\wedge$Real;
> fp—addr : **array**[1—2] **of** Integer **absolute** real—ptr

The Real pointer variable **real—ptr** is stored in memory with four bytes. Then the Integer array **fp—addr**, which also totals four bytes, is stored at the same location, as specified by **absolute**. The variable **fp—addr** occupies the same space as **real—ptr**; **fp—addr** is **real—ptr**. The offset address of variable **real—ptr** is stored in **fp—addr[1]**, and its segment address can be found in **fp—addr[2]**.

You can easily manipulate video memory by declaring an array to overlap video memory. Then all access to video memory is made through the array. On IBM systems, each character sent to the screen also has an attribute (highlighting or underlining) so a record for the array must be declared.

```
type PC_Char = record
                     character : Char
                     attribute : Byte
                 end
var video_mem : array[1..2000] of PC_Char absolute
     $B000:0000;
```

The variable **video_mem** will overlay the memory-mapped video on an IBM PC or compatible using a monochrome video adapter. It gives you direct access to each character on the screen as an attribute byte and a character. If you are using a different computer system that uses memory-mapped video, an interesting project is to determine where in memory the video text image is stored and how the video attributes are controlled.

Part II

EIGHT

Building Include Libraries

In Part I you were introduced to Turbo Pascal and the environment in which it is used. The goal of Part II is to use Turbo Pascal to create a useful application program to analyze loans and print amortization tables. In the next chapter, the Loan Amortization program will be described in detail as you review the design phase of Turbo application development.

Before writing the specific program, it will be helpful to write some general-purpose source code, including constant and type definitions and variable declarations. This code can be saved in include files and used as the building blocks for this Loan Amortization program as well as other applications you will develop yourself. The general-purpose source code you write can be saved as a beginning of a library of practical code that can be reused in many new applications.

The include files you write will contain general-purpose constant and type definitions and variables declarations, as well as miscellaneous global subprograms, controlled keyboard input subprograms, and video display routines. Each subprogram will be presented and discussed individually. You can follow the code along with the discussion. In some cases a subprogram will contain one or more local subprogram definitions; a comment will indicate where the local routine is to be inserted in the source code.

Figure 8-1 lists the subprograms and indicates by listing the level and whether a subprogram is defined within another routine. The code for any local routines will follow the discussion of the subprogram that defines them. As a result you will be able to key in the source code as you go along. In this way you can avoid some of the tedium of entering several pages of code. Of course, it is not necessary to enter the comments or the alternative routines that have been made into comments. At the end of the chapter you will have four include files, each representing a related section of code. Since each include file is made up of a series of subprograms, the first subprogram

STD-CTV.INC

constant definitions
type definitions
variable declarations
constants, types, and variables for keyboard and video I/O routines

STD-UTIL.INC

Beep
Repeat—Char
Strip—Trailing—Char
Strip—Leading—Char
Stripped
Exist

STD-INP.INC
Read—Kbd
Valid—Key
Init—Field
Get—Field—Input

       Process—Control—Character
           BackSpace
           Clear—Field
      Accept—Valid—Character

Valid—Str
Valid—Real
Valid—Int
Valid—Chr

STD-DISP.INC
Clr—Eol
Clear—Prompts
DisplayPrompt
Disp—Error—Msg
Disp—IO—Error
Load—SCR—File
Load—Input—Scrn
Read—Field—Parameters
Check—Status
Load—Help—Text
Disp—Help
Verify—Exit

Figure 8-1. Organization of subprograms in the standard include files

presented will contain comments indicating where the remaining top-level (level 1) routines are to be inserted.

You will find it helpful to have an include file library. A library can help you standardize your programs. The include files can establish a degree of uniformity from one application to another, since all programs will have to conform to the library's style. This results in more productive coding and makes the task of program maintenance easier, especially for large programs.

Some of the include files may not be of any help in other programs, or you may prefer to develop your library in a different way. The user interface, the way a program interacts with the operator, is an area that is subject to wide variations in taste. You can modify any of the library routines to suit your taste, but since these routines will be used later in the Loan Amortization program, changing them may result in the program malfunctioning. Be sure to correct for the program whatever changes you make in the routines. If you plan to modify the routines and to use the Loan Amortization program, you should first get the program running and then make the needed modifications.

Constants, Types, and Variables

The next four listings could be stored in separate include files. But since they will all be used in the program, they can be combined into one include file named STD-CTV.INC.

Constants

The following include file presents a number of general-purpose constant definitions. A description of each constant is included in the comments. Most constants are self-explanatory, except for keyboard constants, which appear to have two versions. The ENTER—KEY, CLEAR—KEY, BS—KEY, and so forth contain the name of the key, while BS, CR, and so forth contain the code for the key. On the IBM PC some keys do not have names but use international symbols for the ENTER, TAB, and BACKSPACE keys.

If your non-IBM PC system has a set of special characters that are produced by the ASCII control codes or the character 128-255, you may want to use them in a similar manner to customize the program to your system. By isolating such custom features in these low-level include files, you can easily make changes if you later decide to convert your programs to run on a different system.

```
{ STD-CTV.PAS General purpose global constants types and variables. }

const  ZERO       = 0;    { Used to clarify code.                      }
       FILL_CHAR  = '_';  { Defines char. used to mark input fields.   }
       SPACE      = ' ';  { Represents the ASCII space character, #32  }
       NULL       = '';   { Represents a null string.                  }

{ Output Control Characters }

       NUL        = #0;   { Null character.                     }
       BELL       = #7;   { Causes a beep when output to a      }
                          { terminal that has sound.            }
       BS         = #8;   { Backspace.                          }
       TAB        = #9;   { Tab character.                      }
       LF         = #10;  { Line Feed.                          }
       CR         = #13;  { Carriage Return.                    }
       FF         = #12;  { Form Feed.                          }
       ESC        = #27;  { Escape character.                   }
       DEL        = #127; { Del or Rubout character.            }

{ Video Limits & Locations }

       MAX_ROW     = 24;  { Maximum number of rows for video.     }
       MAX_COL     = 80;  { Maximum number of columns for video.  }
       MSG_LINE    = 22;  { Line to be used for user messages.    }
       PROMPT_LINE = 23;  { Used for prompts, extended messages   }
                          { and commands.                         }
       CMD_LINE    = 24;  { Primary command input line.           }

{ Input Control Keys:  Keyboard character code and video representation
                       of keys used in Loan_Amortization application.
                       Add others for general purpose use. The definitions
                       shown will work on any Turbo supported system. The
                       alternate definitions, which are commented out, will
                       allow the IBM-PC and compatibles to use function and
                       cursor control keys as indicated. }

       BACKSP      = BS;              { Backspace or left arrow key.        }
{      BS_KEY      = #32#17#196#196#32;   IBM-PC backspace key symbol.      }
       BS_KEY      = ' <BkSpc> ';    { Use text appropriate for keyboard.  }
       ENTER       = CR;             { Return or Enter key.                }
{      ENTER_KEY   = #32#17#196#217#32;   IBM-PC enter key symbol.         }
       ENTER_KEY   = ' <Enter> ';    { Use text appropriate for keyboard.  }
       CLEAR       = TAB;            { Forward tab key or ^I.              }
{      CLEAR_KEY   = #32#196#196#16#221#32;  IBM-PC tab key symbol.        }
       CLEAR_KEY   = ' <Tab> ';      { Use text appropriate for keyboard.  }
       QUIT        = ESC;            { Escape key.                         }
       QUIT_KEY    = ' <Esc> ';      { Use text appropriate for keyboard.  }
{      PREV        = #72;              IBM up arrow key scan code.          }
{      PREV_KEY    = #32#24#32;        IBM-PC up arrow symbol.             }
       PREV        = ^E;             { Use code appropriate for key used.  }
       PREV_KEY    = ' ^E ';         { Use text appropriate for keyboard.  }
{      HELP        = #59;              IBM-PC F1 key scan code.            }
{      HELP_KEY    = ' F1 ';          IBM-PC                              }
       HELP        = ^A;             { Use code appropriate for key used.  }
       HELP_KEY    = ' ^A ';         { Use text appropriate for keyboard.  }
       LEAD_IN     = ESC;            { Lead in char. for IBM function keys. }
                                     { Change as needed for other systems. }

{ ***** Insert general purpose type defintions here. ***** }

{ ***** Insert general purpose variable declarations here. ***** }

{ ***** Insert input/display constants, types and variables here. ***** }
```

Types

User-defined types tend to be specific for each application in which they are being developed. You may find, however, that predefining a set of string types is useful. If your programs tend to be similar in operation—screen displays, calculating routines, and the like—you may want to add some common type definitions. Here again it is worth emphasizing that constant and type definitions do not add to the size of the object code. In fact, type definitions in an include file barely consume memory resources at compile time. The small amount of memory used to store the references to type definitions in the symbol table is a small price to pay for the added clarity that constants and user-defined types add to your programs. Append these type definitions to the constant definition on the STD-CTV.PAS file.

```
{ Insert in STD-CTV.INC - General purpose type definitions. }

{ String types:  General purpose string types. }

type    Str_5      = string[5];
        Str_10     = string[10];
        Str_15     = string[15];
        Str_20     = string[20];
        Str_30     = string[30];
        Str_40     = string[40];
        Str_60     = string[60];
        Str_80     = string[80];
        Str_255    = string[255];
        File_ID    = string[64];
        Drive_ID   = string[2];

{ Set types: }

        Any_Char      = set of Char;        { Defined set of all characters.   }
        Printable_Char = set of ' '..'~';   { Set of printable characters.     }
        Special_Char  = set of #128..#255;  { Set of Non-standard characters.  }
        Control_Char  = set of #0..#127;    { Set of Control characters. This  }
                                            { includes DEL and the IBM-PC      }
                                            { function key scan codes.         }
```

Variables

Very few variables need to be global. It is easy to fall into the trap of declaring unnecessary global variables, but doing so defeats the the advantage of subprograms and modularity.

```
{ Insert in STD-CTV.INC - General purpose global variables. }

var  default,                  { General purpose string buffer.        }
     inp_str      : Str_255;   { Keyboard input string buffer.         }
     i, j, k,                  { Misc. loop counter variables.         }
     io_status    : Integer;   { Global status variable.               }
     inctl,                    { Global control character.             }
     inchr        : Char;      { Global input character.               }
     output_id    : File_ID;   { Store ID of current output file/device.}
     esc_flag,                 { Global logic control flags.           }
     err_flag,
     help_flag,
     quit_flag,
     end_session  : Boolean;
```

Input and Display Constants, Types, And Variables

The constants, types, and variables in the following listing have been isolated, since they are used only in interactive applications. Isolation illustrates the advantage of Turbo Pascal's relaxed rules regarding the placement of the declaration and definition parts of a program. In standard Pascal you are not permitted to have more than one constant definition, type definition, or variable declaration part in each program and subprogram. The advantage of multiple definition and declaration parts is that you can group related definitions and declarations together and then put them in separate include files. The definitions and declarations can be easily included or excluded, depending on the needs of the program you are developing. For example, if you were developing a program that received its input from a disk file and sent its output to a disk file, there would be no need to include the definitions and declarations that handle user interface.

The constants defined in the next listing are self-explanatory. The types and variables, on the other hand, are best explained by example. They are used by the subprograms in the controlled input and display subprograms introduced later in the chapter.

```
{ Additional global constants types and variables required if STD-INP.PAS
  and/or STD-DISP.PAS will be used.
}

const  MAX_FLD     = 32;  { Set maximum number of input fields permitted. }

{ Field input type codes. }

        TEXT_FLD    = 'T';  { Text field. Used for screen doc. only. }
        UC_TEXT     = 'U';  { Upper Case text field.                 }
        NUMERIC     = 'N';  { Numeric field.                         }

{ Field exit type codes. }

        REQUIRED    = 'R';  { Identifies field that requires an entry.     }
        PROTECTED   = 'P';  { Identifies a field to be skipped during input. }
        MANUAL      = 'M';  { Manual exit field. User must press <CR>.     }
        AUTOMATIC   = 'A';  { Automatic exit after last char. is entered.  }

        INCR        = 1;    { INCR & DECR are used to set the }
        DECR        = -1;   { direction indicator variable.   }

{ Define data structure to hold input field parameters. }

type   Fld_Parms   = record
                       xloc       : Integer;  { Video column.             }
                       yloc       : Integer;  { Video row.                }
                       fld_len    : Integer;  { Maximum field length.     }
                       fld_type   : Char;     { See input constants above. }
                       exit_type  : Char;     { See exit constants above.  }
                       fld_msg    : Str_60;   { User prompt message.      }
                     end;

{ Define data structure to hold text for video screens. }

        Scrn        = array[1..MAX_ROW] of Str_80;
```

```
{ Define an array of field parameter records. }

      Inp_Parms    = array[1..MAX_FLD] of Fld_Parms; { Input field parameters.

{ Define pointer and record for help screen text. }

      Help_Pointer = ^Help_Text;

      Help_Text    = record
                        help_txt    : Str_80;
                        next_line   : Help_Pointer;
                     end;

{ Global variables used by standard input and display routines. }

var   fld_cnt,                   { Holds number of fields on current screen. }
      direction      : Integer;  { Increment/Decrement indicator.            }
      top_of_heap    : ^Integer; { Dummy pointer for use by Mark & Release.  }
      first_help     : Help_Pointer; { Pointer to first line of help text.   }
```

This is the last of the code to be inserted in the STD-CTV.INC include file. It should be appended to the variable declarations.

Miscellaneous Global Subprograms

After establishing some standard definitions and declarations, you are ready to define some general-purpose global subprograms. Six subprograms (which beep bells and play with strings) and two forward procedure declarations will be combined into the file named STD-UTIL.INC for standard utility, for the same reason the STD-CTV.INC file was created.

Defining these miscellaneous routines will involve the forward declaration of two error-handling procedures, Disp—Io—Error, for displaying I/O errors, and Disp—Error—Msg, for displaying error messages. These two procedures must be forward declared because they both call some of the miscellaneous subprograms in STD—UTIL.INC and in turn the miscellaneous subprograms call them.

Forward Declarations

When a subprogram calls another subprogram before it can be defined, simply insert the subprogram header as if you were going to define the subprogram, and then append the reserve word **forward**. When the two I/O error procedures are formally defined in the STD-DISP.INC include file, you will see that, other than leaving out the parameter list, the actual definitions are just as they would be if the procedures hadn't been forward declared.

The forward declarations of the I/O procedures are shown next, in what will be the beginning of STD-UTIL.INC. Following the forward declaration will be the miscellaneous utility procedures. You are to replace the insert comments with the subprograms as they are developed.

```
{ STD-UTIL.INC  Miscelaneous global subprograms }

{ Forward declaration of error handling routines which use some of the
  routines in the STD-UTIL.INC file and are also used by some of these
  routines. The formal definition of these forward declared procedures
  is in the STD-DISP.INC Include file, which must be included at some
  point following STD-UTIL.INC. }

    procedure Disp_IO_Error(device_name: File_ID); forward;

    procedure Disp_Error_Msg(err_msg: Str_80); forward;

{ ***** Insert Beep procedure here ***** }

{ ***** Insert Repeat_Char procedure here ***** }

{ ***** Insert Strip_Trailing_Char procedure here ***** }

{ ***** Insert Strip_Leading_Char procedure here ***** }

{ ***** Insert Stripped function here ***** }

{ ***** Insert Read_Kbd procedure here ***** }

{ ***** Insert Valid_Key function here ***** }

{ ***** Insert Exist function here ***** }
```

Beep

The following listing provides two versions of a procedure that will cause the terminal speaker to emit a beep. By simply rearranging the comments, you can select the method appropriate to your system. Note that the non-IBM PC version will work on the IBM PC; however, the sound is considered by many to be annoying. The alternate IBM PC version produces a more acceptable beep. If the system you are using does not beep when it receives an ASCII 7, you may want to devise some other means of getting the operator's attention when the Beep procedure is called.

```
{ Insert in STD-UTIL.INC }

    procedure Beep;
        begin
            Write(BELL);   { Use this statement for non-IBM-PC systems.      }
    (*      begin          { This routine may be substituted on IBM-PC systems. }
                Sound(440); Delay(250); NoSound;
            end;                                                            *)
        end; { Beep }
```

Repeat—Char

Procedure Repeat—Char is a modified version of the Repeat—Char procedure introduced in Chapter 4. Notice that some additions have been made to trap potential I/O errors. Because this routine may be used to send output to any device, there is always the possibility that the device may not be ready to access output. Therefore, you should switch off the compiler's I/O trapping code, using the {$I—} directive, and insert error traps of your own, as illustrated in the listing. Always be sure to use {$I+} to reactivate the internal error trapping as you exit the section of code that you need to control.

You will notice that Repeat—Char expects **io—status**, an integer variable containing the error status, and **output—id**, a string variable containing the device name, to be declared as global variables. An alternative would be to pass them as parameters, with **io—status** as a variable parameter. The primary consideration in deciding whether to use parameters or global variables is modularity versus speed and simplicity. The overhead in passing parameters can be considerable, and using global variables simplifies the interface between the calling routine and the called routine. As defined, Repeat—Char is not a modular subprogram because it depends on the global variable. Excessive use of global variables increases the probability that program modification will produce unexpected side effects.

```
{ Insert in STD-UTIL.INC }

    procedure Repeat_Char(character : Char;      { Character to be output.    }
                          count     : Integer); { Number of times to output. }
      var i     : Integer;

      begin
        io_status := ZERO;
        i := ZERO;
{$I-}
        while (io_status = ZERO) and (i < count) do
          begin
            Write(character);
            io_status := IOresult;
            i := Succ(i);
          end;
{$I+}
        if (io_status <> ZERO) then
          Disp_IO_Error(output_id);
      end; { Repeat_Char }
```

Strip—Trailing—Char

The Strip—Trailing—Char procedure removes trailing characters from the string passed in the **inp—str** parameter. For example, Strip—Trailing—Char will strip the five periods from the string "Hello.....". The **strip** parameter contains the character to be removed beginning at the position indicated by **len**. This is the first of two procedures that are used by the function Stripped. Although the Loan Amortization program accesses Strip_Trailing_Char and Strip_Leading_Char procedures indirectly via calls to the Stripped function, they could be useful in other programs. If the two procedures were defined within the Stripped function, they would not be available to other subprograms. The rules of scope apply to subprograms just as they apply to constants, types, and variables. By defining these procedures separately, they are program global and available to any subprogram.

An alternate implementation is provided for this and the next routine. The reason for this and the trade-offs involved are given later when the Stripped function is discussed.

```
{ Insert in STD-UTIL.INC }

      procedure Strip_Trailing_Char(var inp_str : Str_255; { String to strip.}
                                        len      : Byte;    { Maximum length. }
                                        strip    : Char);   { Char. to strip. }

      { Scan inp_str from len downto 0 until a character <> strip is found.
        Set the length of inp_str equal to the position of the character
        found if any. Note that inp_str is set to null if it contains only
        strip characters. }

        begin
          inp_str[0] := Chr(0);         { Set inp_str length byte to ZERO. }
          while (inp_str[len] = strip) and (len > ZERO) do
            len := Pred(len);
          inp_str[0] := Chr(len);       { Set inp_str length to len. }
        end; { Strip_Trailing_Char }

{ Alternate implementation. See disscussion of Stripped. }

(*    function Trailing_Stripped(inp_str : Str_255;
                                  len      : Byte;
                                  strip    : Char): Str_255;
        begin
          inp_str[0] := Chr(0);         { Set inp_str length to ZERO }
          while (inp_str[len] = strip) and (len > ZERO) do
            len := Pred(len);
          inp_str[0] := Chr(len);       { Set inp_str length to len }
          Trailing_Stripped := inp_str;
        end; { Trailing_Stripped }
*)
```

Strip—Leading—Char

Strip_Leading_Char is the other half of the character-stripping pair; it removes all occurrences of characters matching the **strip** parameter starting at the left end of **inp_str**. This procedure uses Turbo Pascal's Copy function. Copy handles illogical requests gracefully. If you want to copy a string beginning beyond the end of the string, it simply returns a null string. The only way you can upset the Copy function is to indicate a starting position greater than 255; but you can prevent this over-range error by using a Byte type rather than an Integer variable to indicate the starting position.

```
{ Insert in STD-UTIL.INC }

    procedure Strip_Leading_Char(var inp_str : Str_255; { String to strip. }
                                     len      : Byte;    { Maximum length.  }
                                     strip    : Char);   { Char. to strip.  }

        var  i          : Byte;

    { Find the first occurrence, if any, of a character not equal to strip.
      Copy the remainder of inp_str into the new inp_str. Note inp_str is set
      to null if it is null initially or it contains only strip characters. }

        begin
          i := 1;
          While (inp_str[i] = strip) and (i <= len) do
            i := Succ(i);
          inp_str := Copy(inp_str,i,len);
        end; { Strip_Leading_Char }

{ Alternate implementation. See discussion of Stripped. }
(*
    function Leading_Stripped(inp_str : Str_255;
                                  len      : Byte;
                                  strip    : Char): Str_255;
        var  i          : Byte;

        begin
          i := 1;
          While (inp_str[i] = strip) and (i <= len) do
            i := Succ(i);
          inp_str := Copy(inp_str,i,len);
          Leading_Stripped := inp_str;
        end; { Leading_Stripped }
*)
```

Stripped

The Stripped function returns a string based on **inp_str** that has been stripped of any characters that match the **strip** parameter on either the left or right ends. Stripped could have been implemented as a procedure in much the same way as the last two procedures, but it was defined as a function to avoid problems due to **inp_str** being a variable parameter.

You will recall that when calling a procedure with variable string parameters, the actual parameters must be the same type. Unless the compiler directive String Length Checking is disabled ({$V−}), when compiling the calling routines, Strip_Trailing_Char and Strip_Leading_Char could only be used with Str_255 type strings. However, if they were implemented as functions returning a type Str_255 value, the parameter compatibility problem would be circumvented, since functions return the string, as opposed to a parameter, with no type restrictions based on the string type. The function versions of Strip_Leading_Char and Strip_Trailing_Char illustrate this approach. Since the **inp_str** parameter can be passed by value rather than by reference, any string type can be safely passed.

Naturally there are tradeoffs involved: implementation using functions will result in larger, somewhat slower object code. There is no one correct way, but in general, a utility routine should not impose any unnecessary requirements on the programs that will use them.

```
{ Insert in STD-UTIL.INC }

    function Stripped(var inp_str : Str_255;        { String to strip. }
                          len      : Byte;           { Maximum length.  }
                          strip    : Char): Str_255; { Char. to strip.  }

        begin
          Strip_Trailing_Char(inp_str,len,strip);
          Strip_Leading_Char(inp_str,len,strip);
          Stripped := inp_str;
        end; { Stripped }

(* Alternate version of Stripped using functions

        begin
          inp_str := Trailing_Stripped(inp_str,len,strip);
          Stripped := Leading_Stripped(inp_str,len,strip);
        end; { Stripped }
*)
```

Exist

The Exist function is adapted from the Exist function in the Turbo reference manual, except this function closes the file if it exists. It will return TRUE if the file indicated by **file—name** exists; otherwise you'll get a result of FALSE.

```
    function Exist(file_name: File_ID): Boolean;
      var chk_file  : File;

      begin
        Assign(chk_file,file_name);
{$I-} Reset(chk_file); {$I+}
        if (IOresult = ZERO) then
          begin
            Exist := TRUE;
            Close(chk_file);
          end
        else
          Exist := FALSE;
      end; { Exist }
```

Controlled Keyboard Input

The next set of subprograms controls user input and is used in place of Read and ReadLn to accept input from the keyboard. By screening the input on a character-by-character basis, you can make the applications that use these subprograms much simpler. The subprograms should be combined in the STD-INP.INC file.

Read—Kbd

The Read—Kbd procedure is the heart of the controlled keyboard input routines. It allows other routines to examine each keystroke and determine whether a printable character or a control code was generated. Read—Kbd requires two Char type variable parameters: **inctl**, which returns the value of function and control keys, and **inchr**, which returns other characters.

When a function or control key combination is pressed, the parameter **inctl** will contain its ASCII code; however, the relationship between the value of **inctl** and the key that produced it is system-dependent. If the standard control key combinations are used, **inctl** will return a value in the range 1 to 26, where CTRL-A equals 1 and CTRL-Z equals 26. On systems like the IBM PC, function keys and ALT key combinations produce two codes: the first, called the *lead-in character*, is an ASCII 27 followed immediately by a second code called a *scan code*. The relationship between the scan code and the key that produced it can be clarified by constant definitions, as illustrated by the alternate keyboard constant definitions in the input control key section in the STD-CTV.INC file.

Read—Kbd relies on Turbo's KeyPressed function to determine when a key has been pressed. Since the value, either TRUE or FALSE, returned by KeyPressed is based on a call to the operating system's keyboard status function, its action may vary depending on the operating system you are using. As a result, you may have to do some experimenting with KeyPressed if you want to use function keys or dedicated control keys for Read—Kbd on a non-IBM PC system. Two areas of concern are the lead-in character, which is defined as the constant LEAD—IN, and the amount of delay.

The lead-in character may be modified by the Turbo compiler by the time it is received by **inchr**. On the IBMPC, for example, the compiler converts the lead-in character from NUL—CHAR to the ESC character ASCII 27. Some systems do not produce a lead-in character. In those instances **inctl** will contain a character in the ASCII range 1 to 31, or possibly the delete key, or DEL, which is ASCII character 127.

Whether or not a delay is required is determined by how much time the scan code follows the lead-in character. The scan code may be delayed if the I/O driver has a lot of processing to do. For example, if you have enabled the user break directive, {$U+}, a delay will definitely be needed, because the directive adds to the processing time whenever a subprogram is called.

Non-IBM PC systems that offer function keys may or may not need a Delay statement even with the User Break directive disabled. This is an area where you will probably have to dig out the technical reference manual for your system and do some experimenting.

If you use the {$C—} directive to disable the break function completely, you will have to consider the possible results that a key-ahead buffer would produce. A key-ahead buffer is a system-dependent feature that allows the person at the keyboard to type ahead of the program. This commonly occurs when the program is occupied, such as reading from a disk drive, and can't devote its attention to the keyboard when a key is pressed. When this happens, the input from the keyboard is not lost but stored in a keyboard buffer. If the system does not offer buffered keyboard input, input from the keyboard is lost. Because this feature is system-dependent, the Loan Amortization program will not use it; the Loan__Amortization code will be compiled with the default {$C+} directive in effect.

```
{ Insert in STD-INP.INC }

    procedure Read_Kbd(var inchr,inctl: Char);

  {      Keyboard input routine that will allow users of systems with
         'IBM-PC type' function keys to use those keys as control keys.
         It will also work on systems using standard control keys producing
         ASCII characters #1..#31 & #127. The variable parameters will
         be set as follows depending on the key that is pressed.

      inchr  will contain the character value of the key pressed.
             If a control/function key is pressed this will be the
             'lead in' value for the key, if any.  For example the
             lead in character for function keys on many systems is the
             escape character, ASCII #27.
      inctl  will contain NUL or a control/function key value which may be
             used to determine whether a control/function key was pressed
             and if so which key it was. }

        begin
          inctl := NUL;                       { Initialize to inctl to NUL.    }
          Read(Kbd,inchr);                    { Wait for a key to be pressed.  }
          if (KeyPressed and (inchr = LEAD_IN)) then
            begin                             { Get function key scan code.    }
              Delay(0);                       { Increase Delay if needed.      }
              Read(Kbd,inctl);                { Scan code goes in inctl.       }
            end
          else
            if (inchr in [#1..#31,DEL]) then
              inctl := inchr;                 { Trap conventional control chrs.}
        end; { Read_Kbd }


  { ***** Insert the Valid_key function here ***** }

  { ***** Insert the Init_Field procedure here ***** }

  { ***** Insert the Get_Field_Input procedure here ***** }

  { ***** Insert the Valid_Str function here ***** }

  { ***** Insert the Valid_Real function here ***** }

  { ***** Insert the Valid_Int function here ***** }

  { ***** Insert the Valid_Chr function here ***** }
```

Valid —Key

The Valid—Key function is a handy way to accept and verify single key commands. Control is not returned to the calling routine until a valid key, whose range is defined by the parameter **valid—keys**, is pressed. As a result, the calling program is spared the duty of screening the input. Since any character may be a member of the **valid—keys** set, the returned value may be a "control" or "special" character, if you so desire. As defined, this routine does not differentiate between upper- and lowercase characters. If you would prefer that it did, just remove the **inchr:= UpCase(inchr)** statement.

```
{ Insert in STD-INP.INC }

   function Valid_Key(valid_keys: Any_Char): Char;
      var inchr, inctl : Char;

{ Waits for a key to be pressed that is a member of the set valid_keys.
  The ASCII value of the key is returned. Non-control keys are
  displayed. A beep is sounded for invalid keys.

  Note that alpha characters are forced to upper case. }

      begin
        repeat
          Read_Kbd(inchr,inctl);        { Wait for a key to be pressed. }
          if (inctl = NUL) then
            begin                        { If it is not a control key    }
              inchr := UpCase(inchr);    { force it to upper case and     }
              Write(inchr,BS);           { display it, restoring cursor. }
            end
          else                           { If it is a control key then   }
            inchr := inctl;              { pass it through for testing.   }
          if (not (inchr in valid_keys)) then
            Beep;                        { Beep if it's not valid.        }
        until (inchr in valid_keys);
        Valid_Key := inchr;              { Return the valid character.    }
      end; { Valid_Key }
```

Init —Field

The Init—Field procedure and the next group of subprograms are concerned with accepting, screening, and formatting input via the video monitor. Each piece of information is entered into an input field much as you would pencil in answers in boxes next to the questions on an employment form. The data can be verified as it is entered, and the program requests the user to try again for erroneous entries.

The first step in accepting information using input fields is to prepare the field for input and position the cursor. The Init — Field procedure uses Repeat — Char to send a series of **init — char** characters to the current output device. It's purpose is to clear an input field as defined by **parms**, which specifies the video location and length of the field, in characters, to be initialized. You will notice that the parameter **parms** is passed by reference even though Init — Field does not alter its value. This is done to improve the performance of the routine. If an array or record variable is passed by value, the following, time-consuming events take place:

1. The value is passed as an address that points to the first data item in the structure.

2. Space for a local copy of the entire structure is allocated in the local data area of the called subprogram.

3. The actual variable is then copied into this local storage.

The code to do all of this is generated automatically by the compiler, and it is quite efficient. But for larger data structures it still takes a considerable amount of time. As long as you are certain that the subprogram you are writing will not unintentionally alter the value of such a variable, much of this time can be saved by passing the variable by reference rather than by value.

It is also noteworthy that there is a penalty on speed when string, set, or Real variables are passed by value. While in most cases passing a parameter by value protects the values, there are times when you may sacrifice protection for speed.

```
{ Insert in STD-INP.INC }

  procedure Init_Field (init_char : Char;
                        var parms : Fld_Parms);
    var  i   : Byte;

{ Initialize field with init_char based on parms.
  Parameters are:

  init_char  Fill character to be used for field initialization.
  parms      Input field parameters for the field to be initialized. }

    begin
      with parms do
      begin
        GoToXY(xloc,yloc);                   { Position cursor. }
        Repeat_Char(init_char,fld_len);      { Init field with init_char. }
        GoToXY(xloc,yloc);                   { Restore cursor position. }
      end;
    end; { Init_Field }
```

Get_Field_Input

The Get_Field_Input procedure relies on two local procedures, Accept_Valid_Character and Process_Control_Character. In turn, Process_Control_Character has a couple of lower level routines of its own. Here is the pseudo-code for Get_Field_Input:

```
Get_Field_Input
  Initialize variables.
  Repeat
    Get a character from the keyboard.
    If it is a control character then
      Process it.                        { Process_Control_Char }
    Otherwise
      Accept it if it is valid.          { Accept_Valid_Character }
  Until the exit flag is set
  Clear to the end of the field.
End of the Get_Field_Input.
```

A review of the individual subprograms will follow beginning with the Get_Field_Input procedure. Each lower level subprogram will be presented in the order that it appears in Get_Field_Input's definition part. Be sure to note the insert comments and insert the appropriate subprogram code as indicated.

The source code for Get_Field_Input is based on the pseudo-code you just saw. At its heart is a **repeat-until** loop that accepts characters from the keyboard. If a control or function key is pressed, the character is passed to the locally defined procedure Process_Control_Character for further screening. The loop will terminate when the exit flag is set by the Process_Control_Character procedure, which will be described shortly. Notice that Get_Field_Input is composed largely of subprogram statements that call routines defined earlier. As a result, the complex details are hidden, making it easier to see the objective of the procedure.

```
{ Insert in STD-INP.INC }

  procedure Get_Field_Input(var parms    : Fld_Parms;
                            var chr_set  : Printable_Char;
                            var ctrl_set : Control_Char);

     var    count  : Integer; { Number of characters entered. }
            exit   : Boolean; { Local exit flag.              }

  { General purpose keyboard input routine. }
```

```
      Parameters are:
      parms      Input field parameters for the field to be processed.
      chr_set    Set of characters acceptable for input. Beep for others.
      ctrl_set   Set of control/fuction characters acceptable for input. }

   { Global variables used:
               esc_flag    Boolean   Global exit flag.
               inp_str     Str_255   Input buffer string. Note that
                                     Length(inp_str) is set to count on exit.
               direction   Integer   Increment/Decrement indicator. Switched to
                                     DECR if valid control character is PREV.
               inchr       Char      Used to store input character.
               inctl       Char      Used to store input control/function code. }

   { ***** Insert Process_Control_Character procedure ***** }

   { ***** Insert Accept_Valid_Character procedure ***** }

      begin { Get_Field_Input }
        count := ZERO;
        esc_flag := FALSE; exit := FALSE;
        direction := INCR;
        repeat
          Read_Kbd(inchr,inctl);
          if (inctl in ctrl_set) then
            Process_Control_Character
          else
            Accept_Valid_Character;
        until exit;
        inp_str[0] := Chr(count);                  { Set length of input string. }
        Repeat_Char(SPACE,(parms.fld_len - count)); { Clear to end of field. }
      end; { Get_Field_Input }
```

Process—Control—Character

This procedure selects an action based on **inctl**, which contains one of the six globally defined control and function key codes. The Backspace and Clear—Field procedures are local to Process—Control—Character and should be inserted in place of the insert comments.

The action initiated by each control key is self-explanatory with the possible exception of the previous field key, which is defined by the constant PREV key. The PREV, or previous field key, is needed so that the person entering data may jump to a prior field and make a change. All that needs to be done by Process—Control—Character is to let the calling routine know that the PREV key was pressed. This is done by setting the direction indicator to the global constant DECR, which indicates a jump to the previous field. That indicator will then be used to adjust a field pointer, thereby producing the desired effect. This topic will be pursued further when the Modify—Data subprogram is developed in Chapter 11.

```
   { Insert in STD-INP.INC - Get_Input_Field }

      procedure Process_Control_Character;
        var i : Byte;

      { Select action based on control key pressed by user. }
```

```
{ Global variables used:
         esc_flag  : Boolean;  Used to indicate that QUIT key pressed.
         help_flag : Boolean;  Used to indicate that HELP key pressed.
         direction : Integer;  Increment/Decrement indicator. }

{ ***** Insert the BackSpace procedure here ***** }

{ ***** Insert the Clear_Field procedure here ***** }

    begin { Process_Control_Character }
      case inctl of
        BACKSP  : Backspace(FILL_CHAR);
        ENTER   : exit := TRUE;
        QUIT    : begin
                    esc_flag := TRUE;
                    exit := TRUE;
                  end;
        PREV    : begin
                    Clear_Field;
                    direction := DECR;
                    exit := TRUE;
                  end;
        CLEAR   : begin
                    Clear_Field;
                    exit := TRUE;
                  end;
        HELP    : begin
                    help_flag := TRUE;
                    exit := TRUE;
                  end;
        else      Beep;
      end; {case}
    end; { Process_Control_Character }
```

Backspace

The simple procedure shown here performs a backspace on the video screen
and removes the last character from the input string **inp_str** by decrement-
ing the **count** variable. Backspacing out of the field is prohibited by verifying
that the **count** variable is greater than zero. The backspace on the video
screen is called a destructive backspace because the character to the left of
the cursor is replaced with a space.

```
{ Insert in STD-INP.INC - Get_Field_Input - Process_Control_Character }

    procedure Backspace(fill: Char);

  { Perform destructive backspace on video and remove last character
    from inp_str. The parameter is:

    fill   Character to be output in place of character deleted. }

      begin
        if (count > ZERO) then
          begin
            Write(BS,fill,BS);       { Destructive backspace to video.      }
            count := Pred(count);    { Decrement characters entered count. }
          end
        else
          Beep;                      { Beep if count = ZERO initially.      }
      end; { Backspace }
```

Clear —Field

The objective of the Clear —Field procedure is to reinitialize the input field on the video screen and clear the input string **inp —str**. The Clear —Field procedure assumes that when the RETURN key is pressed without entering a new value, the input field variable will remain the value indicated by the global variable **default**. Since pressing the RETURN key indicates that the default value is to be accepted, there needs to be another key that indicates that a field is to be cleared. The TAB key has been designated as the clear field key. The FillChar procedure is used to clear the input string and the Init —Field procedure clears the input field on the video monitor.

```
{ Insert in STD-INP.INC - Get_Field_Input - Process_Control_Character }

      procedure Clear_Field;
        var i : Byte;

   { Initialize video field and clear input string. }

      begin
        Init_Field(FILL_CHAR,parms);              { Clear video field. }
        with parms do
          FillChar(inp_str,fld_len + 1,ZERO);   { Clear inp_str. }
        count := ZERO;                            { Reset count to ZERO. }
      end; { Clear_Field }
```

Accept —Valid —Character

The next listing contains the code for a procedure that validates non-control characters. If a character received by Read —Kbd is not a member of **ctrl —set**, it is passed to the Accept —Valid —Character procedure for further screening. If the parameter **parms** indicates that **fld —type** is UC —TEXT, the character is forced to uppercase. You will recall that the **parms** parameter is passed to Get —Field —Input and is thus available to Accept —Valid —Character. In addition to providing the video screen location of a field, the **parms** record contains codes that indicate the type of the field and whether the operator must press RETURN to exit the field.

The character stored in **inchr** is valid if it is a member of **chr —set**, a parameter from Get —Field, and the end of the field has not been reached. If it passes those hurdles, it is displayed on the video screen and stored in **inp —str**. The Concat procedure or the concatenation operator (+) could have been used to add the character to **inp —str**. Instead it is assigned directly to the element of the character array indicated by **count**. The tradeoff between using concatenation or direct assignment is the speed of direct assignment versus the clarity and portability of the Concat procedure.

Finally, if **parms.exit —type** equals AUTOMATIC and the program is at the last field position, you must make it look as if the RETURN key has been pressed. This is done by setting the exit flag to TRUE and assigning the value of CR to **inctl**. If **parms.exit—type** is MANUAL, a beep is emitted when the user tries to enter characters after reaching the end of the field.

```
{ Insert in STD-INP.INC - Get_Field_Input }

  procedure Accept_Valid_Character;

{ If inchr is a member of chr_set and that the field length has
  not been exceeded, display inchr, increment count
  and store the character in inp_str; otherwise Beep.
  If the end of an AUTOMATIC exit field is reached set the exit
  flag and indicate that a CR has been received by setting inctl to CR. }

    begin
      with parms do
      begin
        if (fld_type = UC_TEXT) then
          inchr := UpCase(inchr);
        if (inchr in chr_set) and (count < fld_len) then
          begin
            Write(inchr);
            count := Succ(count);
            inp_str[count] := inchr;
            if (exit_type = AUTOMATIC) and (count = fld_len) then
              begin
                exit := TRUE; inctl := CR;
              end;
          end
        else
          Beep;
      end;
    end; { Accept_Valid_Character }
```

Valid Input Functions

The next four functions use Get—Field—Input to build controlled input routines for strings, real numbers, integers, and characters. The primary enhancements provided by these functions are the addition of default processing and range checking. These added features are discussed next.

Before using any of these functions, the calling routine should set the global default string to the current value of the field or any other value that you wish to use as a default for the field being input. If the field is numeric, the string representation of the value should be stored in the default string. If the operator presses the RETURN key without entering a new value, this "default" value is returned by the function. This makes it possible for the user to skip through fields that are already set to the desired value.

With the exception of Valid—Str, which is used for free-form text fields, all of the functions require that a range of valid values be specified in the parameter list. (In the case of Valid—Chr a set of valid characters is provided.) If the value (or character) entered doesn't pass the validity test, a descriptive error message is displayed. In addition, the direction indicator is set to ZERO, which forces the re-entry of the field. The end result is that the calling routine is relieved of a great deal of checking.

Rather than review these functions individually, the following discussion of the Valid_Real function will serve to describe the general format of the group.

Valid_Real

The first action in this routine is to convert the global string default to a real numeric value if possible. This is done using the Val procedure. If the conversion of default is unsuccessful, as indicated by the **io_status** parameter, the local variable **real_val** is set to 0.0; otherwise it will contain the result of the conversion. Valid_Real is set equal to **real_val** to provide a default value if the user presses RETURN without making an entry.

Next, Get_Field_Input is called giving the operator an opportunity to enter a new value into the field defined by the **parms** parameter. Note that only the characters 0 through 9, the period, and the minus sign will be accepted due to the definition of the typed constant **chr_set**. If an entry is made to the field or the CLEAR key is pressed, the entry is processed further. If the CLEAR key was pressed, **inp_str** is set to 0.00; otherwise **inp_str** will contain the value entered by the user. The Val procedure is used to convert **inp_str** to a real value. That value is assigned to Valid_Real unless there was a conversion error or the conversion value is not in the range indicated by the **min** and **max** parameters. In either of those cases a descriptive error message is displayed indicating the acceptable range of input values. Notice how the **point** parameter is used to format the error message using the Str procedure and Write parameters.

```
{ Insert in STD-INP.INC }

   function Valid_Real(var parms   : Fld_Parms;
                           point   : Byte;
                           min,max : Real): Real;

      const chr_set   : Printable_Char = ['0'..'9','-','.'];
            ctrl_set  : Control_Char   = [CR,BS,CLEAR,PREV,QUIT];

      var   real_val  : Real;
            min_str,
            max_str   : Str_20;
            err_msg   : Str_80;

   { Accepts field input based on parms. If the user presses <CR> without
     entering anything, the Real value of the global default string is returned.
     Otherwise the string entered is converted to a Real value. If the value
     is not in the range indicated by min and max or a there is an error in
     the conversion, an error message is displayed. }
```

```
begin { Valid_Real }
  Val(Stripped(default,Length(default),SPACE),real_val,io_status);
  if io_status <> ZERO then   { If default is a bad numeric value    }
    real_val := 0.0;          { then return 0.0.                     }
  Valid_Real := real_val;     { Return default if no value is entered. }
  Get_Field_Input(parms,chr_set,ctrl_set);
  if ((inctl = CR) and (Length(inp_str) > ZERO)) or
     (inctl = CLEAR) then
    begin
      if (inctl = CLEAR) then
        inp_str := '0.00';
      Val(inp_str,real_val,io_status);
      if (io_status = ZERO) and
         ((real_val >= min) and (real_val <= max)) then
        Valid_Real := real_val
      else
        begin
          Str(min:parms.fld_len:point,min_str); { The point parameter   }
          Str(max:parms.fld_len:point,max_str); { indicates the position }
          err_msg := 'Value must be from '       { of the decimal point. }
                   + min_str + ' through ' + max_str;
          Disp_Error_Msg(err_msg);
          direction := ZERO;                { Force re-entry of field. }
        end;
    end;
end; { Valid_Real}
```

Valid —Str

```
{ Insert in STD-INP.INC }

  function Valid_Str(var parms: Fld_Parms): Str_80;

    const chr_set     : Printable_Char = [SPACE..'~'];
          ctrl_set    : Control_Char   = [CR,BS,CLEAR,PREV,QUIT];

{ Accepts field input based on parms. If the user presses <CR> without
  entering anything, the value of the global default string is returned.
  Otherwise the characters entered, up to the maximum indicated by
  parms.fld_len, are returned as a string. }

    begin
      Valid_Str := default;    { Returns default if no value is entered. }
      Get_Field_Input(parms,chr_set,ctrl_set);
      if ((inctl = CR) and (Length(inp_str) > ZERO)) or
         (inctl = CLEAR) then
        Valid_Str := inp_str;
    end; { Valid_Str }
```

Valid —Int

```
{ Insert in STD-INP.INC }

  function Valid_Int(var parms   : Fld_Parms;
                         min,max : Integer): Integer;

    const chr_set     : Printable_Char = ['0'..'9','-'];
          ctrl_set    : Control_Char   = [CR,BS,CLEAR,PREV,QUIT];
```

```
            var   int_val      : Integer;
                  min_str,
                  max_str      : Str_20;
                  err_msg      : Str_80;
```

{ Accepts field input based on parms. If the user presses <CR> without
  entering anything, the Integer value of the global default string is returned.
  Otherwise the string entered is converted to an Integer value. If the value
  is not in the range indicated by min and max or a there is an error in
  the conversion, an error message is displayed. }

```
            begin { Valid_Int }
              Val(Stripped(default,Length(default),SPACE),int_val,io_status);
              if io_status <> ZERO then { If default is a bad numeric value    }
                int_val := ZERO;        { then return ZERO.                    }
              Valid_Int := int_val;     { Return default if no value is entered. }
              Get_Field_Input(parms,chr_set,ctrl_set);
              if ((inctl = CR) and (Length(inp_str) > ZERO)) or
                 (inctl = CLEAR) then
                begin
                  if (inctl = CLEAR) then
                    inp_str := '0';
                  Val(inp_str,int_val,io_status);
                  if (io_status = ZERO) and
                     ((int_val >= min) and (int_val <= max)) then
                    Valid_Int := int_val
                  else
                    begin
                      Str(min:parms.fld_len,min_str);
                      Str(max:parms.fld_len,max_str);
                      err_msg := 'Value must be from ' + min_str +
                                 ' through ' + max_str;
                      Disp_Error_Msg(err_msg);
                      direction := ZERO;                { Forces re-entry of field. }
                    end;
                end;
            end; { Valid_Int }
```

Valid —Chr

```
     { Insert in STD-INP.INC }

     function Valid_Chr(var parms : Fld_Parms;
                        valid_set : Printable_Char): Char;

       const. ctrl_set : Control_Char  = [CR,BS,CLEAR,PREV,QUIT];
```

{ Accepts field input based on parms. If the user presses <CR> without
  entering anything, the first character of the global default string is
  returned. Otherwise the user must enter a character that is a member of
  the valid_set parameter. }

```
       begin  { Valid_Chr }
         Valid_Chr := default[1]; { Returns default if no value is entered. }
         Get_Field_Input(parms,valid_set,ctrl_set);
         if ((inctl = CR) and (Length(inp_str) > ZERO)) or
            (inctl = CLEAR) then
           Valid_Chr := inp_str[1]
       end; { Valid_Chr }
```

Video Display Subprograms

The subprograms in the STD-DISP.INC file display user prompts, error messages, and entire video screens of information. Because this code is intended to be portable across the spectrum of CP/M and MS-DOS systems supported by Turbo Pascal, video tricks using memory-mapped systems will not be used.

Clr—Eol, Clear—Prompts, and Display—Prompt

Chances are you have used, seen, or heard about *input program generators*. These are programs that let you design an input screen using an editor of some sort. When you are finished, they generate a program based on the input screen. The keyboard input and video display routines in this section are based on a similar concept; the difference is that *you* do the programming. Chapter 10 will go into detail as to how you can create an input screen using the Turbo editor. For now, Figure 8-2 presents the contents of a text file named LOAN.SCR that will be used by the Loan Amortization program. The top portion is what the operator will see on the screen as data is entered for the amortization table.

The three procedures Clr—Eol, Clear—Prompts, and Display—Prompt shown in the following listing are used to manage three lines on a video screen. These lines, 22, 23, and 24 of the Amortization program, are reserved for prompts and messages. You will find that on most systems with 24 lines available for video text output, the Turbo's ClrEol procedure not only clears the line, but also causes the screen to scroll up one line if it is used on line 24. For that reason, the Clr—Eol procedure is an alternative that will work on all systems. The Clear—Prompts procedure clears the three-line prompt area, while the Display—Prompt procedure outputs a formatted prompt or command message to the line indicated by the **line** parameter. This is an area where personal style comes into play. You may want to modify the cosmetic effects of this routine to suit your style.

```
Loan ID..:

                    Amortization Schedule      Copyright 1985
Tot. Pmts:          Loan Information           Osborne/McGraw-Hill
Interest.:
        Commercial...:
                    Business Name

        Individual...:
                    Last Name       First Name      Title

        Collateral...:

        Principal....:          Interest Rate......:    %
        Payment Amt..:          Payments Per Year..:
        1st Pmt Due..:  /       Number of Payments.:
        Selected Year:          Output to Vid/Print:


19
06,23,01,U,A,Press 'X' if commercial loan otherwise leave blank.
06,26,40,T,M,Enter Business name. Up to 40 characters.
09,23,01,U,P,-{ Computer entry based on field 1 }
09,26,15,T,M,Enter Borrower's Last Name. Up to 15 characters.
09,44,15,T,M,Enter Borrower's First Name. Up to 15 characters.
09,62,10,T,M,Enter Borrower's Title. Up to 10 characters.
12,23,40,T,M,Enter description of the collateral. Up to 40 characters.
14,23,10,N,M,Enter actual amount borrowed at interest.
14,62,06,N,M,Enter the interest rate. Up to 5 digits including decimal.
16,23,10,N,M,Enter payment amount or 0.00 to calculate payment amount.
16,62,02,N,A,Enter the number of payments scheduled annually.
18,23,02,N,M,Enter 2-digit MONTH in which first payment is due.
18,26,04,N,M,Enter 4-digit YEAR in which first payment is due.
18,62,07,N,M,Enter total number of payments scheduled.
20,23,04,N,M,Enter desired year or ZERO for a complete table.
20,62,01,U,M,Enter 'V' for video output or 'P' for printed output.
01,12,11,U,P, -{ Loan ID position. }
03,12,11,N,P, -{ Total Pmts. position. }
04,12,11,N,P, -{ Interest position. }
```

Figure 8-2.   Input screen text file for Loan Amortization program

```
{ STD-DISP.PAS - Requires STD-CTV.PAS and STD-UTIL.PAS }

  procedure Clr_Eol(line: Byte);
    var blank_line : Str_80;

{ Alternate clear to end of line routine for systems that scroll the
  video screen when a Turbo ClrEol is executed on the 24th line. }
```

```
      begin
        FillChar(blank_line,81,SPACE); blank_line[0] := Chr(79);
        GoToXY(1,line); Write(blank_line);
        GoToXY(1,line);
      end; { Clr_Eol }

    procedure Clear_Prompts;

  { Clears the prompt area as defined by the global constants used. }

      begin
        GoToXY(1,MSG_LINE); ClrEol;
        GoToXY(1,PROMPT_LINE); ClrEol;
        GoToXY(1,CMD_LINE); Clr_Eol(CMD_LINE); { Systems with 25 video lines }
      end; { Clear_Prompts }                   { can use ClrEol.            }

    procedure Display_Prompt(line    : Byte;
                             prompt  : Str_10;
                             msg_str : Str_80);

  { Displays prompt & highlighted msg_str at line.
    Parameters are:
    line    The video line on which the prompt and msg_str are displayed.
    prompt  A string that identifies the nature of the message.
    msg_str The message to be displayed.

    Note: The calling routine must preserve and restore the cursor position
          and video intensity as needed.
          Combined length of prompt & msg_str should be less than 76.
  }
      begin { Display_Prompt }
        GoToXY(1,line); Clr_Eol(line);  { Systems with 25 video lines }
        LowVideo;                       { can use ClrEol. }
        Write(Prompt,': '); NormVideo;
        Write(msg_str);
      end; { Display_Prompt }

  { ***** Insert the Disp_Error_Msg procedure here. ***** }

  { ***** Insert the Disp_I/O_Error procedure here. ***** }

  { ***** Insert the Load_SCR_File procedure here. ***** }

  { ***** Insert the Load_Input_Scrn procedure here. ***** }

  { ***** Insert the Disp_Input_Scrn procedure here. ***** }

  { ***** Insert the Load_Help_Text procedure here. ***** }

  { ***** Insert the Disp_Help procedure here. ***** }

  { ***** Insert the Verify_Exit procedure here. ***** }
```

Disp—Error—Msg

The Disp—Error—Msg procedure was forward declared in the STD-
UTIL.INC file. When you make forward declarations, you may find it helpful
to repeat the parameter list in a comment as shown here. Otherwise, you will
have to locate the forward declaration any time you need to see what parameters are passed.

The objective of the routine is to display an error message, located in the **err—msg** parameter, and beep the user. The user is then prompted to press a key. When a key is pressed, the error message is erased. Notice that the calling routine is responsible for restoring the text that the error message erased.

```
{ Insert in STD-DISP.PAS }

  procedure Disp_Error_Msg; { (err_msg: Str_80); }
    var   inchr : Char;       { forward defined in STD-UTIL.PAS }

{ Displays err_msg at MSG_LINE and a 'continue prompt' at PROMPT_LINE.
  Clears both lines when user presses any key.

  Note: The calling routine must preserve and restore cursor position and
        video intensity as well as the contents of the MSG_LINE & PROMPT_LINE. }

  begin
    Display_Prompt(MSG_LINE,'ERR',err_msg); GoToXY(1,PROMPT_LINE);
    Display_Prompt(PROMPT_LINE,
                     'MSG','Press ANY KEY to try again. ==> ');
    Beep;
    Read(Kbd,inchr);                      { Pause until key is pressed }
    GoToXY(1,MSG_LINE); ClrEol; GoToXY(1,PROMPT_LINE); ClrEol;
  end; { Disp_Error_Msg }
```

Disp—IO—Error

The following listing contains the I/O error message display routine. It was also forward declared in STD-UTIL.INC, as noted in the comments. When an I/O error is trapped by the program, the global variable **io—status** is assigned the error number. The Disp—IO—Error procedure uses that number in a case statement to choose an appropriate error message, which is assigned to **IO—Msg**. The error message is combined with the device name, stored in the **device—name** parameter, and then displayed. After the program halts and the message displayed, the user is given the opportunity to either abort the program or ignore the problem. You could add an option that would let the user try again. If you are developing an application in which data integrity is critical, you should review the effect of each error and make modifications as needed to screen the use of the Ignore option.

```
{ Insert in STD-DISP.PAS }

  procedure Disp_IO_Error;   { (device_name: File_ID); }
                             { forward defined in STD-UTIL.PAS }
    var IO_Msg     : Str_80;
        err_str    : string[3];
        valid_keys : Printable_Char;

  { Converts global io_status to a text error message combined with its
    device_name parameter. Displays error message and sets global error_flag. }
```

```
begin
  case io_status of
    $01  :  IO_Msg := 'not found';
    $02  :  IO_Msg := 'not open for input';
    $03  :  IO_Msg := 'not open for output';
    $04  :  IO_Msg := 'not open';
    $05  :  IO_Msg := 'not readable';
    $06  :  IO_Msg := 'not Assigned. Unable to Write';
    $10  :  IO_Msg := 'recieved bad numeric data';
    $20  :  IO_Msg := 'not able to perform operation requested';
    $21  :  IO_Msg := 'not available in Memory mode';
    $22  :  IO_Msg := 'not available for Assign statement';
    $90  :  IO_Msg := 'does not contain matching record type';
    $91  :  IO_Msg := 'does not contain record requested';
    $99  :  IO_Msg := 'end encountered unexpectedly';
    $F0  :  IO_Msg := 'cannot be written to';
    $F1  :  IO_Msg := 'cannot be written due to full Directory';
    $F2  :  IO_Msg := 'has exceeded the maximum file size';
    $FF  :  IO_Msg := 'is no longer on the current disk';
  else        begin
                Str(io_status:3,err_str);
                IO_Msg := 'has experienced I/O error:' + err_str;
              end;
  end; {case}
  Clear_Prompts;
  IO_Msg := 'Device/File ' + device_name + ' ' + IO_Msg;
  Display_Prompt(PROMPT_LINE,'MSG',IO_Msg);
  Display_Prompt(CMD_LINE,'CMD','Ignore | Abort');
  Display_Prompt(MSG_LINE,'INP',
                  'Press CMD: key to enter selection. (I/A) ==> ');
  if (Valid_Key(['A','I']) = 'A') then
    err_flag := TRUE
  else
    io_status := ZERO;
end; { Disp_IO_Error }
```

Load —SCR —File

By using the Load—SCR—File procedure, a text file such as the one in Figure 8-2 may be loaded into a Scrn type data structure. You will recall that the Scrn type is an array of MAX—ROW (24, 80) character strings. This routine opens the file and reads the first MAX—ROW (24) lines into the **text—buf** variable. It does not read the input-field definitions and it does not close **text—file**. Thus, you should be sure that the calling routine closes **text— file** when it is finished.

```
{ Insert in STD-DISP.PAS }

  procedure Load_SCR_File(file_name      : File_ID;
                          var text_buf  : Scrn;
                          var text_file : Text);
      var line_cnt : Byte;

  { Loads up to MAX_ROW lines of text from text_file into text_buf.
    if text file contains more than MAX_ROW lines of text, io_status
    is set to MAX_ROW + 1. Any other value of io_status greater than 0
    should be treated as an I/O error. It is left to the calling routine
    to handle such errors.
    Text_file is left open so that the calling routine may Read additional
    text if necessary. The caller is responsible for closing text_file. }
```

```
        begin
          Assign(text_file,file_name);
     {$I-}
          Reset(text_file); io_status := IOresult;
          line_cnt := 1;
          While (io_status = ZERO) and (not Eof(text_file)) do
            if line_cnt > MAX_ROW then
              io_status := line_cnt
            else
              begin
                ReadLn(text_file,text_buf[line_cnt]);
                io_status := IOresult;
                if (io_status = ZERO) then
                  line_cnt := Succ(line_cnt)
                else
                  Disp_IO_Error(file_name);
              end;
     {$I+}
       end; { Load_SCR_File }
```

Load —Input—Scrn

The Load—Input—Scrn procedure uses Load—SCR—File to load both screen text and input field parameters. This is another subprogram that is best described using pseudo-code. Due to the error-trapping requirements, it looks more complicated than it really is.

```
Load—Input—Screen
    Load text for screen from text file.
    If text file contains additional data then
        Read the next line.
        Convert it to a numeric value indicating the
        number of input fields contained on the screen.
        If the conversion was successful then
            Read a set of input field parameters
            for each field.                        { Read—Field—Parameters }
    Otherwise
            Display an error message and set the error flag.
```

After calling the Load—SCR—File procedure to read the text lines, from a disk, that make up the video screen, this routine checks the file for field parameters. If it doesn't find any field parameters, the program terminates after printing an error message. Otherwise, the next line is read and converted to a numeric value. That value indicates the number of input field definitions that follow. The Read—Field—Parameters procedure, which is described next, is responsible for loading the definitions.

```
{ Insert in STD-DISP.PAS }

procedure Load_Input_Scrn(scrn_id        : File_ID;
                          var scrn_text : Scrn;
                          var fld_dat   : Inp_Parms);
```

```
    type Txt_Num               = string[2];

    var  scrn_file             : Text;
         txt_x, txt_y,
         txt_cnt, txt_len      : Txt_Num;
         i                     : Byte;
         dummy                 : Char;

{ Loads the screen text from file identified by scrn_id into the
  screen buffer pointed to by scrn_text. The input field parameters
  are then loaded into the fld_dat array. }

{ Insert the Read_Field_Parameters procedure here ***** }

    begin { Load_Input_Scrn }
      Load_SCR_File(scrn_id,scrn_text,scrn_file); { Load screen text.    }
      if (io_status = (MAX_ROW + 1)) then
        begin
{$I+}
          ReadLn(scrn_file,txt_cnt);                { Read number of fields. }
          io_status := IOresult;
{$I-}
          if (io_status = ZERO) then
            Val(txt_cnt,fld_cnt,io_status);    { Convert fld_cnt to number.}
          if (io_status = ZERO) then
            Read_Field_Parameters
          else
            begin
              Disp_Error_Msg('Conversion error in screen file.');
              err_flag := TRUE;
            end;
        end

        else
          begin
            Disp_Error_Msg('Invalid input screen file.');
            err_flag := TRUE;
          end;
    end { Load_Input_Scrn };
```

Read — Field — Parameters

The Read—Field—Parameters procedure is used within the Load—Input—
Scrn procedure to initialize an array of **fld—dat** records, each of which describes an input field.

It is critical that the text lines containing the field parameters be formatted as shown in Figure 8-2. The commas separate the items and are skipped
over when the dummy Char variable absorbs them.

Any errors encountered while reading the input field definitions are stored
in a local array called **status**. This reduces overhead by eliminating the I/O
status test that would otherwise be needed following each Read and Val
procedure.

```
{ Insert in STD-DISP.PAS - Load_Input_Scrn }

    procedure Read_Field_Parameters;
      var status : array[1..10] of Integer;  { Used for error trapping. }

{   Reads parameters for fld_cnt fields into fld_dat parameter array.
    The format of the parameter in scrn_file must be:
```

```
            n1,n2,n3,X,Y,Msg

            n1  = 2 digit video screen row of input field.
            n2  = 2 digit video screen col of input field.
            n3  = 2 digit length in characters of input field.
            X   = 1 character field type as defined in global constants.
            Y   = 1 character field exit type as defined in global constants.
            Msg = Up to 60 characters, followed by End Of Line. }

      { ***** Insert the Check_Status procedure here ***** }

            begin { Read_Field_Parameters }
               for i := 1 to fld_cnt do
                  With fld_dat[i] do
                  begin
{$I-}
                     Read(scrn_file,txt_y,dummy); status[1] := IOresult;
                     Read(scrn_file,txt_x,dummy); status[2] := IOresult;
                     Read(scrn_file,txt_len,dummy); status[3] := IOresult;
                     Read(scrn_file,fld_type,dummy); status[4] := IOresult;
                     Read(scrn_file,exit_type,dummy); status[5] := IOresult;
                     ReadLn(scrn_file,fld_msg); status[6] := IOresult;
                     Val(txt_x,xloc,io_status); status[7] := io_status;
                     Val(txt_y,yloc,io_status); status[8] := io_status;
                     Val(txt_len,fld_len,io_status); status[9] := io_status;
                  end;
                  Close(scrn_file); status[10] := IOresult;
{$I+}
                  Check_Status; { Display first error encountered & set error_flag. }
            end; { Read_Field_Parameters }
```

Check — Status

The Check—Status procedure, which is defined within Read—Field—
Parameters, scans the **status** array checking for any errors that may have
occurred. If an error condition is indicated, Disp—IO—Error is called and
the scan is terminated and as a result, only the first error encountered is ever
displayed.

```
      { Insert in STD-DISP.PAS - Load_Input_Scrn - Read_Field_Parameters }
            procedure Check_Status;
               begin
                  i := 1;                         { Set up loop to check status }
                  while (i < 11) do
                     if (status[i] <> ZERO) then
                        begin                     { If error encountered, display }
                           io_status := status[i]; { error message and exit loop. }
                           Disp_IO_Error(scrn_id);
                           i := 11;
                        end
                     else
                        i := Succ(i);
               end; { Check_Status }
```

Disp — Input — Scrn

Displaying an input screen is a simple matter of moving the text from the
inp—scrn array to the video screen. The changes in video intensity are

based on the assumption that the top four video lines will contain a screen header, such as the one illustrated in Figure 8-2, and that the system running the program supports dual-intensity output. The idea is to have the field prompts displayed using LowVideo and the field values displayed using NormVideo, thus making the input values stand out. This is another area that may be modified to suit your taste.

```
{ Insert in STD-DISP.PAS }

  procedure Disp_Input_Scrn(inp_scrn: Scrn);
    var  i   : Byte;

{ Writes text from inp_scrn screen text buffer to video. }

    begin
      NormVideo;
      for i := 1 to 4 do WriteLn(inp_scrn[i]);
      LowVideo;
      for i := 5 to (MAX_ROW -1) do
        WriteLn(inp_scrn[i]);
      Write(inp_scrn[MAX_ROW]); { Required to prevent scrolling on systems }
      NormVideo;                { with MAX_ROW video lines. }
    end { Disp_Input_Scrn };
```

Load—Help—Text

The Load—Help—Text procedure loads lines of text from a disk file into the dynamic storage area known as the heap. The lines are stored as a linked list and the Disp—Help procedure, which will be discussed shortly, is used to display a selected range of these lines of text. This is definitely not the most efficient way to obtain the results. This method of storing and retrieving help screen text was selected so that the use of dynamic storage and pointer variables could be demonstrated.

There are a couple of things that you should know in the Load—Help—Text procedure. First, notice how MemAvail is used to determine the amount of space remaining on the heap. It is a good practice to always leave some free space on the heap. This is because on some systems (CP/M-80 implementations), the heap shares memory with the stack. If you allocate all of the heap space, you may get a run-time **out-of-memory** error should the stack need some extra space later. Finally, the global pointer variable **first—help** is used to point to the first line of text stored on the heap. This is typical of the way that data items stored in dynamic memory are accessed. Once the first item is located, a pointer associated with it can be used to find the next item and so forth.

```
{ Insert in STD-DISP.INC }

  procedure Load_Help_Text(file_name: File_ID);
    const MIN_HEAP = $800;  { Leave at least 2K free on the heap. }
```

```
              var help_file : Text;
                  new_line,
                  last_line : Help_Pointer;

              begin
                Mark(top_of_heap);
                first_help := nil;
                Assign(help_file,file_name);
{$I-}
                Reset(help_file); io_status := IOresult;
                  while ((not Eof(help_file)) and (MemAvail > MIN_HEAP)) and
                         (io_status = ZERO) do
                    begin
                      New(new_line);
                      ReadLn(help_file,new_line^.help_txt);
                      io_status := IOresult;
                      if (first_help = nil) then
                        first_help := new_line
                      else
                        last_line^.next_line := new_line;
                      last_line := new_line;
                      last_line^.next_line := nil;
                    end;
{$I+}
                if (io_status <> ZERO) then
                  Disp_IO_Error(file_name);
                if (MemAvail <= MIN_HEAP) then
                  Disp_Error_Msg('Insufficient memory for complete help file');
              end; { Load_Help_Text }
```

Disp—Help

The Disp—Help procedure is used to display selected lines of text stored by
Load—Help—Text. This text will normally be instructional information for
the user. The parameters identify the first and last lines of text to be displayed. The routine uses the global pointer variable **first—help** to find the
first line. If **first** is greater than 1, the linking pointers are used to find the
first line to be displayed. Then the lines of text are displayed until the line
indicated by **last** has been output. The cosmetic effects (the dashed lines) may
be altered to suit your style.

```
{ Insert in STD-DISP.PAS }

procedure Disp_Help(first, last: Integer);
    var line_ptr  : Help_Pointer;
        line_cnt  : Integer;

{ Displays 'help screen' information from dynamic memory. The information
displayed is determined by first and last, which refer to line numbers
in help_file. Information is displayed starting at row 1 with a dashed
line followed by (last - first + 1) lines of help text and ends on row
(last - first + 3) which is another dashed line.

Note: The calling routine must preserve and restore screen contents.
      Last - first should be less than 20. }
```

```
begin
  GoToXY(1,1); Repeat_Char('-',(MAX_COL - 1)); WriteLn;
  line_ptr := first_help;
  line_cnt := 1;
  while (line_cnt < first) and (line_ptr <> nil) do
    begin
      line_ptr := line_ptr^.next_line;
      line_cnt := Succ(line_cnt);
    end;
  while (line_cnt <= last) and (line_ptr <> nil) do
    begin
      ClrEol;
      WriteLn(line_ptr^.help_txt);
      line_ptr := line_ptr^.next_line;
      line_cnt := Succ(line_cnt);
    end;
  Repeat_Char('-',(MAX_COL - 1));
  Clear_Prompts;
  Display_Prompt(MSG_LINE,'MSG','Press ANY KEY to continue... ');
  Read(Kbd,inchr);
end; { Disp_Help }
```

Verify—Exit

The Verify—Exit procedure allows the users to indicate whether or not they are ready to exit the program. This is needed in case the EXIT key was pressed accidentally.

```
{ Insert in STD-DISP.PAS }

  procedure Verify_Exit;
    begin
      Display_Prompt(MSG_LINE,'INP','Do you want to END this session? (Y/N) ==> ')
      if (Valid_Key(['Y','N']) = 'Y') then
        end_session := TRUE;
    end; { Verify_Exit }
```

NINE

Amortization: Defining the Problem

Throughout the next four chapters, you will be developing a complete Loan Amortization program. Development will begin with defining the problem and then proceed through designing, coding, and finally documenting your work. Even if you do not need such a program as this, you will have created several additional tools for your Turbo tool kit and developed a better understanding of how to use Turbo Pascal.

Program Objectives

The object of building the Loan Amortization program is not solely the program. By constructing a large and complex program you will be better able to see how a typical business problem is transformed into a workable Pascal program. Although the primary and most obvious objective in designing any program is to get the program running properly, you should also be certain that the program has a solid design and incorporates some program features. Most of the features have already been explained in the first part of the book. A quick review before discussing amortization may be helpful.

One of the objectives in developing this application is to illustrate top-down designing and coding, also known as *stepwise refinement*. As discussed earlier, this refers to the process of dividing and subdividing a problem until you reach a point where a solution can be defined with existing tools and building blocks. Using this method to develop a Pascal program, you begin by analyzing the application, determining how it can be divided into modules whose functions are strictly defined. For example, in a word processing program, part of the problem is transferring text from disk to memory and back again. One module can be defined to read the text from disk and another module to write text to the disk. Whether a module should consist of functions or procedures is not important when subdividing a problem, since working out the details will come later. What is important is that you know when a problem is finally subdivided into its most efficient formula—one that can be learned only with experience—and that each module's duty is clearly defined.

A second major consideration is that the interaction between user and machine is handled in a forthright and lucid manner. For example, most interactive programs could use Read and ReadLn for user input. The problem with this approach is that the computer cannot respond to the user's input until the RETURN key is pressed. Being able to monitor every keystroke allows the program to react to function and control keys and to detect obvious errors before the user continues. An example would be screening out non-numeric characters before they are entered into a ZIP code field. The Loan Amortization program will use the controlled input routines developed in the previous chapter for all user input.

On-line help and prompt messages should also be considered part of the user interface. The objective of on-line help is to provide users with information about the operation of the program without forcing them to refer to a manual. On-line help can be implemented in different ways. One method is to provide a *help menu* when a designated HELP key is pressed. The user can then choose the area in which assistance is needed.

Another popular method of making help available is known as context-sensitive help. When that method is employed, pressing the HELP key, even in the midst of the program, will display information pertaining to the current process. For example, if a word processing program prompts the user to enter the name of a file to print and at that point the user presses the HELP key, the program might provide a list of the files available for printing or it might print instructions on how to print a file. A few years ago offering any kind of help in the program was considered nice but not necessary. Now you expect an unfavorable review of your software if you decide to leave such features out of an application.

Error Trapping

Error trapping is another area that complicates life for a software developer. As has been discussed, the run-time error traps provided by the Turbo compiler are meant for programmers, not users. What your program must do is catch these errors before they occur and resolve them as gracefully as possible. The problem lies in anticipating all possible error conditions. However, most run-time errors can be eliminated by screening user input.

The Loan Amortization Program

The first step in system design is to define the problem. Before that step is undertaken, it is important that the person designing the program (the systems analyst) have a good understanding of the subject matter. Before defining the loan amortization problem, let's take a closer look at the subject of amortization.

What is Amortization?

Amortization is a process of paying off a debt. It is the method usually associated with home mortgages and may be used to pay off any relatively large debt. When you borrow money to buy a car, for example, you must repay the amount borrowed plus the interest in equal monthly installments. When the debt and the interest charges are paid in full, the loan is said to be *amortized*. The purpose of an amortization table is to show how much of your monthly payment is applied to the debt and how much is used to pay interest. The amount that you borrowed is called the *principal* amount of the loan and the *interest*, which is usually stated as an annual percentage rate, is the money you pay for the use of the loan. The amount of the periodic payments is calculated from a multitude of factors: the principal of the loan, the percentage rate, the payment period, and the life of the loan. The formula for calculating the periodic rate will be presented in Chapter 11.

As an example, the simplest loan to amortize is one that is paid in full at the end of one year. Since the payment period is annual, the periodic rate is the same as the annual rate. The interest due is then simply the principal amount times the annual rate. For example, if you borrow $1000.00 for one year at 10 percent, the payment would be $1100.00. An amortization table would indicate that $1000.00 of the payment applies to the principal and $100.00 applies to the interest. As you will see, most amortization tables are not this simple.

Defining Program Objectives

Now that you are familiar with amortization, it is time to define the problem. This is often best done by creating a list of objectives. In addition to providing an initial overview of the project, this list will indicate when to quit. You can get carried away in a project by continually adding feature after feature until they become trivial and do no more than slow the program. Here is the objective list for the project:

Table 9-1. Information Fields for the Loan Data Files

Field Description	Size	Type of Path
Collateral	40	Alphanumeric string
Principal	6	Real numeric
Interest rate	6	Real numeric
Payment amount	6	Real numeric
Payments per year	2	Integer numeric
First month due	2	Integer numeric
First year due	2	Integer numeric
Number of payment	6	Real numeric
Selected year	2	Integer numeric
Output device	1	Uppercase character
Not used	9	Alphanumeric string
Commercial	1	Boolean
Business name	40	Alphanumeric string
or		
Last name	15	Alphanumeric string
First name	15	Alphanumeric string
Title	10	Alphanumeric string

1. Allow the user to enter information pertinent to a loan. Table 9-1 defines the required loan data. This information is to be stored in a disk file with a separate file for each loan. The number of loan information files that may be stored is limited only by disk storage space.

2. Allow the user to access and update this information as needed. Whenever data is modified, it should be redisplayed. This allows the user to compare loans with different terms.

3. Allow the user to print an amortization table based on the data in a loan information file. Provision should be made for printing all or part of the table.

In reviewing Table 9-1, notice that the data file allows space for future enhancements. Even if you are not planning for future additions, it is a good idea to allow room for additional record components; however, keep in mind that by leaving space you may prevent a total revision of the program should you need to expand its capacity.

Program Design

There are a number of methods to document the design of an application. Pseudo-code is a flexible alternative because it does not have strict syntax or format requirements. If you are working in an environment that demands stricter standards, you may want to consider HIPO charts or Warnier-Orr diagrams. If you are not familiar with these options, you may want to investigate some textbooks that explain structured programming methods.

Figure 9-1 uses pseudo-code to illustrate the design of the Loan Amortization program. Keep in mind that this documentation is for the top level of the application, which contains the subprograms defined in the main program. The lower levels of the program, the subprograms defined in the top level, will be discussed later.

Top-Level Subprograms

The pseudo-code in Figure 9-1 defines nine level 1 subprograms. Throughout the pseudo-code presented in this chapter, double asterisks are used to identify those statements that represent subprograms defined at the next lower level.

The next step is to take each level 1 subprogram and begin the process of subdivision. That process will inevitably lead to a series of low-level subprograms that may be constructed using the predefined tools provided with Turbo Pascal.

```
Loan Amortization Program { Loan_Amortization }
Initialize global variables and load data as needed.**
While there are no errors and exit is not requested
    Prompt user to enter the name of a loan file.**
    If the user presses the QUIT key then
        Verify that the session is to be ended.**
        If so then set the exit requested flag.
While there are no errors and exit is not requested
    Display the current status of the loan file.**
    Allow the user to select from the following actions:
    Accept, Modify, Print, Help or Quit.**
    Do one of the following based on the user's selection:
        ACCEPT: Write the current values to the disk file.**
        MODIFY: Allow the user to update the loan data.**
        PRINT: Write the current values to the disk file.
               Print an amortization table based on the values.**
        HELP: Display help information based on the user's selection.**
        QUIT: Do housekeeping.**
Clear the screen and display an exit message.
```

Figure 9-1. Pseudo-code for the Loan Amortization program

When producing the pseudo-code for this program you should perform data input and verification using the routines developed in Chapter 8. The controlled field input procedures will be based on the input screen format shown in Figure 9-2. The purpose of an input screen is to make data entry appear to be a process of filling in the blanks on a form. Because this is a familiar process, it is not likely to intimidate the user. Each piece of information is entered at a particular place on the video screen; those places are usually identified by prompts that indicate to the user what input is expected. For example, the last name of an individual borrower will be entered following the **Individual...:** prompt just above the **Last Name** prompt. The input areas are called *input fields* and are defined by input field parameters stored in the LOAN.SCR file. This will be explained in detail in Chapter 10.

Initializing the System

```
Initialize System (Initialize)
    Clear screen and display welcome message.
    Initialize global variables.
    Load input screen data from LOAN.SCR file.
    Load help screen data from LN-HELP.SCR file.
```

Some top-level subprograms, such as the one just illustrated, can be resolved without requiring further subdivision. System initialization is a

```
Loan ID..:
                    Amortization Schedule      Copyright 1985
Tot. Pmts:          Loan Information           Osborne/McGraw-Hill
Interest.:

    Commercial...:
                    Business Name
    Individual...:
                    Last Name      First Name      Title
    Collateral...:
    Principal....:             Interest Rate......:    %
    Payment Amt..:             Payments Per Year..:
    1st Pmt Due..:  /          Number of Payments.:
    Selected Year:             Output to Vid/Print:
```

Figure 9-2. Data entry input screen for the Loan Amortization program

straightforward subprogram. Each of these pseudo-statements can be coded using the tools and building blocks that you have on hand, including those defined in Chapter 8.

You may wonder why these steps are not simply included in the main program rather than being defined in a subprogram. There is certainly no reason that they couldn't be, and the same can be said for the other eight top-level subprograms. The problem is that the program statement block would then become very cluttered, and following its logic would be difficult. As was mentioned earlier, unless speed is a critical factor, you should push as much detail as possible into the lower levels of the program. The payoff will come during debugging and when you are asked to modify the code a few months, or years, later.

Selecting a Loan File

Select Loan File (Select__File)
    Prompt user for a valid file name**
   Unless the user presses ESC
      If such a file exists then
         Open the file**
      Otherwise
         Create a new file.**

In order to keep the size of this book reasonable, the pseudo-code for these lower level subprograms will not be shown. Instead, the actual source code will be presented in chapter 11.

Displaying Current Loan Data

Display Current Loan Data (Display__Current__Data)
    Display data input screen.
   For each data field on the screen
      Display its value based on the current data file.^^

The complexity at this level is hidden in the statement marked with the double circumflex characters, which represent a series of global subprograms. Making these subprograms global is necessary because, as you will see, they will be used by other subprograms at a lower level. Thus, due to Pascal's rules of scope, you must either define them within each subprogram or make them global to make them accessible to all subsequent subprograms.

Prompting the User to Select an Action

Prompt User to Select Action (Select＿Action)
    Set valid selection flag to FALSE.
    Repeat
        Prompt user to Accept, Modify, Print, Help or Exit.**
        Accept user response.
        If user response is valid then
            Set valid selection flag to TRUE.
    Until valid selection flag is TRUE.
    Return user response to calling routine.
end

This is a decision-making module, since at this point, the user must decide what to do with the information selected and displayed in the previous steps. Remember that the program is considered unfriendly if it accepts user input without offering an exit alternative. It is a good idea to have one key designated as an exit key, and in this application the ESC key is assigned to that task. As a general rule, any time input is accepted from the keyboard, the ESC key should be treated as a valid entry, and the result will be to exit to the next higher level of the program. Pressing ESC at the top level takes the user out of the program following a verification prompt. As you will see, this adds to the complexity of the program and verifies the theorem that states: the simpler a program is to use, the more complex it is to write.

Writing Current Values to Disk File

Update the Loan Data File. (Accept＿Data)
    Position record pointer at the beginning of the file.
    If that operation is successful then
        Write the current loan data values to the file.
    If the update is successful then
        set the modified flag to FALSE.
    Otherwise
        display an I/O error.

Looking back at Figure 9-1, you will see that one of five routines is activated based on the selection made by the user. The first of these selections is to accept and record the information as displayed on the video screen.

Updating the Data File

Modify loan data (Modify__Data)
Parameters: first field = First input field to be updated.
     last field = Last input field to be updated.
 Initialize field pointer to first field.
 Repeat
   Accept input for the field indicated by field pointer.**
   Adjust field pointer.
 Until the user requests exit or the last field is updated.
 If exit due to user request then
   Recalculate calculation fields.**
 Set the modified flag to TRUE.

This is the only top-level subprogram that requires parameters to be passed. At the top level, most data sharing can be safely accomplished by using global variables. As you move into the low-level subprograms, parameter passing will play a larger role.

The two low-level modules with double asterisks represent the heart of the input and the calculation part of the program. There is a lot of activity involved in a routine that must accept and edit user input for 16 fields. In addition, there are calculation and display-only fields to be updated. By hiding this detail in low-level routines you can concentrate on the overall design at the top level.

Printing an Amortization Table

Print an Amortization Table. (Print__Amortization__Table)
 If user is ready to print then**
   Initialize local variables.**
   Direct output to the correct output device.**
   Print the Table.**

Printing an amortization program includes four level 2 subprograms that format the amortization table based on the current values in the loan data file. Notice that condition statements can be coded as low-level functions. For example, the "If user ready to print" condition is based on whether or not the printer is selected as the output device. If so, a user prompt is printed; otherwise, it would not be needed. By delegating these details to a low-level function, the code at this level remains clean and easy to follow.

Displaying Help Information

Display User Help Information. (Display—Help)
Allow user to select from the following subjects:
Accept, Modify, or Print**
Do one of the following based on the user's selection:
ACCEPT: Display lines 19-27 of the LN-HELP.SCR text.
MODIFY: Display lines 1-18 of the LN-HELP.SCR text.
PRINT: Display lines 28-36 of the LN-HELP.SCR text.

The user can choose help for three subjects: how to accept the loan data,
how to modify the loan data, and how to print an amortization table.

Depending on what the user selects, a portion of the text that is stored in
the LN-HELP.SCR file will be presented.

The program offers help through menu selection, as opposed to context-
sensitive help, which was described earlier. If you want to implement
context-sensitive help, the program will have to save whatever is displayed on
the video screen and then restore it after the help has been presented. If your
computer uses memory-mapped video, this can be done with relative ease.
Using Turbo Pascal's Move procedure you can move the video image to a
temporary storage area until the help session is finished and then move it
back. Since the Loan Amortization program must run on a variety of
systems—some of which may not offer memory-mapped video—the menu-
driven help method has been used.

Housekeeping

Do Exit Housekeeping (Exit—Housekeeping)
If data has been modified and not accepted then
Display an exit warning and get user verification.**
If exit is requested then
Determine the size of the loan data file.
Close the loan data file.
If the file was empty then
Erase it.
If an I/O error occurred then
Display an error message.

Routines that take care of clean-up chores before exiting the program are
often called *housekeeping routines*. When the user elects to exit at the **Accept
Modify Print** prompt, you need to be sure that any changes have been saved.
If changes have been made but not saved to disk, the user is asked to verify
that the changes are to be abandoned. Notice that empty files are automatically erased. Such files are created when a file is opened using the Rewrite
procedure and then closed without writing to it.

Subdividing the Lower Level Subprograms

Once the top-level subprograms have been defined in pseudo-code, the next step would be to subdivide each of the level 2 subprograms that were identified in the process, which means 11 more subprograms must be described in pseudo-code. After that is done, you will find 17 steps that must be defined as level 3 subprograms. Finally, you would find that seven level 4 subprograms are required. As was mentioned, space considerations make it impractical to illustrate all of these subdivisions.

You may find that there is little to be gained in using pseudo-code below a certain level. When to stop depends on the complexity of the project and the amount of detail required for the design documentation. After you reach a point at which you feel that you, or the programmer that will be doing the coding, have enough detail to get the job done, that is a good point to stop the subdividing process.

Creating a Top-Level Test Program

One advantage of block structured programs is that you can test them as you build them. Based on the top-level design pseudo-code, you can create a test program that replaces the required subprogram definitions with a *stub* subprogram. A stub is basically a placeholder for the actual code that will later replace it. The following listing is an example of a "stubbed" version of the Loan Amortization program. As you can see, in some cases the stub must include a small amount of code to simulate the effect that will be produced by the actual subprogram. The Write statements are not necessary, but they can be useful in analyzing the flow of the program. Notice that the include files defined in Chapter 8 are made a part of the test program. In addition the program statement block uses some constants and variables that are not among those defined in the STD-CTV.INC file. Immediately following the include directives should be the global constants, types, and variables that are specific to the application. This will make them easy to find when additional definitions and declarations are made.

```
program Loan_Amortization;

{$I STD-CTV.INC    Global constants, types and variables }
{$I STD-UTIL.INC   Miscelaneous global subprograms }
{$I STD-INP.INC    Keyboard input subprograms }
{$I STD-DISP.INC   Video display subprograms }

{ Global constants, types and variables specific to the
  the Loan_Amortization program. }

   const  ACCEPT    = 'A';    { Action codes. }
          MODIFY    = 'M';
          PRINT     = 'P';
```

```
              END_INP   = 16;      { Last input field on the input screen.}

    var    action      : Char;
           exit        : Boolean;

{ Subprogram stubs for the Loan_Amortization program. }

    procedure Initialize;
      begin
        ClrScr; WriteLn('Initializing...');
        err_flag := FALSE;
        exit := FALSE;
      end; { Initialize }

    procedure Select_Loan_File;
      begin
        WriteLn('Select Loan File. Press <Esc> to quit.');
        Read(Kbd,inchr);
        if (inchr = QUIT) then
          esc_flag := TRUE
        else
          esc_flag := FALSE;
      end; { Select_Loan_File }

    procedure Display_Current_Values;
      begin
        WriteLn('Display Current Values');
      end; { Display_Current_Values }

    procedure Select_Action;
      begin
        WriteLn('Select Action. Press <Esc> to quit.');
        Read(Kbd,inchr);
        if (inchr = QUIT) then
          esc_flag := TRUE
        else
          esc_flag := FALSE;
        action := UpCase(inchr);
      end; { Select_Action }

    procedure Accept_Data;
      begin
      WriteLn('Accept Data');
    end; { Accept_Data }

    procedure Modify_Data(first_fld, last_fld: Byte);
      begin
        WriteLn('Modify Data');
      end; { Modify_Data }

    procedure Print_Amortization_Table;
      begin
        WriteLn('Print Table');
      end; { Print_Amortization_Table }

    procedure Display_Help;
      begin
        WriteLn('Display Help');
      end; { Display_Help }

    procedure Exit_Housekeeping;
      begin
        WriteLn('Exit Housekeeping')
      end; { Exit_Housekeeping }

begin { Loan_Amortization }
  Initialize;                              { Do initial housekeeping.}
  while (not (err_flag or exit)) do
    begin
      Select_Loan_File;
      if esc_flag then
        Verify_Exit;
```

```
        while (not (esc_flag or err_flag)) do
          begin
            Display_Current_Values;
            Select_Action;
            case action of
              ACCEPT  : Accept_Data;
              MODIFY  : Modify_Data(1,END_INP);
              PRINT   : begin
                          Accept_Data;
                          Print_Amortization_Table;
                        end;
              QUIT    : Exit_Housekeeping;
              HELP    : Display_Help;
            end; {case}
          end; {while}
      end; {while}
  ClrScr; Write('Session Ended');
end. { Loan_Amortization }
```

TEN

Organizing the Data

Once you have defined the problem you are setting out to solve, the next step is to identify and define the global types and variables for the Loan Amortization program. After completing this step, you will have a clear understanding of the data used in the program.

Most of the global definitions have already been made in the STD-CTV.INC include file that was developed in Chapter 8. In addition to examining how these general-purpose types are used, this chapter will define some additional types that are specific to the Loan Amortization program.

After variables have been declared—be it in STD-CTV.INC or in your own declaration—they must be initialized. Remember that Pascal variables, unlike BASIC variables, are not set to any particular value when they are created. A practical method of initializing variables is to define an initialization procedure that is executed at the start of the program. In some instances, text files stored on disk can provide the data for variable initialization. The Turbo editor can be used to create the text files. The advantage of reading from a file, as opposed to initializing the variables directly in the program, is that you can modify the data without having to update the source code and recompile it.

Identifying the Data

The first operation in the pseudo-code outline (Figure 9-1) is to initialize the global variables. However, before this can be done, you must identify the data items to be initialized.

Input Screen Variables

When the initialization step was subdivided in Chapter 9, one of the lower-level steps was to load the input screen from the LOAN.SCR file. This step assumes that the program will be using the data input routines from the STD-INP.INC and STD-DISP.INC include files. You will recall that these routines store the input screen and the input field parameters in a text file. This is but one of many ways to create data input screens. Another way is to code the screen directly in the program, using WriteLn statements for each line in the screen. The drawback to this method is that the program must be modified and recompiled whenever a change is made to the input screen.

Before you can load the input screen from the LOAN.SCR file, you will have to provide a place in memory to store the lines of text and the input field definitions (also called *field parameters*). Figure 10-1 shows the input screen text and the input field definitions as they appear in the LOAN.SCR file. (You will see more about creating this file later.)

What kind of data structure would be best suited to hold this information? Since the first half is lines of text, the string comes to mind as a suitable data type. Knowing that the video screen is made up of 24 lines of text suggests that an array of strings would be an ideal structure for storing an entire screen. One of the global types defined in the STD-CTV.INC file is:

$$Scrn = \textbf{array}[1..MAX\_ROW] \textbf{ of } Str\_80$$

MAX_ROW is a global constant set to 24, indicating the number of video lines; Str_80 is a String type defined in STD_CTV.INC. The structure of the Scrn type may be described as an array of 24 character strings, with each string being 80 characters long. Issuing a variable declaration such as

$$\textbf{var } inp\_scrn : Scrn;$$

will allocate enough memory to store the screen display.

The Load_SCR_File procedure, which loads 24 lines of text from the text file identified by the file name from the STD-DISP.INC include file, will be used to load the LOAN.SCR file.

Now that the input screen has been set, what about the field definitions? The field parameters, which are stored below the screen lines, are also stored as lines of text. The record type Fld_Parms was designed according to the format of the field parameters. By using a record structure you can store the information extracted from the text lines as a series of data items, each of an appropriate type.

Since each Fld_Parms type record will hold the parameters for one screen field, you will need an array of Fld—Parms to store all of the field parameters. The type definition

type Inp—Parms = **array**[1..MAX—FLD] of Fld—Parms;

where MAX—FLD, representing the maximum number of fields, is a con-

```
Loan ID..:
                        Amortization Schedule       Copyright 1985
Tot. Pmts:              Loan Information             Osborne/McGraw-Hill
Interest.:

    Commercial...:
                        Business Name
    Individual...:
                        Last Name       First Name      Title
    Collateral...:
    Principal....:                      Interest Rate......:    %
    Payment Amt..:                      Payments Per Year..:
    1st Pmt Due..:  /                   Number of Payments.:
    Selected Year:                      Output to Vid/Print:




19
06,23,01,U,A,Press 'X' if commercial loan otherwise leave blank.
06,26,40,T,M,Enter Business name. Up to 40 characters.
09,23,01,U,P,—{ Computer entry based on field 1 }
09,26,15,T,M,Enter Borrower's Last Name. Up to 15 characters.
09,44,15,T,M,Enter Borrower's First Name. Up to 15 characters.
09,62,10,T,M,Enter Borrower's Title. Up to 10 characters.
12,23,40,T,M,Enter description of the collateral. Up to 40 characters.
14,23,10,N,M,Enter actual amount borrowed at interest.
14,62,06,N,M,Enter the interest rate. Up to 5 digits including decimal.
16,23,10,N,M,Enter payment amount or 0.00 to calculate payment amount.
16,62,02,N,A,Enter the number of payments scheduled annually.
18,23,02,N,M,Enter 2-digit MONTH in which first payment is due.
18,26,04,N,M,Enter 4-digit YEAR in which first payment is due.
18,62,07,N,M,Enter total number of payments scheduled.
20,23,04,N,M,Enter desired year or ZERO for a complete table.
20,62,01,U,M,Enter 'V' for video output or 'P' for printed output.
01,12,11,U,P,—{ Loan ID position }
03,12,11,N,P,—{ Calculated total payments position }
04,12,11,N,P,—{ Calculated total interest position }
```

Figure 10-1. Input screen combined with input field parameters for Loan Amortization program

stant set to 32 followed at some point by the variable declaration

var fld__dat : Inp__Parms;

will provide storage for the field definitions needed for the entire input screen. The Read__Field__Parameters procedure from the STD-DISP.INC include file will read in the field parameters.

Modify: Press <M> if you want to change any of the information shown. The cursor will move to the first field. To change a field, just type in the new information and press the Return or Enter key.

            To skip a field, leaving it unchanged, press the Return or Enter key without entering a new value. Note that the current value of the field, along with a prompt message, is shown at the bottom of the screen. Check the prompt for instructions on each entry.

            To move to the previous field, for example: to 'back up' and make a correction, press the Previous Field key indicated on the CMD: line.

            To clear a field or a value of 0, press the clear field key indicated on the CMD: line.

            After you have made the modifications you may exit by pressing the exit key as indicated on the CMD: line. This will cause the data input screen to be redisplayed with recalculated values.

Accept: Press <A> when you want to accept the values displayed on the video screen and save them in the LOAN FILE that you are currently working with. This allows you to update the loan information without printing an amortization table.

            If you use the Modify option and then attempt to exit without accepting or printing, you will receive a warning message and you will have to verify that you wish to abandon any changes that may have been made.

Print: Press <P> to accept the values shown and print an amortization table based on those values. The output is sent to the video screen or the printer based on the value of the print or video field. You may elect to print the entire table by entering 0 in the selected year field. Otherwise use that field to designate the year you wish to print.

            Note that whenever print is selected, the LOAN FILE is updated with the information displayed on the screen. Therefore it is not necessary to accept the data prior to selecting print.

Figure 10-2. Text for the LN-HELP.SCR file

Help Screen Variables

The pseudo-code for the Initialize—System procedure indicates that after loading the input screen data, you should load the help screen data from the LN-HELP.SCR file. Figure 10-2 provides a look at the file you should enter now. As you can see, it is a text file containing instructions regarding the three major functions of the program. To allow flexibility in the amount of help text available for an application, the lines of text will be loaded into dynamic storage and accessed using pointer variables.

Fortunately these global types and variables are already defined in the STD-CTV.INC include file, and the Load—Help—Text and Disp—Help procedures, which load and display the help text, are defined in the DISP.INC file. You will recall that Load—Help—Text stores the lines of help text as a linked list structure in dynamic memory. The Disp—Help function scans for the first line and then displays the list.

In Chapter 3 pointers were used to create a stack structure and a sorted linked list. If the subject of pointers and the data structures they create is still not quite clear, you might want to review those examples and compare them to the code for Load—Help—Text and Disp—Help.

Loan File Variables

The next global variable to define stores the file name when the user enters it at the keyboard. It must be global so that it will be accessible to other modules that need to pass it as a parameter to an error-handling routine. The need for this variable is not evident from the pseudo-code until you develop the lower-level routines of the program. You will find that as you work your way into a program using the top-down approach, you will occasionally need to add to the global variable declarations. In the loan program the following global variable is declared:

var file—name : File—ID;

File—ID is defined in the STD-CTV.INC include file.

As you continue to scan through the pseudo-code, the need for another data structure becomes evident after **file—name** is declared. In order to open or create a disk file, you must declare a file type variable. But now you know that the information will be saved on disk, it is a good time to define the properties of amortization in a record structure and then declare the file variable. In the following listing the properties are translated into type definitions and variable declarations:

```
Loan_Record = record
                    collateral        : Str_40;
                    principle         : Real;
                    rate              : Real;
                    payment           : Real;
                    pmts_per_yr       : Integer;
                    first_mo          : Integer;
                    first_yr          : Integer;
                    no_of_pmts        : Real;
                    select_yr         : Integer;
                    out_dev           : Char;
                    unused            : string[9];
                case commercial : Boolean of
                    TRUE              : ( business_name : Str_40);
                    FALSE             : ( borrower      : Full_Name);
                end;

var    loan           : Loan_Record;
       loan_file      : file of Loan_Record;
```

Notice that the Loan—Record type definition illustrates the use of a variant record. The fixed part of the record is represented by all of the fields up through the **unused** field. The next field, **commercial**, of Boolean type, is the tag field. The variant **case** statement uses this tag field as the case selector. When **commercial** is TRUE, the variant part will contain **business— name**, which is a 40-character string. If it is FALSE, the variant part will contain a Full—Name type variable. (Full—Name was defined in the STD-CTV.INC file.)

Other Variables

As you scan the rest of the pseudo-code you will find that only a few more global variables are necessary. When the user selects an action (ACCEPT, MODIFY, PRINT, and so on), it needs to be stored in a variable. A character variable, as declared here, is all that's needed:

var action : Char;

The last two variables are Boolean types. One is used as an exit flag and the other is used to keep track of whether the current loan data has been modified without having been saved to the disk file. These can be declared as follows:

var exit—flag,
modified : Boolean;

The following listing summarizes the global types and variables that are needed in addition to those provided by the STD-CTV.INC include file. Some global constants have also been defined. This listing should be entered with the Turbo editor with a file name of LN-CTV.INC. (Notice that the previous listing has been added.)

```
{ Global constants, types & variables specific to
  the Loan_Amortization program. }

const   ACCEPT    = 'A';      { Action codes. }
        MODIFY    = 'M';
        PRINT     = 'P';

        VIDEO     = 'V';      { Output device codes. }
        PRINTER   = 'P';

        MIN_LOAN  = 100.0;        { Program limits. }
        MAX_LOAN  = 9999999.99;   { These values may be reset to }
        MIN_RATE  = 0.0;          { impose stricter range checking. }
        MAX_RATE  = 99.999;
        MIN_PMT   = 5.00;
        MAX_PMT   = 9999999.99;
        MAX_TERM  = 360;          { Stated as number of payments. }
        END_INP   = 16;          { Last user input field on LOAN.SCR }

        Loan_Record = record
                        collateral    : Str_40;
                        principle     : Real;
                        rate          : Real;
                        payment       : Real;
                        pmts_per_yr   : Integer;
                        first_mo      : Integer;
                        first_yr      : Integer;
                        no_of_pmts    : Real;
                        select_yr     : Integer;
                        out_dev       : Char;
                        unused        : string[9];
                      case commercial : Boolean of
                          TRUE        : ( business_name : Str_40);
                          FALSE       : ( borrower      : Full_Name);
                      end;

var     loan          : Loan_Record;
        loan_file     : file of Loan_Record;
        file_name     : File_ID;
        inp_scrn      : Scrn;
        fld_dat       : Inp_Parms;
        action        : Char;
        exit_flag,
        modified      : Boolean;
```

Next you can update the LOAN.PAS file created in the last chapter by replacing the constant and variable parts of the program with the include directive:

{$I LN-CTV.PAS}

You will find that when you are developing a program, the definitions and declarations part may not be complete until you have finished writing the source code, since as you write the code, you may have to create more variables and definitions. Consequently, it is usually easier to leave the definitions and declarations in the main program file until the program is complete. In the case of the Loan Amortization program, there will be no need to add to the declaration. Therefore, you can clean up the main file by moving these details into an include file.

Input and Information Screens

Input screens form the primary interface between your program and the user. You can use Turbo Pascal's editor to enter and modify the input screen in Figure 10-1 and the help screen in Figure 10-2. In fact, that is what you should do now for the input screen. Load the Turbo editor as usual and specify a file name of LOAN.SCR. The screen lines and the field parameters in Figure 10-1 should both be entered into this file. The screen text should begin on line 1 and end on line 20. The format of the field parameter data lines is very important. First of all, the field count number, indicating the number of field parameters for a screen (in this case 19), must always be on line 25. This is easily confirmed when entering the number by checking the line number displayed at the top of the screen. The column numbers at the top of the screen will also be helpful in aligning the input fields and determining their position for the field parameters.

The Line and Col numbers at the top of the editor screen should correspond to the first two numbers in the field definition line for that field. For example, after entering the screen text, position the cursor as if you were going to enter a value for the Collateral field as noted by the X:

Collateral...: X

The editor Line indicator should be 12 and the Col indicator should be 23.

The sequence in which the field parameters are defined determines the display sequence used when the field values are output to the video monitor. As you will see in the next chapter, the field input routine has total control over the input sequence. However, that routine will be easier to write and maintain if the field definition sequence follows the input sequence. Finally, you can determine which field definition goes with which field based on the field message prompts. That is why messages are included for the display-only fields.

The input screen is often the source of requests for program changes. The input screens used in this program have been developed to make many of these changes very simple. For example, assume that the users decide that they would prefer to see the copyright notice on the left side of the heading and the calculated fields on the right and the total interest above the total payments. Figure 10-3 illustrates the four screen lines and three field parameter lines that would have to be changed. After using your Turbo editor to make these changes, the program will produce the desired results. It is not necessary to change the source code or recompile the program.

Entering text for the help screens is even easier. After entering and saving

```
Copyright 1985             Amortization Schedule        Loan ID..:
Osborne/McGraw-Hill          Loan Information
                                                        Interest.:
                                                        Tot. Pmts:


01,65,11,U,P,-{ File ID position }
04,65,11,N,P,-{ Calculated total interest position }
03,65,11,N,P,-{ Calculated total payments position }
```

Figure 10-3.   Modified input screen and field parameters

the screen and field data, create a file named LN-HELP.SCR. Then, type in the text as shown in Figure 10-2. The only other thing you must do is note the line number that marks the beginning of each help subject. Those numbers will be used to determine the parameters passed to the Disp—Help procedure indicating the first and last lines to be displayed. If you wanted to get fancy, you could devise a scheme for letting the program figure the first and last line of text for each subject. That will be left as a do-it-yourself project to be added later if you so desire.

The method used to load and display the help screen text is somewhat contrived. It was done this way so that the program would include an example using pointers and dynamic storage. While it works fine for this application, you could have space problems with a large program that needed a lot of help text. Developing an alternate method that would avoid such problems would make another good project for future consideration.

The design work and data organization are now taken care of. In the next chapter you will actually build the application. In a step-by-step, procedure-by-procedure process, you will construct a complete, commercial-quality Loan Amortization program.

ELEVEN

Building the
Loan Amortization Program

The Loan Amortization program is made up of 46 subprograms in addition to the include files created in Chapter 8. In terms of compiled code, the routines in this chapter represent about 60 percent of the Loan Amortization program. This statistic illustrates one advantage of Pascal's block structured approach to programming: every time you develop a program that uses the include files, you will have a large part of the program finished with just four include directives.

In most cases, the code for the procedures and functions described in this chapter will be presented one subprogram at a time. After you enter the subprograms, the related ones will be combined into include files, as was done in Chapter 8. The code for the first top-level procedure in each group will indicate at what point other routines should be inserted.

Figure 11-1 provides an organization chart for the subprograms. The subprograms at level 1 should be saved in an include file using the file name indicated. Whenever a subprogram contains comments for a level 2, 3, or 4 subprogram, that additional code is to be inserted in place of the comment. After you have entered the code for the last routine in a particular include file, that file will be complete and should be saved. As you create some of the larger files, it would be prudent to stop occasionally and save the code as you go along.

When you are finished you will have nine include files. These will replace the stub definitions in the LOAN.PAS file you created in Chapter 9. The final result will be a program for evaluating loans and printing amortization tables. In order to keep the code as uncluttered as possible, it will be presented with limited comments.

Initialize

Use the Turbo editor to enter the following routine into a work file named
LN-INIT.PAS. The objective of this routine is to see that the program's global variables are properly initialized. After a variable is declared, its value is
undefined until you assign it a value.

(Include file name) Level 1	Level 2	Level 3	Level 4
(LN-INIT.INC) Initialize			
(LN-FILE.INC) Select_Loan_File	Get_FileSpec Open_Loan_File Make_New_File	Valid_FileID Make_Loan_File	Set_Default_Values
(LN-DISP.INC) Current_Value Disp_Field_Value Display_Current_Values			
(LN-SLCT.INC) Select_Action			
(LN-ACPT.INC) Accept_Data			
(LN-MOD.INC) Modify_Data	Payment_Amt Input_Field	Rate_Factor Payment_Cnt Get_Pmts_Per_Yr Get_Select_Yr	End_Yr
(LN-PRNT.INC) Print_Amortization	Ready_To_Print Init_Variables Init_Output_Device Print_Table	New_Page Continue_Prompt Calc_Month Calc_Year Calc_Detail_Line Print_Detail_Line Check_EndOfPage Check_EndOfYear Check_UsrQuit End_Table Print_Final_Totals	Print_Header End_Loan_Year End_Select_Year End_Loan Print_Annual_Totals
(LN-HELP.INC) Display_Help	Select_Subject		
(LN-EXIT.INC) Exit_Housekeeping	Disp_Exit_Warning		

Figure 11-1. Organization chart of subprograms in the Loan Amortization
program

Some of Turbo Pascal's predefined subprograms are used to initialize complex variables. For example, the statement

FillChar(loan,SizeOf(loan),ZERO);

illustrates how the FillChar procedure and the SizeOf function initialize **loan**, which is a complex variant record structure, to zeros. The amount of memory occupied by **loan** is determined by the SizeOf function, and FillChar assigns the value to **loan**, which is 0. This method is faster and more compact than initializing each element individually using an assignment statement. However, sometimes you will need to set variables to a specific value. If the variable you are setting is large and complex, you can store the values in a file and have a routine read them and initialize the variable. This is done in the loan program with **inp—scrn** and **fld—dat**, two record type variables:

Load—Input—Scrn('LOAN.SCR',inp—scrn,fld—dat);

In this example data will be loaded into the **inp—scrn** and **fld—dat** variables from the LOAN.SCR file on disk. The Load—Input—Scrn procedure is defined in the STD-DISP.INC include file developed in Chapter 8. Storing initialization data in disk files reduces the size of the program code and makes it easy to find the values when changes need to be made. The tradeoff is slower execution of the initialization part of the program. Since the initialization routines are usually executed once, the time penalty is not too great.

```
procedure Initialize;

  begin
    ClrScr; Write('Initializing...');
    FillChar(loan,SizeOf(loan),ZERO);
    output_id := 'Video Screen';
    help_flag := FALSE;
    err_flag := FALSE;
    esc_flag := FALSE;
    quit_flag := FALSE;
    exit_flag := FALSE;
    modified := FALSE;
    end_session := FALSE;
    Load_Input_Scrn('LOAN.SCR',inp_scrn,fld_dat);
    Load_Help_Text('LN-HELP.SCR');
  end; { Intitialize }
```

Select—Loan—File

What sounds like a fairly simple task will require seven subprograms spanning four levels; however, all of the routines are short and simple. The overall objective is to allow the user to select a file that will be used to store information pertaining to a specific loan. The following seven subprograms should be stored in LN-FILE.INC.

If the user enters a file that already exists, the values in the file are used to initialize the loan record. Otherwise a new file must be created and the loan record will be initialized with default values. The code for the lower level subprograms should be inserted between the Select—Loan—File procedure header and its statement part, as indicated by the insert comments.

```
{ LN-FILE.INC  Include file }

  procedure Select_Loan_File;

{ ***** Insert Get_FileSpec ***** }

{ ***** Insert Open_Loan_File ***** }

{ ***** Insert Make_New_File ***** }

    begin { Select_Loan_File }
      Get_FileSpec(file_name);
      if (not esc_flag) then
        if Exist(file_name) then
          Open_Loan_File(file_name)
        else
          Make_New_File(file_name);
      ClrScr;
    end; { Select_Loan_File }
```

Get—FileSpec

From the operator's perspective, the Get—FileSpec displays a prompt requesting a valid file name for a loan file. The only options are to enter a valid file name or press the QUIT key, which is assigned to the ESC key. Of particular interest from a programming perspective is the extensive use of typed constants. As you will recall, this is a Turbo Pascal specialty that gives you initialized variables. In this example both set type and record type structures are created and initialized. Notice that the values assigned to the fields of a record structure must be enclosed in parentheses. Also notice that the formatting of the source code helps clarify the purpose and action of the code. Using typed constants in situations such as this will result in faster, more compact object code.

After displaying a prompt and a message to the user, Get—FileSpec uses the typed constants as parameters for the Init—Field and Get—Field— Input routines. This illustrates how these controlled input procedures are used when the field parameters are not provided as part of an input screen.

Upon return from the Get—Field—Input procedure, an if statement determines whether the user pressed the QUIT key. If not, the validity of the file name is verified in a lower level function. This demonstrates that a Boolean function may be used wherever a relational expression is called for. In addition to pushing the detail to a lower level, replacing a relational expression with a function permits you to improve the readability of the source code.

```
{ LN-FILE.INC   Level 2 }

    procedure Get_FileSpec(var file_name: File_ID);
      const chr_set      : Printable_Char = [':','0'..'9','A'..'Z'];
            ctrl_set     : Control_Char   = [CR,BS,QUIT];
            cmd_fld      : Fld_Parms      =
                           ( xloc         : 56;              { Column }
                             yloc         : MSG_LINE;        { Row }
                             fld_len      : 10;              { Length }
                             fld_type     : UC_TEXT;         { Upper Case }
                             exit_type    : MANUAL;          { <CR> Require(
                             fld_msg      : '');             { None }

      var   inp_ok       : Boolean;

{ ***** Insert  Valid_FileID ***** }

      begin { Get_FileSpec }
        esc_flag := FALSE;
        inp_ok := FALSE;
        ClrScr;
        Repeat
          Display_Prompt(CMD_LINE,'MSG',
                'Up to 8 characters beginning with a letter. | ' +
                QUIT_KEY + 'to Exit');
          Display_Prompt(MSG_LINE,'INP',
                'Enter LOAN FILE NAME to be created or updated ==> ');
          Init_Field(FILL_CHAR,cmd_fld);
          Get_Field_Input(cmd_fld,chr_set,ctrl_set);
          if (not esc_flag) then
            if Valid_FileID then
              begin
                inp_ok := TRUE;
                file_name := inp_str + '.LDT';
              end
            else
              Disp_Error_Msg((inp_str + ' is not a valid file name.'));
        Until (inp_ok or esc_flag);
        GoToXY(1,CMD_LINE); ClrEol;
      end; { Get_FileSpec }
```

Valid—FileID

Valid—FileID should be inserted in the Get—FileSpec procedure as indicated by the insert comment. The objective of Valid—FileID is to be sure that the drive identifier, if any, is valid. The screening performed by the Get—Field—Input procedure will catch any other errors.

Valid—FileID also shows how the Pos function locates a colon in the file name and stores its position in a variable. As a rule, if the value of a function is used more than once, it should be saved. If Pos returns 0, no colon was detected, hence no drive identifier was specified.

```
{ LN-FILE.INC   Level 3 }

    function Valid_FileID: Boolean;
      var  col_pos : Byte;

      begin
        col_pos := Pos(':',inp_str);
        if (col_pos = ZERO) and (inp_str[1] in ['A'..'Z']) then
          Valid_FileID := TRUE
        else
          if (col_pos = 2) and (inp_str[3] in ['A'..'Z']) then
```

```
        if (inp_str[1] in ['A'..'P']) then
            Valid_FileID := TRUE
        else Valid_FileID := FALSE
    else
        Valid_FileID := FALSE;
end; { Valid_FileID }
```

Open — Loan — File

Looking back at Select—Loan—File, you will see that Open—Loan—File is the second level 2 subprogram to be inserted in the Select—Loan—File procedure. Its purpose is to open an existing loan file and read its contents into the variable **loan**. Following the Reset statement the record pointer for the file is implicitly set to record 0, which is the first and only record stored in a user-created loan file. Therefore, after verifying that Reset was successful, a simple Read statement is all that is needed to perform the data transfer.

```
{ LN-FILE.INC  Level 2 }

    procedure Open_Loan_File(file_name: File_ID);
        begin
            Assign(loan_file,file_name);
{$I-}
            Reset(loan_file); io_status := IOresult;
            if (io_status = ZERO) then
                Read(loan_file,loan); io_status := IOresult;
{$I+}
            if (io_status <> ZERO) then
                Disp_IO_Error(file_name);
        end; { Open_Loan_File }
```

Make — New — File

If the user enters a file name that does not exist, the Make—New—File procedure is called to verify that the operator does in fact want to create a new file. If so, the Make—Loan—File procedure at level 3 is activated.

```
{ LN-FILE.INC Level 2 }

    procedure Make_New_File(file_name: File_ID);

{ ***** Insert Make_Loan_File ***** }

        begin { Make_New_File }
            Display_Prompt(CMD_LINE,'INP',
                        'Do you want to create a NEW loan file? (Y/N) ==> ');
            if (Valid_Key(['Y','N']) = 'Y') then
                Make_Loan_File
            else
                esc_flag := TRUE;
        end; { Make_New_File }
```

Make — Loan — File

Make—Loan—File uses the Rewrite procedure to create a new file and then calls the level 4 procedure Set—Default—Values to initialize the loan variable. I/O error trapping is performed here as it is in all of the routines involving file I/O. The code for Make—Loan—File should be inserted between the Make—New—File header and its statement part.

```
{ LN-FILE.INC   Level 3 }

      procedure Make_Loan_File;

{ ***** Insert Set_Default_Values ***** }

      begin
        Assign(loan_file,file_name);
{$I-}
        Rewrite(loan_file); io_status := IOresult;
{$I+}
        if (io_status = ZERO) then
          Set_Default_Values
        else
          Disp_IO_Error(file_name);
      end; { Make_Loan_File }
```

Set—Default—Values

The FillChar procedure and assignment statements are used by Set—Default—Values to initialize the loan variable. The default values for the new file are arbitrary and may be changed as you wish. The only exception is that **no—of—pmts** and **pmts—per—yr** must be greater than 0 to prevent divide-by-zero errors.

This is the last subprogram in the LN-FILE.PAS include file. After it is inserted in the Make—Loan—File procedure you should save the include file.

```
{ LN-FILE.INC Level 4 }
      procedure Set_Default_Values;
        begin
          FillChar(loan,SizeOf(loan),ZERO);
          with loan do
          begin
            principle    := MIN_LOAN;
            rate         := MIN_RATE;
            no_of_pmts   := 12;
            first_mo     := 1;
            first_yr     := 1980;
            pmts_per_yr  := 12;
            select_yr    := ZERO;
            out_dev      := VIDEO;
            commercial   := FALSE;
          end;
        end; { Set_Default_Values }
```

Current—Values

Current—Values returns the current value of any of the 19 input fields on the input screen as a formatted string. It is used by the routines that display the initial values, the default values, and the formatted echo of the user's input. The calling routine passes the field parameter to indicate which field value is needed. The case statement uses the field parameter as its selector variable. Some of the actions are described here:

Field parameter	**Action**
1 or 3	The Boolean value **commercial** is converted to X or SPACE.
2 or 4-6	If the condition tested by the if statement is FALSE, Current—Value will return its initial value of NULL.
8-15	Here are several examples of how the Str procedure can be used to convert a numeric value to a formatted string. Note the use of the local variable **num—str**.
17	The Copy function is used here to return the file name up to but not including the period (.) that precedes the file extension added by the program.
18 or 19	This code illustrates the fact that numeric parameters may be expressions. Notice the parameters to the Str procedure. Also note that Current—Value will return the word "Invalid" if the values used to calculate these display-only fields do not produce a meaningful result.

```
{ LN-DISP.INC   Include file }
   function Current_Value(field: Byte): Str_80;
      var num_str : Str_80;
          len     : Byte;

      begin
        Current_Value := NULL;
        len := fld_dat[field].fld_len;
        with loan, fld_dat[field] do
        case field of
              1         : if commercial then
                             Current_Value :='X'
                          else
                             Current_Value := ' ';
              2         : if commercial then
                             Current_Value := business_name;
              3         : if (not commercial) then
                             Current_Value :='X'
                          else
                             Current_Value := ' ';
              4         : if (not commercial) then
                             Current_Value := borrower.last_name;
              5         : if (not commercial) then
                             Current_Value := borrower.first_name;
              6         : if (not commercial) then
                             Current_Value := borrower.title;
              7         : Current_Value := collateral;
              8         : begin
                             Str(principle:len:2,num_str);
                             Current_Value := num_str;
                          end;
```

```
   9      : begin
              Str(rate:len:3,num_str);
              Current_Value := num_str;
            end;
  10      : begin
              Str(payment:len:2,num_str);
              Current_Value := num_str;
            end;
  11      : begin
              Str(pmts_per_yr:len,num_str);
              Current_Value := num_str;
            end;
  12      : begin
              Str(first_mo:len,num_str);
              if (first_mo < 10) then
                num_str[1] := '0';
              Current_Value := num_str;
            end;
  13      : begin
              Str(first_yr:len,num_str);
              Current_Value := num_str;

            end;
  14      : begin
              Str(no_of_pmts:len:2,num_str);
              Current_Value := num_str;
            end;
  15      : begin
              Str(select_yr:len,num_str);
              Current_Value := num_str;
            end;
  16      : Current_Value := out_dev;
  17      : Current_Value :=
              Copy(file_name,1,(Pos('.',file_name) - 1));
  18      : begin
              if ((no_of_pmts * payment) > 0.0) then
                begin
                  Str((no_of_pmts * payment):len:2,num_str);
                  Current_Value := num_str;
                end
              else
                Current_Value := '   Invalid';
            end;
  19      : begin
              if ((no_of_pmts * payment - principle) > 0.0) and
                 (rate > 0.0) then
                begin
                  Str((no_of_pmts * payment - principle):len:2,
                      num_str);
                  Current_Value := num_str;
                end
              else
                Current_Value := '   Invalid';
            end;
    end; {case}
  end; { Current_Value }

{ ***** Insert Disp_Field_Value ***** }

{ ***** Insert Display_Current_Values ***** }
```

Display＿Field＿Value

The purpose of Display＿Field＿Value is to display the current value of the field indicated by the parameter field. It uses the Current＿Value function to obtain the string to be displayed. If Current＿Value returns a null string, the field is initialized using Init＿Field. The location at which the output will be displayed is determined by the **fld＿dat** record for the field. The with

statement is used to allow direct access to the field parameters stored in
fld—dat[field]. Notice too how Repeat—Char is used to blank out the
unused portion of the field if it is not filled by the input value.

```
{ LN-DISP.INC  Level 1 }

  procedure Disp_Field_Value(field: Byte);
    var fld_str : Str_80;

    begin
      fld_str := Current_Value(field);
      if fld_str <> NULL then
        with fld_dat[field] do
        begin  { Display fld_str and clear to end of field. }
          GoToXY(xloc,yloc); Write(fld_str);
          Repeat_Char(SPACE,(fld_len - Length(fld_str)));
        end
      else
        Init_Field(FILL_CHAR,fld_dat[field]);
    end; { Disp_Field_Value }
```

Display—Current—Values

This routine redisplays the input screen and all of the current field values.
This procedure also shows how straightforward your program is when
details such as this routine are moved out of the way.

```
{ LN-DISP.INC  Level 1 }

  procedure Display_Current_Values;
    var  fld_no  : Byte;

    begin
      ClrScr; Disp_Input_Scrn(inp_scrn);
      for fld_no := 1 to fld_cnt do
        Disp_Field_Value(fld_no);
    end; { Display_Current_Values }
```

Select—Action

Select—Action prompts the user to select one of five activities (accept the
loan data, modify the loan data, print the loan data, quit the program, or ask
for help) by pressing a single key. Then Valid—Key assigns a character corresponding to one of the five valid keys. Save this code in LN=SLCT.INC.

```
{ LN-SLCT.INC  Include file }

  procedure Select_Action;
    var   cmd_msg    : Str_80;
```

```
begin
  cmd_msg := 'Accept   |   Modify   |   Print   | ' + HELP_KEY +
               'HELP   | ' + QUIT_KEY + 'Exit';
  Display_Prompt(CMD_LINE,'CMD',cmd_msg);
  Display_Prompt(MSG_LINE,'INP'
                 ,'Press a CMD: key to enter selection ==> ');
  action := Valid_Key(['A','M','P',HELP,QUIT]);
end; { Select_Action }
```

Accept—Data

If the user elects to accept the data from the input screen, Accept—Data readies the disk for updating. First the record pointer is positioned at the first record in the file with the Reset statement.

After the disk file is updated using a Write statement, the global variable **modified** is set to FALSE. This indicates that there have been no changes to the loan variable since the disk file was updated. This is true because the disk file has just been updated by the Write statement. Store this procedure in a file named LN-ACPT.INC.

```
{ LN-ACPT.INC   Include file }

  procedure Accept_Data;
    begin
{$I-}
      Reset(loan_file);
      io_status := IOresult;
      if (io_status = ZERO) then
        begin
          Write(loan_file,loan);
          io_status := IOresult;
        end;
{$I+}
      if (io_status = ZERO) then
        modified := FALSE
      else
        Disp_IO_Error(file_name);
    end; { Accept_Data }
```

Modify—Data

The Modify—Data procedure along with its seven subprograms should be stored in the LN-MOD.INC include file. Its purpose is to allow the operator to modify the loan information on the input screen. It also changes the global variable **modified** to TRUE. The parameter **fld—no** is used as a field pointer. When the user has the cursor on field 3 in the input screen, **fld—no** is 3.

After each field is input, **fld__no** is adjusted by the value of the global variable **direction**. If the user presses the ENTER key, the value of **direction** is set to 1; however, if the user presses the PREV key, which is assigned to the UP ARROW key, **direction** is set to −1. Then the direction is added to **fld__no**. As you will see, the Input__Field procedure, a subprogram of Modify__Data, controls the input sequence and assigns **direction** its value.

After a field value has been entered using procedure Input__Field and the field pointer has been adjusted, the Modify__Data routine checks if the user pressed the QUIT key to terminate input. If so, it is necessary to recalculate the loan payment to reflect any changes that may have been made. This is handled by the Payment__Amt function, which is described next.

```
{ LN-MOD.INC   Include file }

procedure Modify_Data(fld_no,last_fld: Byte);
   var periodic_rate      : Real;

{ ***** Insert Payment_Amount ***** }

{ ***** Insert Input_Field ***** }

  begin { Modify_Data }
    repeat
      Input_field;
      fld_no := fld_no + direction;
      if (fld_no < 1) then
        fld_no := 1;
    until (esc_flag or (fld_no > last_fld));
    if esc_flag then
      begin
        esc_flag := FALSE;
        with loan do
          periodic_rate := rate / pmts_per_yr / 100.0;
        loan.payment := Payment_Amt
      end;
    modified := TRUE;
  end; { Modify_Data }
```

Payment__Amt

Payment__Amt calculates the payment amount of a loan based on the term, principal, and periodic interest rate. Before the payment amount is calculated, a rate factor based on the periodic rate must be calculated. This is done in the local function Rate__Factor (presented next). Figure 11-2 shows the step-by-step calculations that provide the payment amount returned by the Payment__Amt function.

In the program, notice that the test, **factor**=1.0, will be TRUE when the interest rate is set to 0.0. In that case the payment amount is simply the principal divided by the number of payments. The last two statements round the value to the nearest cent and assign the result to the function identifier.

```
{ LN-MOD.INC   Level 2 }

  function Payment_Amt: Real;
    var cents,
        pmt_amt,
        int_factor : Real;

{ ***** Insert Rate_Factor ***** }

    begin { Payment_Amt }
      with loan do
      begin
        int_factor := Rate_Factor;
        if (int_factor = 1.0) then
          pmt_amt := principle / no_of_pmts
        else
          pmt_amt := (principle * periodic_rate) / (1 - int_factor);
        cents := Frac(pmt_amt);
        Payment_Amt := pmt_amt - cents + (Round(cents * 100.0) * 0.01);
      end;
    end; { Payment_Amt }
```

Payment Calculations

principal	=	100.00
rate	=	10.00
pmts _ per _ yr	=	12 (monthly payments)
no _ of _ pmts	=	3 (loan paid in full in 3 months)
periodic _ rate	=	rate/pmts _ per _ yr/principal = 10 / 12 / 100 = .0083333
accum	=	1.0
factor	=	accum + periodic = 1.0 + .008333 = 1.0083333
Payment loop 1		
accum	=	accum/factor = 1.0 / 1.0083333 = .9917355
Payment loop 2		
accum	=	accum/factor = .9917355 / 1.0083333 = .9835393
Payment loop 3		
accum	=	accum/factor = .9835393 / 1.0083333 = .9754109
Rate _ Factor	=	.9754109
pmt _ amt	=	principal * periodic _ rate/(1−accum) = 100 * .0083333 / (1 − .9754109) = 33.890219
cents	=	Frac (pmt _ amt) = .890219
Payment _ Amt	=	pmt _ amt - cents + Round (cents) = 33.890219 − .890219 + .89 = 33.89

Figure 11-2. Example of calculating the payment amount

Rate—Factor

The Rate—Factor function returns a value that is used in the calculation in Payment—Amt. If the number of payments is an integer, Rate—Factor does not have to be adjusted for a final partial payment. If the number of payments has a fractional part (when you enter a payment amount and allow the number of payments to be calculated), the Frac function will detect the need for a partial payment, the compound statement within the if-then statement will be executed, and it will adjust the value returned by Rate—Factor to reflect the effect of the partial payment.

```
{ LN-MOD.INC   Level 3 }
    function Rate_Factor: Real;
        var i        : Byte;
            adj,
            accum,
            factor   : Real;

        begin
          accum := 1.0; factor := 1.0 + periodic_rate;
          for i := 1 to Trunc(loan.no_of_pmts) do
            accum := (accum / factor);
          if Frac(loan.no_of_pmts) > 0.0 then
            begin
              adj := accum - (accum / factor);
              adj := adj * Frac(loan.no_of_pmts);
              accum := accum - adj;
            end;
          Rate_Factor := accum;
        end; { Rate_Factor }
```

Input—Field

The Input—Field procedure prompts the user, accepts and verifies keyboard input, and adjusts the **direction** variable. The three user prompt lines are used as follows:

CMD—LINE   The constant strings that identify the valid command keys, which are printed at the bottom of the screen, combine with prompts to create the message for the command line. Note that the + symbol is used as the string concatenation operator.

PROMPT—LINE   The prompt message that is stored with the field parameters in the input screen file is displayed with the prompt line. You will recall that the program global variable **fld—dat** is an array of field parameters, which is initialized with data from the LOAN.SCR file. Each element of the array is a record made up of the parameters for a single field. Using **fld—no** to indicate the current field, this identifier:

fld—dat[fld—no].fld—msg

is used to access the prompt message for the field.

MSG—LINE   This line is used to indicate the value that will be assigned to a field if the RETURN key is pressed without entering a new value. This is called the default value for the field. The Current—Value function is used to make the current contents of a field the default for that field. This permits the operator to skip quickly through the input fields to get to a particular field that is to be modified.

The operator input is accepted and verified in the case statement part of the Input—Field procedure. For the most part, verification is taken care of by the input functions defined in STD-INP.INC. Most of the code for the individual fields is concerned with adjusting the direction variable or seeing that either the **payment** or **no—of—pmts** field is calculated as needed.

The best way to understand how the input sequence is controlled is to review the Input—Field procedure after you get the program running. Then you can experiment, changing the status of the commercial field and moving from field to field both forward and backward. Also you will be able to see how the input sequence changes when a payment amount is entered, as opposed to clearing with zero.

The processing for fields 11 and 15 in the case statement has been moved into lower level subprograms. This is recommended whenever a long or complex statement is required for a particular case selector value. The reasons are to clarify the purpose of the statement and to avoid cluttering the subprogram with detail. The Payment—Cnt routine, which calculates the number of payments, has been defined as a local function for the same reasons.

```
{ LN-MOD.INC   Level 2 }

  procedure Input_Field;
    var parms      : Fld_Parms;
        err_msg,
        cmd_msg    : Str_80;
        last_yr    : Integer;
        len, i     : Byte;

{ ***** Insert Payment_Cnt ***** }

{ ***** Insert Get_Pmts_Per_Yr ***** }
```

```
{ ***** Insert Get_Select_Yr ***** }

    begin { Input_Field }
      default := Current_Value(fld_no);
      Clear_Prompts;
      cmd_msg := PREV_KEY + ' Prev Fld  | ' +
                 CLEAR_KEY + ' Clear Fld  | ' +
                 QUIT_KEY + ' Exit ';
      Display_Prompt(CMD_LINE,'CMD',cmd_msg);
      Display_Prompt(PROMPT_LINE,'MSG',fld_dat[fld_no].fld_msg);
      Display_Prompt(MSG_LINE,ENTER_KEY,default);
      parms := fld_dat[fld_no];
      len := parms.fld_len;
      Init_Field(FILL_CHAR,parms);
      with loan do
      case fld_no of
          1  : begin
                  inchr := Valid_Chr(parms,['X',SPACE]);
                  commercial := (inchr = 'X');
                  if (not commercial) then
                    begin
                      Init_Field(FILL_CHAR,fld_dat[2]);
                      FillChar(business_name,Length(business_name),ZERO);
                      direction := 2;
                    end;
               end;
          2  : begin
                  business_name := (Valid_Str(parms));
                  if (direction = INCR) then
                    begin
                      direction   := 5;
                      for i := 3 to 6 do
                        Init_Field(FILL_CHAR,fld_dat[i]);
                    end;
               end;
          3  : begin
                  Write('X'); direction := INCR;
               end;
          4  : begin
                  borrower.last_name := (Valid_Str(parms));
                  if (direction = DECR) then
                    direction := (-3);
               end;
          5  : borrower.first_name := (Valid_Str(parms));
          6  : borrower.title := (Valid_Str(parms));
          7  : begin
                  collateral := (Valid_Str(parms));
                  if (commercial and (direction = DECR)) then
                    direction := (-5);
               end;
          8  : principle := (Valid_Real(parms,2,MIN_LOAN,MAX_LOAN));
          9  : rate := (Valid_Real(parms,3,MIN_RATE,MAX_RATE));
          10 : payment := (Valid_Real(parms,2,0.0,MAX_PMT));
          11 : Get_Pmts_Per_Yr;
          12 : first_mo := (Valid_Int(parms,1,12));
          13 : begin
                  first_yr := (Valid_Int(parms,1900,2040));
                  if (payment > 0.0) and (direction = INCR) then
                    begin
                      no_of_pmts := Payment_Cnt;
                      Disp_Field_Value(14);
                      direction := 2;
                    end;
               end;
          14 : begin
                  no_of_pmts :=
                    (Valid_Real(parms,2,1.0,MAX_TERM));
                  if (direction = INCR) then
                    begin
                      payment := Payment_Amt;
                      Disp_Field_Value(10);
                    end;
```

```
               end;
        15   : Get_Select_Yr;
        16   : out_dev := Valid_Chr(parms,['V','P']);
     end; {case}
     Disp_Field_Value(fld_no);   { Redisplay formated input }
end; { Input_Field }
```

Payment—Cnt

Function Payment—Cnt determines how many payments are required to pay off a loan at a specified interest rate. If the interest rate is 0 or the payment is equal to the loan amount plus interest for one period, the condition tested by the if statement will be TRUE and calculating the number of payments would entail dividing the principal by the payment.

Few loans will be this generous; however, the program must test for these cases as an interest rate of 0 will result in an error in the more complex formula. The more complex formula accounts for an interest rate. This formula is

$$N = -Log_e (1 - PR/A))/Log_e (1 + R)$$

where P = principal amount, R = periodic rate, and A = payment amount.

```
{ LN-MOD.INC   Level 3 }

   function Payment_Cnt: Real;
     begin
       with loan do
         if (Ln((1.0 + periodic_rate)) = 0.0) then
           Payment_Cnt := (principle / payment)
         else
           Payment_Cnt := -(Ln(1.0 - (principle * periodic_rate / payment))
                          / Ln((1.0 + periodic_rate)));
     end; { Payment_Cnt }
```

Get—Pmts—Per—Yr

Get—Pmts—Per—Yr accepts an integer between 1 and 52 from the operator and then verifies that the number entered represents a valid payment period based on the typed constant PMT—TERMS. This allows payment periods from annual to weekly. The number of payments per year is used to calculate the periodic interest rate. If the user has specified a payment amount, the program must verify that the payment amount will at least cover the interest. If not, an error message is displayed and the direction indicator is set to −1, causing the cursor to move to the previous field, so that the user will be prompted to re-enter the payment amount.

```
{ LN-MOD.INC  Level 3 }

    procedure Get_Pmts_Per_Yr;
      type Term_Set   = set of 1..52;

      const  pmt_terms : Term_Set = [1..4,6,12,24,26,52];

      begin
        with loan do
        begin
          pmts_per_yr := (Valid_Int(parms,1,52));
          if (pmts_per_yr in pmt_terms) then
            begin
              periodic_rate := rate / pmts_per_yr / 100.0;
              if (payment > 0.0) and
                ((periodic_rate * principle) >= payment) then
                begin
                  Disp_Error_Msg(
                  'Payment amount insufficient to pay interest');
                  direction := (-1);
                end;
            end
          else
            begin
              Disp_Error_Msg(
              'Valid entries are 1 2 3 4 6 12 24 26 52');
              direction := ZERO;
            end;
        end;
      end; { Get_Pmts_Per_Yr }
```

Get—Select—Yr

If the user wants only part of the amortization table to be printed, Get—
Select—Yr verifies that the user selected a year in which payments are due.
The local function End—Yr, to be presented next, identifies the last calendar
year in which payments are scheduled. The Valid—Int function is used to
limit the user's response to a value from 0 to End—Yr. An entry of 0 will
print the entire table.

```
{ LN-MOD.INC  Level 3 }

    procedure Get_Select_Yr;

{ ***** Insert End_Yr ***** }

      begin { Get_Select_Yr }
        last_yr := End_Yr;
        if (last_yr > ZERO) then
          with loan do
          begin
            select_yr := (Valid_Int(parms,ZERO,last_yr));
            if (select_yr > ZERO) and (select_yr < first_yr) then
              begin
                Disp_Error_Msg('No payments due in year entered.');
                direction := ZERO;
              end;
          end; {with}
      end; { Get_Select_Yr }
```

End—Yr

End—Yr determines the last calendar year in which payments are scheduled based on the terms of the loan. First, the number of months is calculated. The result, plus the number of months during the first year in which the loan was not in effect, is divided by 12. The last year of the loan will be the first year plus the result of the previous calculations. Since the first year for a loan has been arbitrarily restricted to the year 2040 and a maximum of 360 payments, even if the payment period is annual, the End—Yr function will never return a value greater than 2400.

```
{ LN-MOD.INC   Level 4 }

     function End_Yr: Integer;
       var mo_cnt,
           last_yr   : Integer;

       begin
         with loan do
         begin
           if (pmts_per_yr * no_of_pmts) = 0.0 then
             mo_cnt := ZERO
           else
             mo_cnt := Trunc(12 / pmts_per_yr * no_of_pmts + 0.99);
           End_Yr := Trunc((mo_cnt + first_mo - 1) div 12 + first_yr);
         end; {with}
       end; { End_Yr }
```

Print—Amortization

A quick review of Figure 11-1 shows that the Print—Amortization procedure relies on 20 lower level subprograms. The good news is that most of the low-level subprograms have fewer than 20 lines of code. The Print—Amortization procedure and its subprograms should be stored in the LN-PRNT.INC include file.

When developing a lengthy or complex routine like Print—Amortization, you will find that pushing the detail to a lower level keeps the top level simple and descriptive. This speeds up the development process. In return the object code is less efficient. If speed and size are important, you can move the critical portions from a lower level routine into the calling routine after the program is running. But unless the routine is in a loop that executes frequently, the overhead involved in calling lower level routines is insignificant.

Before looking at the lower levels of Print—Amortization, you may be curious about some of the type definitions and variable declarations. First of all, take a look at the definition of the Address type. As an array of two integers it will hold both 16- and 32-bit addresses. This is important because the program will run on any system supported by Turbo Pascal. The variable **hold_out_ptr**, which is declared to be of type Address, stores the address of the I/O driver for the console output device. Totals is an enumerated type that describes the variable **total_ptr**. It also provides the descriptive constants for the bounds of the **year_total** and **final_total** arrays.

```
{ LN-PRNT.INC   Include file }

procedure Print_Amortization
   const PRINT_PAGE = 58;    { Number of print lines per page. }
         VIDEO_PAGE = 20;    { Number of print lines on video screen. }
         TOF        = #12;   { Printer top of form control code. }
         ADDR_SIZE  = 4;     { Number of bytes required to store an Address }
                             { CP/M-80 systems replace 4 with 2. }

   type  Address = array[1..2] of Integer;
         Totals  = (Payments,Principle,Interest);

   var   hold_out_ptr    : Address;
         total_ptr       : Totals;
         month_offset,
         offset_factor,
         calc_pmt,
         periodic_rate,
         loan_balance    : Real;
         final_total     : array[Payments..Interest] of Real;
         year_total      : array[Payments..Interest] of Real;
         line_cnt        : Integer;
         pmt_no,
         max_line        : Byte;

{ ***** Insert Ready_To_Print ***** }

{ ***** Insert Init_Variables ***** }

{ ***** Insert Init_Output_Device ***** }

{ ***** Insert Print_Table ***** }

   begin { Print_Amortization }
     if Ready_To_Print then
       begin
         Init_Variables;
         Init_Output_Device;
         Print_Table;
       end;
   end; { Print_Amortization }
```

Ready_To_Print

When the user selects the Print option, Ready_To_Print is activated. If the user directs the output to the printer, a prompt is displayed reminding the user to check the printer; it also offers an opportunity to cancel the print selection.

```
{ LN-PRNT.INC   Level 2 }

  function Ready_To_Print: Boolean;
    begin
      if (loan.out_dev = PRINTER) then
        begin
          Clear_Prompts;
          Display_Prompt(CMD_LINE,'CMD', QUIT_KEY + ' Cancel Printing ');
          Display_Prompt(MSG_LINE,'INP','Press ' + ENTER_KEY +
                         'when PRINTER is READY. ==> ');
          Ready_To_Print := (Valid_Key([CR,QUIT]) = CR);
          Display_Prompt(MSG_LINE,'MSG','Printing amortization table...');
        end
      else
        Ready_To_Print := TRUE;
    end; { Ready_To_Print }
```

Init—Variables

Variables for the Print—Amortization procedure are initialized with Init—
Variables. The number of months that have been paid and the offset factor,
which equals 12 divided by the number of payments per year, will be used to
keep track of the calendar month and year, which are output with each payment line of the amortization table. The variable **pmt—no** is used to keep
track of which payment is being processed. The remaining variables are
accumulators to hold the yearly totals, the final totals, and intermediate
calculations.

```
{ LN-PRNT.INC   Level 2 }

  procedure Init_Variables;
    var i : Byte;

    begin
      month_offset := 0.0;
      offset_factor := 12 / loan.pmts_per_yr;
      calc_pmt := loan.payment;
      periodic_rate := loan.rate / loan.pmts_per_yr / 100.0;
      loan_balance := loan.principle;
      for total_ptr := Payments to Interest do
        begin
          year_total[total_ptr] := 0.0;
          final_total[total_ptr] := 0.0;
        end;
      pmt_no := ZERO;
    end; { Init_Variables }
```

Init—Output—Device

Init—Output—Device illustrates how easy it is to redirect output using
Turbo Pascal. When a Write or WriteLn statement is used without specifying
an output file, the output is directed to the standard console output device,
which is almost always assigned to your video monitor. Init—Output—

Device reassigns the standard console output device to the printer by substituting the address of the printer I/O driver for that of the console driver. Turbo Pascal's Move procedure is used to transfer the address. As a result, the output will go to the printer. Variable **hold__out__ptr** temporarily stores the address of the console driver so that it can be restored when the program is finished printing.

On CP/M-80 systems the address is stored in 16 bits (2 bytes), while 32 bits (4 bytes) are required for MS-DOS and CP/M-86 systems. The ADDR__SIZE constant should be defined for the system you are using by setting the number of bytes to 2 or 4. You must make the assignment depending upon your system.

There are other ways to send information to the printer, but this is the easiest to implement. It does have one drawback: if the program terminates abnormally while the output is directed to the printer, all output intended for the video will show up on the printer. The only way to correct the situation is to reset the system. This means it is very important that you trap any potential errors so that the program terminates normally.

Note: If your system uses a serial printer, you may have to replace the statement

$$Move(LstOutPtr,ConOutPtr,ADDR\_SIZE);$$

with

$$Move(AuxOutPtr,ConOutPtr,ADDR\_SIZE);$$

This will replace the console output driver with the serial output driver that controls your printer, assuming that the address of the serial driver is stored in AuxOutPtr.

```
{ LN-PRNT.INC   Level 2 }

  procedure Init_Output_Device;
    begin
      Move (ConOutPtr,hold_out_ptr,ADDR_SIZE); { Save console device addr. }
      if loan.out_dev = PRINTER then
        begin
          Move (LstOutPtr,ConOutPtr,ADDR_SIZE);
          max_line := PRINT_PAGE;
        end
      else
        max_line := VIDEO_PAGE;
    end; { Init_Output_Device }
```

Print__Table

Like Print__Amortization, Print__Table hides most of its detail in lower level routines. This procedure also provides another example of a typed constant array that will convert the current month from a numeric to a string value for output.

The last statement in Print__Table, the Move procedure, restores the output to the console device. This statement should be executed even if output was directed to the screen or if the routine is exited due to an error condition.

```
{ LN-PRNT.INC   Level 2 }

  procedure Print_Table;
    type  Month_Str    = string[3];

    const month_id     : array[1..12] of Month_Str =
                          ('Jan','Feb','Mar','Apr',
                           'May','Jun','Jul','Aug',
                           'Sep','Oct','Nov','Dec');

    var   interest_amt,
          principle_amt : Real;
          current_year  : Integer;
          current_month : Byte;
          user_quit     : Boolean;

  { ***** Insert New_Page ***** }
  { ***** Insert Continue_Prompt ***** }
  { ***** Insert Calc_Month & Calc_Year ***** }
  { ***** Insert Calc_Detail_Line ***** }
  { ***** Insert Print_Detail_Line ***** }
  { ***** Insert Check_EndOfYear ***** }
  { ***** Insert Check_EndOfPage ***** }
  { ***** Insert Check_UsrQuit ***** }
  { ***** Insert End_Table ***** }
  { ***** Insert Print_Final_Totals ***** }

    begin { Print_Table }
      user_quit := FALSE;
      err_flag := FALSE;
      New_Page(loan.out_dev);
      repeat
        Calc_Detail_Line;
        Print_Detail_Line;
        if (not err_flag) then
          begin
            Check_EndOfPage;
            Check_EndOfYear;
            Check_UsrQuit;
            pmt_no := Succ(pmt_no);
          end;
      until (End_Table or err_flag);
      if (not (err_flag or user_quit)) then
        Print_Final_Totals;
      Move(hold_out_ptr,ConOutPtr,ADDR_SIZE); { Restore console device addr. }
    end; { Print_Table }
```

New—Page

Depending on its parameter, set to video or printer, New—Page will either clear the video screen or send a top-of-form signal to the printer. Then, in most cases the header that defines the column of values for the loan will be output at the top of screen. The top-of-form signal will not be output if **pmt— no** = ZERO and the output device is the printer, preventing a sheet of paper from being wasted each time a table is printed. Note also that the quit flag is used to inhibit output of the header.

```
{ LN-PRNT.INC   Level 3 }

    procedure New_Page(device: Char);

{ ***** Insert Print_Header ***** }

    begin { New_Page }
      if (device = VIDEO) then
        ClrScr
      else
        if (pmt_no > ZERO) then
          Write(TOF);
      if (not user_quit) then
        Print_Header;
    end; { New_Page }
```

Print—Header

Except for I/O error trapping, Print—Header is very simple. Assuming there are no I/O errors, the header will be output and the line counter initialized.

```
{ LN-PRNT.INC   Level 4 }

      procedure Print_Header;
        begin
{$I-}
          WriteLn(' Payment        Remaining   Total of    Principle    Interest'`·
          io_status := IOresult;
{$I+}
          if (io_status = ZERO) then
            WriteLn(' No./Date      Principle   Payments   Payment      Payment')
          else
            Disp_IO_Error('Printer');
          if (not err_flag) then
            begin
              Repeat_Char('-',62); WriteLn;
              line_cnt := 3;
            end;
        end { Print_Header };
```

Continue—Prompt

Here is another simple routine. Continue—Prompt permits the user to review each full screen of output and then either continue or quit as requested.

```
{ LN-PRNT.INC   Level 3 }

   procedure Continue_Prompt;
     begin
       Display_Prompt(CMD_LINE,'CMD', QUIT_KEY + ' Cancel Printing ');
       Display_Prompt(PROMPT_LINE,'INP',
                      'Press ANY KEY to continue. ==> ');
       Read(Kbd,inchr);
       GoToXY(1,PROMPT_LINE); ClrEol;
       if (inchr = QUIT) then
         user_quit := TRUE;
     end; { Continue_Prompt }
```

Calc—Month and Calc—Year

Calc—Month keeps track of the calendar month; Calc—Year keeps track of the year as each detail line is calculated and output. The basis for the calculations is the value stored in **month—offset**, which is initialized to 0.0 in the Init—Variables procedure. As each payment period is processed, **month—offset** is incremented by the value stored in **offset—factor**, which is 12 divided by the number of payments per year. For example, if 6 payments are scheduled each year, **offset—factor** will be 2. On the other hand, if there are 24 payments per year, **offset—factor** will be 0.5.

```
{ LN-PRNT.INC   Level 3 }

   function Calc_Month: Integer;
     begin
       Calc_Month := Round(loan.first_mo +
                     month_offset - 1.49) mod 12 + 1;
     end; { Calc_Month }

   function Calc_Year: Integer;
     begin
         Calc_year := loan.first_yr +
                      ((Round(month_offset) + loan.first_mo - 1) div 12);
     end; { Calc_Year }
```

Calc—Detail—Line

Calc—Detail—Line calculates and outputs the values including the payment number, payment date, remaining principal, total payment, principal payment, and interest payment. The calculations are straightforward; however, you should be aware that rounding the value of **interest—amt** in the fifth statement:

$$interest\text{—}amt := interest\text{—}amt - cents + (Round(cents * 100.0)*0.01);$$

is just as workable. An alternative method is

$$Trunc(interest\text{—}amt) + (Round(cents * 100) * 0.01);$$

This statement does the job unless the integer part of **interest—amt** exceeds

MAXINT. Because Trunc returns an Integer type value, this will cause an overflow error.

Incidentally, the variable **cents** is not necessary; the Frac function could replace it in the calculation. It is used solely to clarify the code.

Another interesting point is that

$$(\text{Round}(cents * 100) / 100)$$

takes about 20 percent longer to execute than

$$(\text{Round}(cents * 100) * 0.01)$$

because division is slower than multiplication. As a rule you should replace division with multiplication whenever possible.

The first if statement in the procedure calculates the final payment when it is less than the rest of the payments. There will still be occasions when a balance of a few cents will remain after the final payment. If you wish, an additional test can be added to adjust the final payment in those cases. That will be left as another do-it-yourself project.

The remaining calculations adjust the annual and final total accumulators. This illustrates how enumerated types can be used to clarify your source code. The **if** statement is used to see to it that yearly totals are accumulated only when the entire table is being printed or the selected year is being processed.

```
{ LN-PRNT.INC   Level 3 }

    procedure Calc_Detail_Line;
      var cents        : Real;

    begin
      current_month := Calc_Month;
      current_year := Calc_Year;
      interest_amt := (loan_balance * periodic_rate);
      cents := Frac(interest_amt);
      interest_amt := interest_amt - cents +
                    (Round(cents * 100.0) * 0.01);
      if ((loan_balance + interest_amt) < calc_pmt) then
        calc_pmt := (loan_balance + interest_amt);
      principle_amt := calc_pmt - interest_amt;
      loan_balance := loan_balance - principle_amt;
      final_total[Payments] := final_total[Payments] + calc_pmt;
      final_total[Principle] := final_total[Principle] + principle_amt;
      final_total[Interest] := final_total[Interest] + interest_amt;
      if (loan.select_yr = ZERO) or (loan.select_yr = current_year) then
        begin
          year_total[Payments]   := year_total[Payments] + calc_pmt;
          year_total[Principle] := year_total[Principle] + principle_amt;
          year_total[Interest]  := year_total[Interest] + interest_amt;
        end;
    end; { Calc_Detail_Line }
```

Print—Detail—Line

Print—Detail—Line outputs the values calculated by Calc—Detail—Line. The values are not output unless the year being processed equals the selected year or the selected year is zero. After a line is output, the line counter is incremented using the Succ function.

```
{ LN-PRNT.INC   Level 3 }

    procedure Print_Detail_Line;
      begin
        with loan do
        if (select_yr = 0) or (select_yr = current_year) then
          begin
{$I-}
            WriteLn((pmt_no + 1):3,month_id[current_month]:5,
                  current_year:5,loan_balance:11:2,final_total[Payments]:12:2,
                  principle_amt:12:2,interest_amt:12:2);
            io_status := IOresult;
            line_cnt := Succ(line_cnt);
          end;
{$I+}
        if (io_status <> ZERO) then
          Disp_IO_Error('Printer')
      end; { Print_Detail_Line }
```

Check—EndOfPage

As each line is printed Check—EndOfPage verifies that there is space on the screen or page for another line. When the screen or page is full, the New—Page procedure is called.

```
{ LN-PRNT.INC   Level 3 }

    procedure Check_EndOfPage;
      begin
        if line_cnt > max_line then
          begin
            if (loan.out_dev = VIDEO) then
              Continue_Prompt;
            New_Page(loan.out_dev);
          end;
      end; { Check_EndOfPage }
```

Check—EndOfYear

The Check—EndOfYear procedure prints the annual summary totals following the payment detail for each year. If the user has selected a specific year to be output, the totals will be for a calendar year. If the entire table is being output, totals will be shown after each loan year. The first if statement prevents annual totals from appearing for loans with only one payment per year.

The next **if** statement uses lower level functions to test the three conditions that determine when annual totals should be output. If any of the conditions are true, totals are printed or displayed.

```
{ LN-PRNT.INC  Level 3 }

    procedure Check_EndOfYear;
      var  next_year,
           next_month,
           current_month : Integer;

{ ***** Insert End_Loan_Year, End_Select_Year, End_Loan ***** }

{ ***** Insert Print_Annual_Totals ***** }

      begin { Check_EndOfYear }
        current_month := Calc_Month;
        month_offset := month_offset + offset_factor;
        next_month := Calc_Month;
        next_year := Calc_Year;
        if (loan.pmts_per_yr > 1) then
          if (End_Loan_Year or End_Select_Year) or End_Loan then
            Print_Annual_Totals;
      end; { Check_EndOfYear }
```

End—Loan—Year, End—Select—Year, and End—Loan

The relational test in End—Loan—Year will be TRUE if **month—offset** is divisible by 12 (based on integer division) and the month will change for the next payment. If you are unfamiliar with the **mod** operator, you will find that it is useful for tests such as this.

```
{ LN-PRNT.INC  Level 4 }

      function End_Loan_Year: Boolean;
        begin
          End_Loan_Year :=
            ((Round(month_offset) mod 12) = ZERO) and
            (next_month <> current_month);
        end; { End_Loan_Year }

      function End_Select_Year: Boolean;
        begin
          with loan do
            if (select_yr > ZERO) and (next_year = (select_yr + 1)) then
              begin
                End_Select_Year := TRUE;
                pmt_no := Trunc(no_of_pmts + 0.99);
              end
            else
              End_Select_Year := False;
        end; { End_Select_Year }

      function End_Loan: Boolean;
        begin
          End_Loan :=
            ((pmt_no + 1) = Trunc(loan.no_of_pmts + 0.99));
        end; { End_Pmts }
```

Print—Annual—Totals

Print—Annual—Totals outputs the values accumulated in the **year—total** array, formatted on a single line following a line header of **Total for Yr**. Note the use of a Write parameter with a SPACE to cause 11 spaces to be output. The **for—do** loop in this routine illustrates the use of enumerated type constants as loop limits. The two **if** statements are used to control the line spacing differences when output is directed to the printer.

```
{ LN-PRNT.INC   Level 4 }

    procedure Print_Annual_Totals;
      begin
        if (loan.out_dev = PRINTER) then
          WriteLn;
        Write('Total for Yr.',SPACE:11);
        for total_ptr := Payments to Interest do
          begin
            Write(year_total[total_ptr]:12:2);
            year_total[total_ptr] := 0.0;
          end;
        WriteLn; line_cnt := Succ(line_cnt);
        if (loan.out_dev = PRINTER) then
          begin
            WriteLn; line_cnt := line_cnt + 2;
          end;
      end; { Print_Annual_Totals }
```

Check—UserQuit

After each detail line is printed this routine is called to see whether the user has pressed the QUIT key. If so, the global **quit—flag** is set to TRUE, which will force an exit of the Print—Table routine.

```
{ LN-PRNT.INC }

    procedure Check_UsrQuit;
      begin
        if KeyPressed then
          begin
            Read(Kbd,inchr);
            if (inchr = QUIT) then
              user_quit := TRUE;
          end;
      end; { Check_Usr_Quit }
```

End—Table

If all payments have been output or the user presses the QUIT key, this routine will return TRUE. It also makes sure that there is room on the video screen for the final totals if the output is going there.

```
{ LN-PRNT.INC   Level 3 }

    function End_Table: Boolean;
      begin
        if (user_quit or (pmt_no >= Trunc(loan.no_of_pmts + 0.99))) then
          begin
            End_Table := TRUE;
            if (loan.out_dev = VIDEO) and (line_cnt > (max_line - 3)) then
              begin
                Continue_Prompt;
                New_Page(VIDEO);
              end;
          end
        else
          End_Table := FALSE;
      end; { End_Table }
```

Print—Final—Totals

The values accumulated in the **final—total** array are output by this routine unless the output is for a selected year, in which case not all the totals have been displayed by the Print—Annual—Totals procedure. Again, note the use of the constants from the Totals enumerated type.

That wraps up the LN-PRNT.INC include file. The code that you have entered in this file illustrates the power of modular design. You have completed a relatively complex operation involving several variable factors. Yet, as you review the code in each subprogram, you will find that in each case it represents a simple solution to a simple problem. The block structured nature of Pascal makes it ideal for breaking complex problems into a number of simple problems.

```
{ LN-PRNT.INC   Level 3 }

    procedure Print_Final_Totals;
      begin
        if (loan.select_yr = ZERO) then
          begin
            WriteLn;
            WriteLn('Loan Totals ',SPACE:12,final_total[Payments]:12:2,
                    final_total[Principle]:12:2,final_total[Interest]:12:2);
          end;
        if (loan.out_dev = PRINTER) then
          Write(TOF)
        else
          Continue_Prompt;
      end; { Print_Final_Totals }
```

Display—Help

The Display—Help procedure is used to display text on the video screen explaining a subject selected by the user. The subject selection is handled with the Select—Subject procedure described next. A **case** statement selects the parameters to be passed to Disp—Help, defined in the STD-DISP.INC file. As you entered the text for the help screens in Chapter 10, you were asked to note the line number for the start of each subject. Here those numbers are used to determine the parameters for the Disp—Help procedure.

```
{ LN-HELP.INC   Include file }

  procedure Display_Help;
     var    help_msg  : Str_80;
            action    : Char;

{ ***** Insert Select_Subject ***** }

     begin { Display_Help }
       Select_Subject;
       case action of
         ACCEPT  : Disp_Help(19,27);
         MODIFY  : Disp_Help(1,18);
         PRINT   : Disp_Help(28,36);
         QUIT    : esc_flag := FALSE;
       end {case}
     end; { Display_Help }
```

Select—Subject

Select—Subject is kept simple and easy to follow by using a number of the controlled input routines developed in Chapter 8. This demonstrates the value of creating and using such routines consistently. Without such conventions, it would certainly not be possible to code a help screen facility with only two simple procedures.

```
{ LN-HELP.INC   Level 2 }

  procedure Select_Subject;
     begin
       Clear_Prompts;
       help_msg := 'Accept  |  Modify  |  Print  | '
                 + QUIT_KEY + 'Exit';
       Display_Prompt(CMD_LINE,'HLP',help_msg);
       Display_Prompt(MSG_LINE,'INP'
                   ,'Press a HLP: key to select subject ==> ');
       action := Valid_Key([ACCEPT,MODIFY,PRINT,QUIT]);
     end; { Select_Subject }
```

Exit—Housekeeping

The main goal of the housekeeping routines is to be sure the loan file is properly closed, thus assuring that it is updated if any changes have been made. It also makes sure that the user is warned if an exit is attempted after the loan information has been modified but before it has been written to the disk file. The warning is handled by the lower level routine that follows.

Before closing the file, its size is determined using the FileSize function that is provided by Turbo Pascal. This is because it is possible that the user has created an empty file as follows:

1. A new file is created on entering the program.

2. Information is entered but not accepted or printed.

3. Exit is selected and the user elects to abandon modifications.

This might occur if the program were used to determine the payment amount or term of a loan. The resulting file will be empty but it will still exist and use space on the disk. That is why the exit routine should check for this condition and erase these empty files.

```
{ LN-EXIT.INC   Include file }

   procedure Exit_Housekeeping;
      var size : Integer;

{ ***** Insert Display_Exit_Warning ***** }

      begin { Exit_Housekeeping }
         io_status := ZERO;
         if modified then
            Display_Exit_Warning
         else
            esc_flag := TRUE;
         if esc_flag then
            begin
{$I+}
               size := FileSize(loan_file);        { Get size of file. }
               io_status := IOresult;
               if (io_status = ZERO) then
                  begin
                     Close(loan_file);             { Close the file. }
                     io_status := IOresult;
                     if (io_status = ZERO) then
                        if (size = ZERO) then       { If it was empty then }
                           Erase(loan_file);        { delete it from the disk }
                  end;
            end;
{$I+}
         if (io_status <> ZERO) then
            Disp_IO_Error(file_name);
         end; { Exit_Housekeeping }
```

Disp—Exit—Warning

This procedure gives the user an opportunity to return to the program if the QUIT key is pressed accidentally. The routines used here are very similar to those used in the Select—Subject procedure. You will find that this sequence occurs frequently in most interactive applications.

That completes the final include file. In the next chapter all the parts will be put together to create a working program.

```
{ LN-EXIT.INC   Level 2 }

  procedure Display_Exit_Warning;
    var   action   : Char;

  begin
    Clear_Prompts;
    Display_Prompt(CMD_LINE,'CMD',
                   '<Y> Abandon Changes | <N> Return to Input Screen');
    Display_Prompt(MSG_LINE,'INP',
                   'Do you want to abandon modifications? ( Y/N ) ==> ');
    action := Valid_Key(['Y','N']);
    if (action = 'Y') then
      esc_flag := TRUE
    else
      esc_flag := FALSE;
  end; { Display_Exit_Warning }
```

TWELVE

Assembling the Parts
And Program Documentation

In the previous chapter you created nine include files, containing a total of 44 subprograms, for the Loan Amortization program. Now it's time for the main program to create a file to call the include files. The main program should be saved with the name LOAN.PAS.

```
program Loan_Amortization;

{$I STD-CTV.INC    Standard constants, types and variables. }
{$I STD-UTIL.INC   Standard utility subprograms. }
{$I STD-INP.INC    Standard keyboard input subprograms. }
{$I STD-DISP.INC   Standard video display subprograms. }
{$I LN-CTV.INC     Loan constants, types & variables. }
{$I LN-INIT.INC    Initialization procedure. }
{$I LN-FILE.INC    Select Loan File. }
{$I LN-DISP.INC    Display current values from loan file. }
{$I LN-SLCT.INC    Select Accept | Modify | Print | Help | Quit. }
{$I LN-ACPT.INC    Accept current values and update disk file. }
{$I LN-MOD.INC     Modify loan record data. }
{$I LN-PRNT.INC    Print amortization table. }
{$I LN-HELP.INC    Select and display 'help' information. }
{$I LN-EXIT.INC    Do Exit housekeeping. }

begin { Loan_Amortization. }
  Initialize;                         { Do initial housekeeping.}
  while (not (err_flag or end_session)) do
    begin
      Select_Loan_File;
      if esc_flag then
        Verify_Exit;
      while (not (esc_flag or err_flag)) do
        begin
          Display_Current_Values;
          Select_Action;
          case action of
            ACCEPT : Accept_Data;
            MODIFY : Modify_Data(1,END_INP);
            PRINT  : begin
                       Accept_Data;
                       Print_Amortization;
                     end;
```

```
            QUIT    : Exit_Housekeeping;
            HELP    : Display_Help;
          end; {case}
        end; {while}
      end; {while}
    ClrScr; Write('Session Ended');
  end. { Loan_Amortization }
```

After you have entered the main program, you are ready to compile it using the .COM compiler option. The result will be stored in an executable file named LOAN.COM. Here is a quick review of the procedure:

1. From the main menu press O for compiler options.

2. Press C at the Compiler Options menu to select the .COM file option.

3. Press Q to return to the main menu.

4. Before beginning the compilation, press M and enter LOAN as the main program file. You will find this helpful any time you compile a program with include files.

5. Press C to start the compilation process.

6. If any errors are encountered during compilation, make corrections and recompile.

After a successful compilation, note the size of the program as indicated by the compiler statistics. This value will be compared with a modified version of the program later. You are now ready to test the program. Exit the Turbo system and execute the program by typing LOAN and pressing RETURN at the operating system command prompt. If you are using a CP/M-80 system, you can execute the program using the Execute option without leaving Turbo.

Testing the Program

When a program is large and complex, testing should be performed as each subprogram is developed. This is done by using a main program with stubs representing the top-level subprograms. The LOAN.PAS file created in Chapter 9 is an example of such a program. The stubs are replaced with working code in a sequence that makes it possible to compile and test run the main program. You will often save time and trouble by testing subprograms as they are developed rather than testing them when they are assembled into the main program.

In this example, your primary concern is to locate and eliminate errors that may have been introduced as you entered the source code from listings in the previous chapters. The range-checking compiler directive {$R+} is included in the main program to detect indexing errors. Once you are confident that the program is free of errors, you can recompile the program with range-checking disabled ({$R−}), which speeds up program execution.

There are many formal procedures for testing programs, but it is beyond the scope of this book to list them all. However, you should make a few test runs of the program and compare the results to an amortization schedule produced by a financial institution. If the comparison looks good, try testing the program by inputting extreme and erroneous loan data. Programs of this complexity are rarely if ever totally free of bugs for every possible combination of input values. If you suspect you have found a bug, please write the author in care of the publisher so that it can be eliminated from future editions.

Overlays for Loan Amortization

There are some modifications you can make to the loan program that will illustrate how Turbo Pascal can be used to create very large programs. You may recall that when a series of subprograms is declared as overlays, the object code for those routines is stored in a file separate from the main program code. When the main program is loaded into memory, space is reserved for the largest of the routines in the overlay file. As the program executes and an overlay subprogram is activated, its code is loaded from the overlay file into the reserved section of memory. The objective is to reduce the memory requirements of the program.

The loan program lends itself well to the use of overlays. The case statement in the main program will activate procedures Accept_Data, Modify_Data, Print_Amortization, Display_Help, or Exit_Housekeeping, depending upon the user's selection. (Notice that when the User selects the Print option, Accept_Data and Print_Amortization are called in sequence.) The loan program was designed so that each procedure could be defined in an include file. In order to combine the object code for these routines into an overlay file, here's all you have to do:

1. Load an include file into the Turbo editor.

2. Insert the reserved word **overlay** in front of the first procedure header in each file. For example, the first line in the LN-ACPT.INC file would be **overlay procedure** Accept_Data;

3. Exit the editor and save the modified file.

4. Repeat the process for the files LN-ACPT.INC, LN-MOD.INC, LN-PRNT.INC, LN-HELP.INC, and LN-EXIT.INC.

After the modifications are made, recompile the main program, LOAN. PAS, as a .COM file. Note the code size when the compilation is complete. You will see that 3500 to 3800 fewer bytes are consumed for the object code when overlays are used. The savings will vary depending on the system you are using. Since you can have multiple overlay areas in a program and an overlay procedure may itself define a series of overlay procedures, you can see that a very large program can be packed into a relatively small amount of storage.

To see the price you pay for saving space, exit Turbo and run the program. The program functions just as before, except for a brief pause while the program reads the overlay file from each disk when you select one of the five options. Notice that except for the Print selection, the other selections can be repeated consecutively without causing the disk drive to activate. Can you figure out why? (Hint: the overlay is not loaded if it is already resident in the overlay area.)

Chain Programs for Loan Amortization

Before modifying the Loan Amortization program for chain programs, go back and remove the overlay directives. Since implementing chain programs requires more extensive changes than overlays, you may want to make a copy of LOAN.PAS and LN-PRNT.INC.

The loan program is not as well suited for chain programs as it is for overlays. Chaining usually works better for large systems composed of related programs that function independently except for sharing data. In fact, when you convert a subprogram to a chain program, it is compiled as a separate program. The following listing shows the changes to make LN-PRNT.INC a chained program.

```
program Print_Amortization    { Change header from procedure to program }

{$I STD-CTV.INC}              { Add these include directives }
{$I STD-UTIL.INC}            { following the header. }
{$I STD-INP.INC}
{$I STD-DISP.INC}
{$I LN-CTV.INC}

    exec_file : File;          { Add to variable declaration part. }
  begin { Print_Amortization }
    if Ready_To_Print then
      begin
        Init_Variables;
        Init_Output_Device;
        Print_Table;
      end;
    Assign(exec_file,'LOAN.COM');  { Add this line. }
    Execute(exec_file);            { Add this line. }
  end. { Print_Amortization }      { Change semicolon to period following end.}
```

When a chained program shares data with another program, the shared variables must have identical declarations and must be declared in the same sequence. Do this by using the same include files for the definitions and declarations. The routines in this program also rely on some of the routines in the STD-UTIL.INC, STD-INP.INC, and STD-DISP.INC files, so they are also included using include directives. Finally, the Assign and Execute statements at the end of LN-PRNT.INC cause it to execute the LOAN.COM program file.

After the changes are made, compile the program using the .CHN compiler option. The procedure is the same as that for creating a .COM file with two exceptions.

1. Select H for .CHN from the compiler Options menu instead of C for .COM.

2. The main program should be renamed LN-PRNT.INC rather than LOAN.PAS.

When the compilation is complete, you must make note of the size of both the code and data areas. This information will be needed when the main loan program is recompiled.

The following listing shows the changes you must make to the LOAN.PAS file so that it will chain to the LN-PRNT.CHN program:

```
program Loan_Amortization;

{$I STD-CTV.INC    Standard constants, types and variables. }
{$I STD-UTIL.INC   Standard utility subprograms. }
{$I STD-INP.INC    Standard keyboard input subprograms. }
{$I STD-DISP.INC   Standard video display subprograms. }
{$I LN-CTV.INC     Loan constants, types & variables. }
{$I LN-INIT.INC    Initialization procedure. }
{$I LN-FILE.INC    Select Loan File. }
{$I LN-DISP.INC    Display current values from loan file. }
{$I LN-SLCT.INC    Select Accept | Modify | Print | Help | Quit. }
{$I LN-ACPT.INC    Accept current values and update disk file. }
{$I LN-MOD.INC     Modify loan record data. }
(* {$I LN-PRNT.INC   Print amortization table. } THIS LINE COMMENTED OUT *)
{$I LN-HELP.INC    Select and display 'help' information. }
{$I LN-EXIT.INC    Do Exit housekeeping. }

procedure Print_Amortization;                  { Add this procedure. }
  var chain_file : File;

  begin
    Assign(chain_file,'LN-PRNT.CHN');
    Chain(chain_file);
  end; { Print_Amortization }
```

Note that the Print—Amortization subprogram has been redefined to execute the LN-PRNT.CHN file. Be sure to delete or make into a comment the LN-PRNT.INC include directive. After the changes have been made, you should again compile LOAN.PAS into a .COM file. If you are using an MS-

DOS or CP/M-86 version of Turbo, there are two additional steps that are required when compiling .CHN programs. After you have pressed C to select the .COM compiler Options menu, you should

1. Indicate the minimum code segment size by pressing O for code and entering the code size (in paragraphs) as noted when the chain program was compiled. If you are compiling a .COM program that will chain to more than one chain program, the size you enter should be equal to or greater than the largest chain program.

2. Indicate the minimum data segment size by pressing D for data and entering the data size (in paragraphs) as noted when the chain program was compiled. As before, if the .COM program will chain to more than one chain program, the size you enter should be equal to or greater than the largest chain program.

CP/M-80 users need not be concerned with this unless either the start or the end address of the chain program has been altered. If these addresses are changed, the same changes must be made when the .COM file is created.

After changing the source code and compiling the LN-PRNT.CHN and LOAN.COM files, enter into DOS and test the loan program. This time the program experiences a slight pause when the Print selection is made. If you are using an MS-DOS or CP/M-86 version of Turbo prior to version 3.0, you will also notice that the screen clears even when the output is directed to the printer. In the earlier versions of Turbo the ClrScr procedure is executed whether you want it to or not when a new program is executed. This was changed in version 3.0.

Another difference becomes apparent when the output is complete and control is returned to the LOAN.COM file. Unlike the original program or the overlay version, you start from the beginning of the program when the output is finished. As was mentioned earlier, the design of the loan program is not conducive to the use of chaining. However, this does not mean that chaining is not a useful concept. For very large systems, chaining or a combination of chaining and overlays will often prove to be the best way to implement the system.

Documenting the Program

Because microcomputer software documentation is so widely maligned, it might be a good idea to review the requirements for good documentation. There are two types of documentation: *system documentation*, which covers the design and implementation of the program, and *user documentation*, which covers the operation of the program. User documentation for the loan program will be discussed rather than system documentation.

In general you program should be documented both on-line, a method using help screens and user prompts to assist the user while running the program, and in writing. Obviously, on-line documentation must be designed into the program. As the loan program is a relatively simple application, the help screens are not context-sensitive. A program with context-sensitive help screens allows the user to interrupt a program by pressing a designated key at virtually any point for help. For example, if the loan program had context-sensitive help screens and the user pressed the designated HELP key at the payment prompt, a help screen such as the one shown in Figure 12-1 would appear. Similar information would be available any time the user is prompted to make an entry.

The manual that you provide to users of your programs may serve as a tutorial and a reference guide, or both, depending on the nature of the program. The following guidelines may help you determine what sections to include in your manual, if you intend to distribute the program commercially.

If you want the payment amount to be calculated, enter 0 in this field.

If you enter a payment amount, the amount should be the amount due each payment period. The payment period is determined by the payments per year specified in the next field. For example, if you specify 12 payments per year, the payment amount should indicate the monthly payment due.

When a payment amount is specified, the total number of payments will be calculated by the program and the number of payments field will be skipped.

```
        Principal....:  4000.00      Interest
                                     Rate......:  8.000 %
        Payment Amt..: _____     Payments Per Year..:  12
        1st Pmt Due..:  04/1986      Number of Payments.:  24.00
        Selected Year:  0            Output to Vid/Print:  V

     <Enter>:  180.91
   MSG: Enter payment amount or 0.00 to calculate payment amount.
   CMD: ^E  Prev Fld  |  <Tab>  Clear Fld  |  <Esc>  Exit
```

Figure 12-1. Example of a context-sensitive help screen

- Installation section
- Overview section
- Tutorial section
- Reference section
- Index.

The Installation Section

The purpose of the installation section is to explain to the user that a working system disk is needed and also how to create it. With the proliferation of hard disk systems you may need to include a discussion of how to transfer the required files to a hard disk.

The installation section for the loan program should instruct the user to create a system disk—one which holds the operating system and the loan program—by copying LOAN.COM, LOAN.SCR, and LN-HELP.SCR from the distribution disk.

Hard disk users should be instructed to copy these three files to the same directory or user area on their hard disk. The amount of detail in the Installation section depends on whether the program is intended for a specific system or if it will be running on a variety of computers. If your program will run only under PC-DOS on an IBM PC with one floppy disk drive, the instructions can be very specific. On the other hand, since the loan program must run on a wide variety of systems, the installation instructions will have to cover installation for all systems. You might refer users to the DOS documentation for details on specific DOS commands like copying files.

The Overview Section

A good manual should include a short, accessible section outlining the essentials of the program. The first thing the overview should do is direct the user to the installation section. That will reduce the number of phone calls you get from users wondering why they got an error when they tried to start up the computer using just the distribution disk. Next, briefly outline the objectives of the program and explain how to get started, and then Review the operation of the program, including the data input menu routine.

The Tutorial Section

Most successful tutorials assume that the user is inexperienced with the computer and the subject matter. There are exceptions, of course. You may feel safe in assuming that the user of a quantum physics theorem program has an understanding of the subject; however, it would be unwise to assume that all users of the loan program understand the financial terminology.

A tour of the operation is usually an effective way to help the user feel comfortable with the program. This can be a step-by-step description, based on a specific example, demonstrating how the program is used. Here again the nature of the program may dictate a better way of getting the user up to speed, but a step-by-step example is often effective.

The Reference Section

If your program uses a lot of commands or has a complicated operating procedure, you should include a reference section. The commands should be organized so that a user who needs a refresher can find the information quickly. You may review each command in alphabetical order or group them based on function.

The Index

All but the most trivial manuals should be indexed. This makes the documentation much more usable as a reference guide. You may find that if you are going to be doing a lot of indexing, a program that assists in the process will be helpful.

APPENDIX A

Some Optional Turbo Tools

Borland International packages software tools that enhance the power of Turbo Pascal. These packages fall into two categories. The first is a source code library of ready-to-use subprograms that solve general programming problems, such as sorting and file access, and that add graphics or serial communications capabilities to Turbo. The other category of Turbo tools is utility programs that add new functions to the Turbo environment. These include programs such as Borlands Sidekick and SuperKey as well as similar products from other vendors. The following information will provide specific examples of some of the available source code libraries and utility programs.

Turbo Toolbox

Borland's Turbo Toolbox offers two source code libraries and one utility program. The source code libraries provide an indexed file access method and a general-purpose sort procedure. The utility program is used to generate terminal installation programs that are in turn used to install your Turbo Pascal programs for use with a particular terminal.

Turbo ISAM

Business applications often must control data files containing thousands of records stored on disk. A program that handles thousands of files for an accounts receivable program or a hundred patient files for a medical office system must be able to access the information in a specific record quickly to be useful.

ISAM, for *indexed sequential access method*, retrieves selected records stored in a data file. When ISAM searches a file, the sequence of the records is not important since it uses an index to locate and retrieve a record. For example, a customer file might have one index based on account numbers and another based on customer names. The last name and the first name in the customer name index would be the key information, with duplicate entries allowed, while the account number would be the key information in a customer account index without duplicates. The keys, while based on information in the data file, do not have to match that information in terms of type or format. For example, a key could be composed of the first six characters of a last name or the last four digits in an account number. This gives you a great deal of flexibility in creating keys.

Turbo ISAM is an enhanced version of the ISAM concept because it uses a sophisticated data structure called a *B+ tree* to store and maintain key information in the index files. Because of this, a single record can be located from a file of over 32,000 records in less than two seconds on most systems. Because the details and complexities of the access method are hidden in the lower levels of the ISAM include files, you can take advantage of this performance even if you've never heard of a B+ tree. On the other hand, if you are curious, you can poke about in the source code to learn more about this advanced data structure.

Files in the Turbo ISAM routines are effectively limited to 32,767 records. Although the manual indicates that 64,000 records may be stored in a data file, the index files may not reference more than 32,767 records.

Each fixed-length record in the file being indexed must be at least 8 and no more than 65,535 bytes long. The keys stored in index files may be from 1 through 255 bytes long and must be stored as string type data items.

Turbo Quicksort

The Turbo Toolbox also includes a library of routines that will sort up to 32,767 data items using the *quicksort* method. Turbo's Quicksort may be viewed as a magical black box. Unsorted data items of any type along with instructions for sorting and formatting are poured into the box, sorted, and then poured out. Before you can use the quicksort routine you must write three routines that input the items to be sorted, compare two items, indicating the sequence, and output the sorted items to a file or device formatted, as you wish.

Like any general-purpose routine, you will find that Turbo QuickSort is somewhat slower than a routine you might write to sort specific type data items under specific circumstances. However, for most purposes its performance is more than adequate.

Terminal Installation Utility

Unlike Turbo ISAM and Turbo Quicksort, the Terminal Installation utility is not a source code library. It is a pre-compiled utility program that creates a program similar to the TINST.COM program that you used to install Turbo Pascal on your system. Its primary value is for software developers who are writing programs for CP/M systems or MS-DOS systems that are not IBM PC compatible. Its purpose is to allow users of your program to indicate what type of terminal they are using with their system. The result is that your program can take advantage of such terminal features as character highlighting. It is not of much value for IBM PC users, since the available screen modes can be controlled by the program itself when you use the IBM PC version of the Turbo compiler.

Operation of the utility is very simple. Using a copy of your Turbo Toolbox disk, enter GINST to run the program. You will be asked to enter the name of your program and the name you want to use for the installation program. Using the loan program as an example, you could enter LOAN as the program name and LINST as the installation name. After a few seconds of disk activity you will be advised that your installation program is complete. When you exit to DOS, a review of the file directory shows that LINST.COM, LINST.MSG, and LINST.DTA have been created. To use these files, copy them to a disk containing the LOAN.COM file. To run the installation program, enter LINST. When the screen appears, it will offer the choice of quitting or selecting a screen. When you press S, a list of supported terminals appears, just as when you installed Turbo itself. The procedure is exactly as described in the Turbo reference manual. In fact Borland even gives permission for you to copy or paraphrase that part of their manual to provide documentation for users of your program.

Sidekick

Borland International's Sidekick (for IBM PCs and compatibles only) is sold as a desktop organizer. Its purpose is to allow the user to have access to a number of useful programs, even as another program is being used. The functions provided by Sidekick are

- A notepad
- A calculator
- A table of ASCII codes and their video representation
- A telephone dialer
- An appointment calendar.

The first three items are what makes Sidekick very valuable as a programmer's utility; each will be examined in more detail.

The Notepad

When working on a complex project, you often need to take a quick look at another file. For example, assume you are working on an include file and you need to check the global variables declared in a different include file. Sidekick's notepad feature makes this possible without leaving the file you are editing.

Pressing ALT-CTRL takes you from your program into Sidekick in an instant. Once there you can load and edit files using the notepad. The notepad editor is virtually identical to the Turbo editor including a few added features. You can print blocks of code, sort any or all of the lines in the notepad, and even import text from another file. This last feature is handy when it's time to write the documentation. As you run the program, you can flip back and forth between the program and the notepad containing the documentation. If you want to include all or part of an input screen in the documentation, just press the F4 key, which specifies the import function, and the notepad disappears so you can mark any part of the screen text to be transferred.

The notepad also comes in handy when you are using input screen files, like those in the Loan Amortization program. If you are testing an input program and decide to change the screen layout, you can load it into the notepad and make the modifications immediately.

The Calculator

Sidekick's calculator function does all of the things you would expect a four-function pocket calculator to do. Results are accurate to 18 places, and four decimal places are always displayed. What makes this calculator especially useful for programmers is that you can choose a number base of 2, 10, or 16 with a single keystroke, thus selecting binary, decimal, or hexadecimal representations of the values being calculated. For example, you can enter 155 in decimal and press H, causing the value to be displayed in hexadecimal as 9B; pressing B will cause the value to be displayed in binary 10011011.

Another feature of the calculator assigns the results of the calculator to any key. For example, suppose you need to calculate a value for a document you are creating in the notepad editor. At any time while you are using the notepad, a single key combination, ALT-C, will cause the calculator to appear instantly. After you have made the calculation, press P followed by any other key (preferably an unused function key or an ALT key combination), and the result will be assigned to that key combination. Then press ESC and the calculator will disappear, leaving you at your previous position in the notepad. From then on, pressing the key associated with the result will cause that value to appear as if you had typed it.

The ASCII Table

Just about every programmer keeps a copy of the ASCII codes handy for quick reference. However, when you need a copy, it's almost always lost. If you've got Sidekick, an extended ASCII table is never more than a couple of keystrokes away. The table includes the special characters and line-drawing sets for the IBM PC, using the non-standard codes 128-255. For codes greater than 31, the decimal code, the hexadecimal code, and the character representation are displayed in groups of 32 codes. Codes less than 32, known as *control codes*, are displayed in two groups of 16, showing the control code (^G, ^M) and the ASCII mnemonic (BEL, CR) in addition to the other information. The UP ARROW and DOWN ARROW keys allow you to scan the groups.

Superkey

Programming naturally involves a lot of time at the keyboard. Superkey is another Borland International product that helps make your time at the keyboard more productive. It is a utility program that, among other things, allows you to convert a single keystroke into a series of keystrokes. A simple example would be to assign the various Pascal reserve words—such as **for**, **while**, and **begin** and **end**—to a series of control keys. From then on you could press a function key to cause a **begin-end** pair to appear with **begin** and **end** vertically aligned and the cursor below the "g" in **begin** on an intervening blank line. You have replaced 16 keystrokes with one.

Superkey also has facilities for file encryption, display protection (after a specified time period the screen goes blank if there is no activity), and keyboard input control. All in all most programmers who use IBM PC or compatible systems should find Superkey a worthwhile addition to their tool kit.

APPENDIX B

Turbo Quick Reference

This section contains eighteen tables outlining Turbo Pascal's predefined types, subprograms, identifiers, and symbols. With the exception of Table B-8, each table contains three or more columns of information identified as follows:

Identifier   This column will list the Pascal identifier or symbol.

Procedure/ Function   If the identifier is a subprogram, the Procedure/Function column will indicate whether it is a procedure or a function.

Standard   This column will indicate whether the identifier is defined in standard Pascal. If so, the letter Y will appear; otherwise N indicates that it is a Turbo Pascal feature. An asterisk (∗) indicates that the identifier is a reserved word. A plus (+) sign indicates that Turbo Pascal offers an enhanced version over standard Pascal, and a minus (−) indicates a restricted version.

System   This column indicates which versions of Turbo Pascal support the identifier. The following abbreviations are used:

All	Available in all versions.
C-80	Available only in CP/M-80 versions.
C-86	Available only in CP/M-86 versions.
MS	Available only in MS-DOS versions (including PC-DOS).
16	Available in MS-DOS and CP/M-86 versions.
None	A standard Pascal feature not used in Turbo Pascal.

If 3+ follows the system abbreviation, the identifier is available only in version 3.0 or later.

Description   This column contains a brief description of the identifier.

The format of Table B-8 for write parameters is an exception; its column headings and notes should make its meaning clear.

Tables B-10 through B-18 describe predefined subprograms. If the subprogram requires parameters, a generic parameter list will follow the identifier. The following variable identifiers are used in these parameter lists to represent actual parameters:

```
any    : Any_Typ; {can be of any type}
byt    : Byte;
bool   : Boolean;
chr1   : Char;
fil    : file of Any_Typ; {except file of File_Typ}
fp     : Real;
int1   : Integer;
pntr   : ^Any_Typ; {pointer variable of any type}
scalar : Scalar_Typ;
str1   : Any_String;
txt    : Text;
```

In these above declarations, Any_Typ represents any type, Scalar_Typ represents any scalar type, Any_String represents any string type, and File_Typ represents any file of Text type. Where more than one variable of the same type is required, ascending numbers are used to make each one unique. For example, *int1*, *int2*, and *int3* would be Integer types.

A parameter surrounded by the left and right bracket ([and]) is optional, the vertical bar (|) between two parameters means either parameter, but not both, is acceptable, and any variable followed by an elipse may be repeated.

Table B-1.   Block Component Identifiers

Identifier	Standard	System	Description
program	Yes*	All	Marks start of program block (optional)
label	Yes*	All	Marks start of label declarations
const	Yes*	All	Marks start of constant definitions
type	Yes*	All	Marks start of type definitions
var	Yes*	All	Marks start of variable declarations
procedure	Yes*	All	Marks start of a procedure definition
function	Yes*	All	Marks start of a function definition
begin-end	Yes*	All	Marks the statement part of a program or subprograms. (See Table B-6 for another usage)

Table B-2.   Predefined Constants

Identifier	Standard	System	Description
MAXINT	Yes	All	Represents the integer value 32767
NIL	Yes*	All	Pointer type value that points to nothing
PI	No	All	Contains the real value 3.1415926536 for Pi
Numbers and Letters	Yes+	All	All literal constants for Integer, Real, and Char types
TRUE and FALSE	Yes	All	Literal constants for Boolean type

Table B-3. Predefined Types

Identifier	Standard	System	Description
Boolean	Yes	All	Composed of FALSE and TRUE
Byte	No	All	Composed of integers from 0 to 255
Char	Yes+	All	Composed of ASCII characters, plus character set defined from #128 to #255
Integer	Yes	All	Composed of integers from −32768 to 32767
Real	Yes	All	Composed of real values from 1E−38 to 1E+38
Text	Yes+	All	External file of Char type structure
Text[*nn*]	No	16 3+	Same as Text, with buffer size specified by *nn* number of 128-byte blocks

Table B-4. Type Definitions Statements

Identifier	Standard	System	Description
array of	Yes*	All	Used to define array type structures
file of	Yes*	All	Used to define file type structures
packed	Yes*	None	Not used in Turbo Pascal
record-end	Yes*	All	Used to define record type structures
set of	Yes*	All	Used to define set type structures
string	No*	All	Used to define string type structures

Table B-5.   Predeclared Variables

Identifier	Standard	System	Description
			Text File Variables
			(assignment may vary depending upon system)
Aux	No	All	Assigned to a serial communication device
Con	No	All	Assigned to system console I/O devices
Input	Yes	All	Assigned to standard input device
Kbd	No	All	Assigned to system console input device
Lst	No	All	Assigned to the system printer
Output	Yes	All	Assigned to standard output device
Trm	No	All	Assigned to system console I/O device
Usr	No	All	Available for user assignment
			I/O Driver Vector Address Variables
			16-bit addresses on 8-bit systems; 32-bit addresses on 16-bit systems
AuxInPtr	No	All	Points to Aux input procedure
AuxOutPtr	No	All	Points to Aux output procedure
ConInPtr	No	All	Points to Con input procedure
ConOutPtr	No	All	Points to Con output procedure
ConStPtr	No	All	Points to Con status function
ConLstPtr	No	All	Points to Lst output procedure
UsrInPtr	No	All	Points to Usr input procedure
UsrOutPtr	No	All	Points to Usr output procedure
			Memory and Port Array Variables
Mem[ ]	No	All	Array of Byte; overlays all of memory
MemW[ ]	No	16	Array of Word; overlays all of memory
Port[ ]	No	All	Array of Byte; overlays all I/O ports
PortW[ ]	No	16	Array of Word; overlays all I/O ports

Note: Byte arrays must be indexed by integer values. Word arrays must be indexed by *segment:offset* values.

			System Level Variables
BufLen	No	All	Maximum characters accepted by the Read procedure
HeapPtr	No	All	Address of top of heap
RecurPtr	No	All	Address of top of recursion stack
StackPtr	No	All	Address of top of stack

Note: Address on 8-bit systems are integer values. Addresses on 16-bit systems are *segment:offset* values.

Table B-6.   Control Statements

Identifier	Standard	System	Description
begin-end	Yes*	All	Marks a compound statement (See Table B-1)
case of-else	Yes*+	All	Multi-way branch, **else** is optional
exit	No	All 3+	Forces immediate return to calling routine
for-do	Yes*	All	Predetermined loop with test at top
goto	Yes*−	All	Transfers control to a labeled statement
if-then-else	Yes*	All	Two way branch, **else** is optional
repeat-until	Yes*	All	Conditional loop with test at bottom
while-do	Yes*	All	Conditional loop with test at top
with-do	Yes*	All	Permits access of field identifiers for a record without having to specify the record identifier

Table B-7.   Operators

Identifier	Standard	System	Description
Boolean and Arithmetic Operators			
− {unary minus}	Yes	All	Reverse sign of Real or Integer type operand
not	Yes+	All	Boolean or Integer type logical **not**
*	Yes	All	Integer or Real type number multiplication
/	Yes	All	Real type number division
div	Yes	All	Integer type division
mod	Yes	All	Modulus operation; result is remainder after integer division
and	Yes+	All	Boolean and Integer type logical **and**
shl	No	All	Bitwise Integer shift left
shr	No	All	Bitwise Integer shift right
+	Yes	All	Integer or Real number addition
−	Yes	All	Integer or Real number subtraction
or	Yes+	All	Boolean and Integer logical **or**
xor	No	All	Boolean and Integer logical exclusive **or**

continued

Table B-7. Operators (*continued*)

Identifier	Standard	System	Description
		Relational Operators	
val1 = *val2*	Yes	All	TRUE if values are equal
val1 <> *val2*	Yes	All	TRUE if values are not equal
val1 < *val2*	Yes	All	TRUE if *val1* less than *val2*
val1 <= *val2*	Yes	All	TRUE if *val1* less than or equal to *val2*
val1 > *val2*	Yes	All	TRUE if *val1* greater than *val2*
val1 >= *val2*	Yes	All	TRUE if *val1* greater than or equal to *val2*

Note: Val1 and *val2* must be compatible types.

Identifier	Standard	System	Description
		Set Operators	
set1 * *set2*	Yes	All	Set intersection; result contains members common to both sets
set1 + *set2*	Yes	All	Set union; result contains all members from both sets
set1 − *set2*	Yes	All	Set difference; result contains members from *set1* that are not in *set2*
set1 = *set2*	Yes	All	Set equality − TRUE if sets are identical
set1 <> *set2*	Yes	All	Set inequality − TRUE if sets are not identical
set1 <= *set2*	Yes	All	TRUE if *set1* is a subset of *set2*
set1 >= *set2*	Yes	All	TRUE if *set2* is a subset of *set1*
set1 in *set2*	Yes	All	Same as <= except that *set1* may be a single data item of the base set type

Note: The base type of *set1* and *set2* must be compatible.

Table B-8.   Write Parameters

Data Type	Parameter	Example	Output
Boolean	None	Write('*',TRUE,'*');	*TRUE*
Boolean	:n	Write('*',TRUE:6,'*');	* TRUE*
Char	None	Write('*','A','*');	*A*
Char	:n	Write('*','A':3,'*');	* A*
Integer	None	Write('*',99,'*');	*99*
Integer	:n	Write('*',99:5,'*');	* 99*
Real	None	Write('*',33.6,'*');	* 3.3600000000E+01*
Real	:n	Write('*',33.6:10,'*');	* 3.36E+01*
Real	:n:m	Write('*',33.6:6:2,'*');	* 33.60*
String	None	Write('*','Turbo','*');	*Turbo*
String	:n	Write('*','Turbo':7,'*');	* Turbo*

Note: n represents an integer expression with a value of 0 to 255. m represents an integer expression with a value of 0 to 24.

Table B-9.   Special Symbols

Identifier	Standard	System	Description
#	No	All	Precedes an integer between 0 and 255 representing an ASCII or special character
$	No	All	Precedes a hexadecimal value
'	Yes	All	The apostrophe (single quote) delimits string and character constants
( )	Yes+	All	Encloses subprogram parameters, enumerated type definitions, field declarations for variant record type definitions, value assignments to structured, typed constants, and modifies precedence of operators
,	Yes	All	The comma separates identifiers in a number of contexts
.	Yes	All	The period marks the end of the main program
..	Yes	All	Double periods indicate a subrange of values

(continued)

Table B-9.   Special Symbols (*continued*)

Identifier	Standard	System	Description
:	Yes	All	Precedes the type identifier in variable declarations, parameter lists, and function definitions
:=	Yes	All	The assignment statement
;	Yes	All	Separates statements and terminates declarations, definitions, and headers
=	Yes+	All	Binds type and constant definitions to respective identifiers (See Operators for other usages.)
[ ] or (. .)	Yes+	All	Delimits set type constant identifiers, as **chr1** in ['0'..'9','−','.'] or indicates a reference to an array element
∧	Yes+	All	Defines and identifies pointer type data items and precedes the characters 'A' to 'Z', [, \,], ∧ or __ to indicate a control character
{ } or (* *)	Yes+	All	Encloses a comment

Table B-10.   Video and Keyboard Subprograms

Identifier (parameters)	Procedure/ Function	Standard	System	Description
ClrEol	P	No	All	Clear from cursor to end of line
ClrScr	P	No	All	Clear video screen and home cursor
CrtExit	P	No	All	Output terminal reset string
CrtInit	P	No	All	Output terminal initialization string
DelLine	P	No	All	Delete line at cursor position
GoToXY (*int1,int2*)	P	No	All	Position cursor at column *int1*, row *int2*
HighVideo	P	No	All	Subsequent output in high intensity

(continued)

Table B-10. Video and Keyboard Subprograms (*continued*)

Identifier (parameters)	Procedure/ Function	Standard	System	Description
InsLine	P	No	All	Insert line at cursor position
IOresult	F	No	All	Returns I/O status for error trapping
KeyPressed	F	No	All	TRUE if character waiting in Kbd buffer
LowVideo	P	No	All	Subsequent output in low intensity
NormVideo	P	No	All	Same as HighVideo
Page	P	Yes	None	Not included in Turbo Pascal

Table B-11. External Device and File I/O Subprograms

Identifier	Procedure/ Function	Standard	System	Description
Append(*txt*)	P	No	MS 3+	Open an exiting Text file, positioning the file pointer at the end of the file
Assign (*fil,str1*)	P	No	All	Associate file name in *str1* with *fil*
BlockRead (*fil,any,int1, [int2...]*)	P	No	All	Untyped transfer from disk to memory
BlockWrite (*fil,any,int1, [int2...]*)	P	No	All	Untyped transfer from memory to disk
Chain(*chn1*)	P	No	All	Load and execute a Turbo .CHN file
Close(*fil*)	P	No	All	Close external file
Eof(*fil*)	F	Yes	All	TRUE if file pointer at end of file
EoLn(*txt*)	F	Yes	All	TRUE if Text file at end of line
Erase(*fil*)	P	No	All	Remove file from directory
Execute(*fil*)	P	No	All	Load and execute a .COM file
FilePos(*fil*)	F	No	All	Returns position of file pointer — not valid for Text files

(continued)

Table B-11. External Device and File I/O Subprograms (*continued*)

Identifier	Procedure/ Function	Standard	System	Description
FileSize(*fil*)	F	No	All	Returns size of non-Text file—not valid for Text files
Flush(*fil*)	P	No	All	Forces sector buffer out to disk—not valid for Text files
Get	P	Yes	None	Low level input—not used in Turbo
LongFilePos (*fil*)	F	No	MS	Returns file pointer positions larger than 32K—not valid for Text files
LongFileSize (*fil*)	F	No	MS	Returns non-Text file size larger than 32K—not valid for Text files
LongSeek (*fil,fp*)	P	No	MS	Positions file pointer in files larger than 32K—not valid for Text files
Put	P	Yes	None	Low level output—not used in Turbo
Read*[fil]*, any₁[any₂...]	P	Yes	All	Input data from external disk file
ReadLn(*[txt]*, str1,[str2...])	P	Yes+	All	Input data from Text file or device
Rename(*fil*)	P	No	All	Rename disk file
Reset(*fil*)	P	Yes	All	Open existing external disk file
Rewrite(*fil*)	P	Yes	All	Create and open new disk file
Seek(*fil,int1*)	P	No	All	Position file pointer in non-Text file—not valid for Text files
SeekEof(*fil*)	P	No	All 3+	Skips tabs and blanks before Eof test
SeekEoln(*txt*)	P	No	All 3+	Skips tabs and blanks before Eoln test
Truncate(*fil*)	P	No	MS 3+	Truncate file at the record indicated by the current file pointer value
Write(*[fil]*,str1, [str2...])	P	Yes	All	Output data to external disk file
WriteLn (*[txt]*,str1, [str2...])	P	Yes	All	Output data to Text file or device

Table B-12. String-Handling Subprograms

Identifier	Procedure/ Function	Standard	System	Description
Concat (*str1,str2 [,str3...]*)	F	No	All	Concatenate two or more string parameters
Copy(*str1,int1, int2*)	F	No	All	Extract *int2* characters from *str1* starting at position *int1*
Insert(*str1, str2,int1*)	P	No	All	Insert *str1* into *str2* at position *int1*
Length(*str1*)	F	No	All	Returns current length of *str1*
Pos(*str1,str2*)	F	No	All	Returns position of *str1* in *str2*
UpCase(*chr1*)	F	No	All	Returns uppercase of *chr1*, if it is in the range 'a'..'z'
Str(*int1, str1*)	P	No	All	Convert Integer or Real value of *int1* or *fp* to a string returned in *str1*
Val(*str1,int1, int2*)	P	No	All	Convert *str1* to a numeric value returned in *int1* or *fp*. Status is returned in *int2*

Table B-13. Memory Manipulation Subprograms

Identifier	Procedure/ Function	Standard	System	Description
		Memory Allocation		
Dispose(*pntr*)	P	Yes	All	Free memory allocated to *pntr*
FreeMem (*pntr,int1*)	P	No	All	Free *int1* bytes starting at *pntr*
GetMem (*pntr,int1*)	P	No	All	Allocate *int1* bytes starting at *pntr*
Mark(*pntr*)	P	No	All	Save top-of-heap address in *pntr*
MaxAvail	F	No	All	Returns largest contiguous space on heap
MemAvail	F	No	All	Returns total space remaining on the heap
New(*pntr*)	P	Yes	All	Allocates space based type of *pntr*
Pack	P	Yes	None	Not used in Turbo Pascal
Ptr(*int1*)	F	No	C-80	Returns a pointer value based on *int1*
Ptr(*int1,int2*)	F	No	16	Returns a pointer value. *int1* is the segment address, *int2* is the offset address
Release(*pntr*)	P	No	All	Restore top of heap to address in *pntr*
		Memory Manipulation		
Addr(*any*)	F	No	C-80	Returns the address of *any* variable or entry address for a subprogram
Addr(*any*)	F	No	16	Returns the address of *any* variable
Cseg	F	No	16	Returns code segment base address
Dseg	F	No	16	Returns data segment base address

(continued)

Table B-13.   Memory Manipulation Subprograms (*continued*)

Identifier	Procedure/ Function	Standard	System	Description
		Memory Allocation		
FillChar (*memloc*, *int1*,*chr1*)	P	No	All	Fills *int1* bytes of memory starting at the address of *memloc* with *chr1* or *byte*
Hi(*int1*)	F	No	All	Returns value of high-order byte of *int1*
Lo(*int1*)	F	No	All	Returns value of low-order byte of *int1*
Move (*memloc1*, *memloc2*, *int1*)	P	No	All	Move block of *int1* bytes from the address of *memloc1* to the address of *memloc2*
Ofs(*any*)	F	No	16	Returns offset address of *any*, which may be a variable or subprogram identifier
Seg(*any*)	F	No	16	Returns segment address of *any*, which may be a variable or subprogram identifier
SizeOf(*any*)	F	No	All	Returns storage requirement of *any*, which may be a variable or type identifier
Sseg	F	No	16	Returns stack segment's base address
Swap(*int1*)	P	No	All	Exchange high- and low-order bytes of *int1*

Table B-14. Conversion and Scalar Functions

Identifier	Standard	System	Description
Chr(*int1*)	Yes*	All	Returns *int1* as a Char type data item
Odd(*int1*)	Yes	All	Returns TRUE if *int1* is odd
Ord(*scalar*)	Yes	All	Returns ordinal value of *scalar*
Ord(*pntr*)	No	C80	Returns integer address pointed to by *pntr*
Pred (*scalar*)	Yes	All	Returns *scalar* decremented by 1
Succ (*scalar*)	Yes	All	Returns *scalar* incremented by 1
Scalar_Typ (*scalar*)	No	All	Returns the literal constant of Scalar_Typ that corresponds to *scalar*. Scalar_Typ represents any scalar type identifier

Table B-15. Arithmetic Functions

Identifier	Standard	System	Description
Abs(*int1* | *fp*)	Yes	All	Returns absolute value of *int1* or *fp*
ArcTan(*int1* | *fp*)	Yes	All	Returns angle based on *int1* or *fp* tangent
Cos(*int1* | *fp*)	No	All	Returns cosine of *int1* or *fp* angle
Exp(*int1* | *fp*)	Yes	All	Returns exponential of *int1* or *fp*
Frac(*int1* | *fp*)	No	All	Returns fractional part of *int1* or *fp*
Int(*int1* | *fp*)	No	All	Returns integer part of *int1* or *fp*
Ln(*int1* | *fp*)	Yes	All	Returns natural log of *int1* or *fp*
Random	No	All	Returns a pseudo-random value greater than or equal to 0 and less than 1
Random(*int1*)	No	All	Returns a pseudo-random value greater than or equal to 0 and less than *int1*
Sin(*int1* | *fp*)	Yes	All	Returns sine of *int1* or *fp* angle
Sqr(*int1* | *fp*)	Yes	All	Returns *int1* or *fp* squared
Sqrt(*int1* | *fp*)	Yes	All	Returns the square root of *int1* or *fp*
Trunc(*fp*)	No	All	Returns integer part of *fp*

Notes: The angle parameter for the trigonometric functions Sin and Cos must be in radians. One radian equals .017453 degrees. One degree equals 57.2957795 radians. The tangent of an angle may be calculated as Sin(angle) / Cos(angle). The Ln and Exp functions use the natural logarithmic base, which is 2.718282.

Table B-16.   System Control Subprograms

Identifier	Procedure/ Function	Standard	System	Description
Bdos(*int1,* *[int2]*)	P	No	C-80	Invoke CP/M-80 BDOS routine *int1* using optional parameters *int2* as required
Bdos(*int1,* *[int2]*)	F	No	C-80	Invoke CP/M-80 BDOS function *int1* using optional parameters *int2* as required; result is returned in register A
BdosHL(int1, *[int2...])*	F	No	C-80	Invoke CP/M-80 BDOS function *int1* using optional parameters *int2* as required; result is returned in register pair HL
Bdos(*dos__reg*) (See Note)	P	No	C-86	Perform CP/M-86 BDOS function calls based on *dos__reg*; result returned in *dos__reg*
Bios(*int1,* *[int2...]*)	P	No	C-80	Invoke CP/M-80 BIOS routine *int1* using optional parameters *int2* as required
Bios(*int1,* *[int2...]*)	F	No	C-80	Invoke CP/M-80 BIOS function *int1* using optional parameters *int2* as required; result returned in register A
BiosHL(*int1,* *[int2...]*)	F	No	C-80	Invoke CP/M-80 BIOS function *int1* using optional parameters *int2* as required; result is returned in register pair HL
ChDir(*str1*)	P	No	MS 3+	The current directory is changed to the directory indicated by *str1*
GetDir(*int1,* *str1*)	P	No	MS 3+	*str1* is set to current directory path on drive *int1*

(continued)

Table B-16.   System Control Subprograms (*continued*)

Identifier	Procedure/ Function	Standard	System	Description
Intr(*dos__reg*) (See Note)	P	No	16	Causes an MS-DOS or CP/M-86 software interrupt based on *dos__reg*
MkDir(*str1*)	P	No	MS 3+	Creates a new subdirectory specified by path string *str1*
MsDos (*dos__reg*) (See Note)	P	No	MS	Performs an MS-DOS system call based on *dos__reg*
OvrDrive(*int1*)	P	No	16 3+	Indicates overlay files are on drive *int1*
OvrPath(*str1*)	P	No	MS 3+	Indicates overlay files are in directory indicated on *str1*
ParamCount	F	No	All 3+	Returns the number of parameters in the operating system command line buffer
ParamStr (*int1*)	F	No	All 3+	Returns parameter string *int1* from the operating system command line buffer
Delay(*int1*)	P	No	All	Causes a pause of *int1* milliseconds
Halt	P	No	All	Terminates program execution
Randomize	P	No	All 3+	Reseeds the random number routine; has no effect in versions prior to 3.0
RmDir(*str1*)	P	No	MS 3+	Removes the subdirectory indicated by path string *str1*, if it is empty

Note: The *dos__reg* parameter is a record type that may be declared using this type:

```
type Registers = record
            ax,bx,cx,dx,bp,si,di,ds,es,flags: Integer;
        end;
```

Dos__reg is a variable parameter and may be used by MS-DOS to return values to the calling routine.

Table B-17. IBM PC System Subprograms

Identifier	Procedure/ Function	Description
Graphics Board Not Required		
NoSound	P	Stop sound generation routine
Sound(*int1*)	P	Start sound generation using pitch *int1*
TextBackground(*int1*)	P	Select background color *int1* for text
TextColor(*int1*)	P	Select foreground color *int1* for text
TextMode	P	Select text mode using current screen format
TextMode(*int1*)	P	Select text mode using screen format *int1*
WhereX	F	Returns current column position of the cursor
WhereY	F	Returns current row position of the cursor
Window(*int1,int2,int3,int4*)	P	Define text window. Upper-left corner at *int1,int2,* lower-right corner at *int3, int4*
Requires Graphics Board		
Draw(*int1,int2,int3,int4,int5*)	P	Starting at point *int1,int2* draw a line to point *int3,int4* using color *int5*
GraphBackground(*int1*)	P	Select background color *int1* for graphics
GraphColorMode	P	Select the color graphics mode
GraphWindow(*int1,int2,int3,int4*)	P	Define graphics window. Upper-left corner at *int1,int2,* lower-right corner at *int3, int4*
HiRes	P	Select 640 × 200 pixel resolution
HiResColor(*int1*)	P	Same as HiRes, plus select foreground color
Palette(*int1*)	P	Select color combinations for 320 × 200 resolution graphics
Plot(*int1,int2,int3*)	P	Set pixel at *int1,int2* to color *int3*

(continued)

Table B-17. IBM PC System Subprograms (*continued*)

Identifier	Procedure/ Function	Description
Requires Graphics Board and Turbo Version 3.0		
Arc(*int1,int2,int3,int4,int5*)	P	Starting at point *int1,int2* draw an arc of *int3* degrees with a radius of *int4* using color *int5*
Circle(*int1,int2,int3,int4*)	P	Draw a circle with center point *int1,int2* and radius *int3* using color *int4*
ColorTable(*int1,int2,int3,int4*)	P	Define color translation table using colors *int1* to *int4*
FillScreen(*int1*)		Clear graphics window using color *int1*
FillShape(*int1,int2,int3,int4*)	P	Fill area at *int1,int2* with color *int3* until border color *int4* is encountered
FillPattern(*int1,int2,int3,* *int4,int5*)	P	Fill rectangle with upper-left corner at *int1,int2* and lower-right corner at *int3,int4* with current pattern using color *int5*
GetDotColor(*int1,int2*)	F	Returns the color code of the pixel at *int1, int2*
GetPic(*any,int1,int2,int3,int4*)	P	Stores the graphics image with upper-left corner *int1,int2* and lower-right corner *int3, int4* in buffer defined by *any*
Pattern(*ptrn*) (See Note)	P	Define pattern used by FillPattern using bit map in *ptrn*
PutPic(*any,int1,int2*)		Display the graphics image in buffer *any* at position *int1,int2*

Note: The *ptrn* parameter is an array of 7 bytes. The status of individual bits determines the pattern.

(*continued*)

Table B-17.   IBM PC System Subprograms (*continued*)

Identifier	Procedure/ Function	Description
Turtle Graphics **Requires Graphics Board and Turbo Version 3.0**		
Back(*int1*)	P	Move turtle back *int1* steps
ClearScreen	P	Clear turtle graphics window and move turtle to position 0,0
Forward(*int1*)	P	Move turtle forward *int1* steps
Heading	F	Returns the direction of forward in degrees
HideTurtle	P	Makes the turtle invisible
Home	P	Moves the turtle to the center of the current turtle window (Position 0,0)
NoWrap	P	Prevents the turtle from appearing on the opposite side of the window when it moves out of the window boundaries
PenDown	P	Causes a line to be drawn as the turtle moves
PenUp	P	Allows the turtle to move without drawing a line
SetHeading(*int1*)	P	Sets the direction to forward in degrees (0 is up or North, 180 is down or South.)
SetPenColor(*int1*)	P	*int1* determines the color of the line drawn as the turtle moves
SetPosition(*int1,int2*)	P	Moves turtle to coordinates *int1,int2*
ShowTurtle	P	Makes the turtle visible as a small triangle
TurnLeft(*int1*)	P	Rotate the turtle *int1* degrees counterclockwise from its current heading
TurnRight(*int1*)	P	Rotate the turtle *int1* degrees clockwise from its current heading

(continued)

Table B-17. IBM PC System Subprograms (*continued*)

Identifier	Procedure/ Function	Description
Turtle Graphics **Requires Graphics Board and Turbo Version 3.0**		
TurtleWindow(*int1,int2,int3,int4*)	P	Define turtle graphics window. Center at *int1,int2,* with width *int3* and height *int4*
TurtleThere	F	Returns TRUE if the turtle is in the current turtle window
Wrap	P	Causes the turtle to appear on the opposite side of the window when it moves out of the window boundaries
Xcor	F	Returns the turtle's current horizontal coordinate
Ycor	F	Returns the turtle's current verticle coordinate

Table B-18. Subprogram Definition Directives and a Variable Declaration Directive

Identifier	Standard	System	Description
absolute	No*	All	Declared variable at a specific memory location
external 'FILE'	No *	All	Load object code for the preceding sub-program from a disk file indicated by the string constant
forward	Yes*	All	The preceding subprogram header is a forward declaration
overlay	No*	All 2+	Compile subprogram to an overlay file

Index